Single-Camera Video Production

FIFTH EDITION

Single-Camera Video Production

FIFTH EDITION

Robert B. Musburger

AMSTERDAM • BOSTON • HEIDELBERG • LONDON
NEW YORK • OXFORD • PARIS • SAN DIEGO
SAN FRANCISCO • SINGAPORE • SYDNEY • TOKYO
Focal press is an imprint of Elsevier

Focal Press is an imprint of Elsevier
30 Corporate Drive, Suite 400, Burlington, MA 01803, USA
The Boulevard, Langford Lane, Kidlington, Oxford, OX5 1GB, UK

Notices

Knowledge and best practice in this field are constantly changing. As new research and experience broaden our understanding, changes in research methods, professional practices, or medical treatment may become necessary.

Practitioners and researchers must always rely on their own experience and knowledge in evaluating and using any information, methods, compounds, or experiments described herein. In using such information or methods they should be mindful of their own safety and the safety of others, including parties for whom they have a professional responsibility.

To the fullest extent of the law, neither the Publisher nor the authors, contributors, or editors assume any liability for any injury and/or damage to persons or property as a matter of product liability, negligence or otherwise, or from any use or operation of any methods, products, instructions, or ideas contained in the material herein.

Library of Congress Cataloging-in-Publication Data
Musburger, Robert B.
   Single-camera video production / Robert B. Musburger. — 5th ed.
      p. cm.
   Includes bibliographical references and index.
   ISBN 978-0-240-81264-9 (pbk. : alk. paper) 1. Video tape recorders. 2. Video recordings–Production and direction. 3. Camcorders. I. Title.
   TK6655.V5M88 2010
   778.59–dc22

                                                                                      2009040290

British Library Cataloguing-in-Publication Data
A catalogue record for this book is available from the British Library.

ISBN: 978-0-240-81264-9

For information on all Focal Press publications
visit our website at www.elsevierdirect.com

10 11 12 13 5 4 3 2 1

Printed in the United States of America

DEDICATION

To my mother, Mary Tomazina Wemple Musburger Houska, for teaching me the value of integrating art and technology.

Contents

Introduction xii
Additional Comments on the Fifth Edition xiv
Acknowledgments xv

Chapter One
Production Philosophy 2
  The Production Process 2
  Importance of Goals-Audience Analysis 4
  Importance of Workflow 6
  Difference between Studio and Field Production 8
  Importance of Technology 10

Chapter Two
The Technology 12
  Connecting the Real World to the Digital World 12
    Limitations of Equipment 12
  Audio Signals 14
    Frequency 14
    Amplitude 16
  Measuring Audio Signals 18
  Compression 20
  Video Signals 22
    Changing Light into Electrons 22
  Synchronization 24
    Scan Systems 28
  Measuring Video Signals 30
    Video Compression 32

Chapter Three
The Equipment 34
  Equipment Development 34
  Cameras 36
    Camera Types 37
    Handheld Cameras 38
    HDV Professional Camera 39

Broadcast Camera 41

Digital Cinema Camera 42

Specialized Digital Cameras 43

Image Sources and Optics 44

Tubes 44

Chips 44

Optics 45

Focal Length 46

Focus 47

Aperture 48

Depth of Field 49

Viewfinder and Camera Controls 50

Viewfinder 50

Camera Controls 52

Bars/Gain Selector 52

Color Temperature Control/Filter Selector 53

White Balance 54

Camera Supports 56

Tripods and Body Mounts 56

Cranes, Dollies, and Pedestals 58

Handholding the Camera 60

Digital Recording 63

Recording 63

Recorder Operation 66

Connecting Equipment 69

Cable Coiling 70

Power Connectors and Plugs 71

Audio Connectors 72

Video Connectors 74

Digital Connectors 76

Audio 78

Microphone Types 79

Electronic Impedance 79

Element Construction 80

Pickup Pattern 82

Mounting Devices 84

Nonmicrophone Audio Sources 87

Which Audio Track to Use 88

Lighting 89

Floodlights 90

Focusing Spotlights 92

Fixed-Focus Instruments 93

Controlling Light 95

Power Sources 96

Color Temperature 98

Measuring Light Intensity 100

Lighting Ratio 101

Contrast Ratio 102

Chapter Four

The Production Process: Preproduction 105

Preliminary Forms 106

The Proposal 106

Treatment 108

Legal Considerations 112

Script Formats 112

Scene Script 112

Shooting Script 114

Script Formats 114

Single-Column Format 116

Dual-Column Format 118

Organizing Forms 120

Storyboards 120

Location Scouting 122

Site Survey 124

Organizing Equipment and Crew 126

Chapter Five

The Production Process: Production 129

Production Stages and Setup 129

Setting Up 129

Field Equipment Considerations 131

Camera Setup 132

Audio Preparation 134

Prompting Devices 136

Sets and Properties 138

Lighting Preparation 140

Controlling Color Temperature 142

Controlling Light Intensity 144

Contrast Range 146

Basic Three-Point Lighting 148

Backlight 148

Key Light 149

Fill Light 149

Kicker and Set Lights 150

Multiple or Moving Subjects 152

Creative Lighting 154

Mood Lighting 154

Lighting for Time, Date, and Location 154

Directing and Rehearsing 156

Directing Talent 156

Rehearsal 157

Shooting 160

Shooting and Framing 162

Standard Shot Names 163

Framing Principles 166

Aspect Ratio 166

Critical Area 168

Lead Room or Edge Attraction 169

The Rule of Thirds 170

Creating Movement 172

Subject Movement 172

Camera Movement 174

Movement through Zooms 174

Z-Axis Movement 176

Graphic Force Movement 178

The Third Movement: Editing 181

Shoot to Edit 181

Continuity of Action 182

Continuity of Direction 182

Continuity of Location 183

Cover Shots 184

In-Camera Effects 186

Iris Fades 186

Roll or Rack Focus 187

Swish Pans and Zooms 187

Reversing Polarity 188

Digital In-Camera Effects 188

Logging and Striking 190

Striking 192

Chapter Six

The Production Process: Postproduction 195

The Soul of Production 195

Editing Depends on Aesthetic and Equipment Knowledge and Skills 196

Editing Concept 198

Basic Process 198

Process Background 200

Nonlinear Film 200

Linear Electronic 202

Nonlinear Electronic 204

Hardware 206

Editing Equipment 206

Accessories 208

Software 210

Physical Process 211

Choices and Decisions 211

Technical Process 216

Editing Operating Methods 220

Basic Editing 221

Transitions 222

Titles 224

Adding Audio 225

Rendering 226

The Aesthetic Process 228

Output-Distribution 233

Preparing to Output/Export 233

Output Process 234
Destination Choices 236

Chapter Seven
Your Future 237
Introduction 237
Internship 240
The Application Process 242
Résumé Writing 243
Composing a Cover Letter 243
The Portfolio 246
The Interview 248
Summary 250

Glossary 253

Further Reading 287

Index 289

Introduction

This text has been written to provide three groups of video enthusiasts with enough information to produce acceptable single-camera video productions: the media production student, the professional who needs a refresher on the basics, and the first-time video camera owner. It is a basic, introductory book designed to point the beginner in the right direction. This is not an advanced book in preproduction research and writing, nor is it a book on advanced techniques in electronic editing. Each of those subjects deserves its own title.

I wrote this book from three points of view: first, from that of an instructor introducing the techniques that lead to quality video productions utilizing a single video camera; second, from that of a practitioner who has spent 50 years working in professional media and learning the contents of this book the hard way—by making mistakes until I finally got it right; and third, from that of an academic fielding 20 phone calls a week from people new to electronic production who desperately want information about single-camera video production.

This book outlines the process of working with a single video camera from beginning to end, with an emphasis on the actual production process. First, though, you must lay some groundwork before you pick up your camera. The video camera and the recording medium used remain two complex pieces of equipment, despite efforts to simplify them. The process by which a video image is created is also complex, and you must understand it in order to properly utilize the benefits and master the restrictions of the medium.

The first chapter of the book outlines the production process, emphasizes the importance of goals and audience analysis, explains the production workflow process, and discusses the importance of technology. The second chapter contains a simplified explanation of how and why video and audio signals are created. It also describes the technical restrictions of a digital system. The third chapter describes the equipment: cameras; recorders; and audio, lighting, and mounting equipment. With the first three chapters providing a firm base, the fourth chapter carries you through the production process from preproduction planning (much more important than most beginners realize) to setting up, rehearsing, shooting, and striking. The fifth chapter details the digital process by exploring lighting and audio techniques. The sixth chapter concentrates on the digital nonlinear editing process, techniques, aesthetics, and the importance of shooting for the editing process. The final chapter outlines methods to move your career beyond the classroom: finding and earning an internship, preparing for the interviewing and job search process, and approaching your first and next job.

As the media production world rapidly moves toward an all-digital environment, I have included those changes that are critical for single-camera production. From experience, I am aware that the rapid changes require new information on virtually a weekly basis. I have attempted to anticipate some of those changes, but at the same time, I have avoided making any wild guesses as to the next level of production developments. There are too many new concepts and proposals in the works—some of them will be working years from now, others will be gone within 6 months. All we can do is watch, take advantage of what the field has to offer, and remember that it isn't the paintbrush that makes the difference, it's the mind and the hands of the artist.

Additional Comments on the Fifth Edition

The layout of this text includes major changes from the old format, in which editorial copy was placed on one page with illustrations on the facing page. In the new format presented here, figures and photographs are interspersed with the editorial copy as needed to illustrate or clarify a point. More than 100 new figures and photographs replace drawn figures.

The emphasis will expand on the concentration of digital equipment and production techniques applicable to field video production and nonlinear postproduction. New sections on production workflow, audience analysis, modern formats, distribution methods, and career planning extend the value of this book.

A key factor in the move of media to an "all-digital" production format is the realization that all media must start in an analog format, and for humans to comprehend the messages, the messages must be returned to an analog format. Media converted to a digital format may be easily manipulated without loss of quality but cannot be viewed or listened to until converted into a form a person's eye and ear can interpret. For that reason, some analog theory and technology remain as critical parts of this book and will remain so until humans can directly interpret a digital signal.

Acknowledgments

One cannot work in the video business without relying on many other people. This is not a solitary business, and throughout the years many people have made major contributions to my knowledge and career. Here are a few of many: Parks Whitmer and Sam Scott, who started me in media production and kept me going; Art Mosby, who paid my first television paycheck; Bob Wormington, who let me develop my directing skills; the thousands of students at Avila College, University of Missouri at Kansas City, Kansas University, Florida State University, the University of Houston, and Central Washington University who constantly reminded me that I don't know everything there is to know about media production; and my wife, Pat, who lets me think that I do.

Credit for the illustrations for this book I share with more than 30 manufacturers of equipment who provided photographs, ideas, and illustrations for this text. Thanks also to all of the helpful people at Focal Press who have guided and prodded me through my publishing efforts for the past 19 years: Karen, Philip, Mary, Trish, Marie, Maura, Tammy, Tricia, Lilly, Jennifer, Amy, Elinor, Cara, and, for this edition, Michele Cronin and Laura Aberle.

Chapter One
Production Philosophy

The Production Process

Despite the general public's attitude toward digital media production as a simple activity, in reality you will find that although digitizing has made the equipment lighter, smaller, more powerful, and full of technology that offers greater creativity to you as a producer, director, camera operator, or editor, the process actually has gotten more complex. When you replace controls and functions necessary to operate analog video and audio equipment with digital equipment, it appears to make operations simpler, and in some ways that has occurred. But the nature of digital technology and equipment provides you a greater opportunity for more choices in operations. Those opportunities require you to meet a broader range of decisions, setting specific operational criteria for each shot or setup. You may point and shoot, but that alone is not professional.

To give you the best means to take advantage of all that digital equipment offers, this text is organized to lead you through the entire production process from beginning to end. The first step is for you to understand that production is actually a three-stage process: preproduction, production, and postproduction. The three stages are unique and separate to a point, but they are dependent on each other for the success of the complete project, and all are also dependent on the final plans for distribution of the project. The three steps are equally important—without all three you will not be able to complete a professional production (see Figure 1.1).

You will use the preproduction stage to prepare the production, organize and research your thoughts on what you want to do with it, and complete the many sets of written materials from proposals through completed scripts.

During the production stage before you actually start shooting, you still must perform some preparation steps before you may remove the lens cap and record data. You must take as much care with logging and striking equipment as you did with setting and shooting.

Once the data are recorded on tape, disc, or solid-state media, you then are faced with organizing the material again in the postproduction stage. Data must be entered, and you must choose the shots you want and trim them into a final form before adding sound, effects, and completing your final project.

SINGLE-CAMERA VIDEO PRODUCTION
THREE-STEP PRODUCTION PROCESS

PREPRODUCTION	PRODUCTION	POSTPRODUCTION
Concept Research Planning	Organizing Crew Cast Equipment	Acquisition Organizing
Proposal Treatment Budget Storyboard	Constructing Sets Props Communication Prompting	Ingesting Logging Formatting
Draft Script Scene Script Shot Script	Setting up Lights Audio Camera(s)	Rough Cut Final Cut Audio Mix
Location Scouting Site Survey Plot Drafting	Rehearsal Rough Cast Camera Final	Effects Color Correction Audio Correction Rendering
Hiring Crew Cast Equipment	Recording Logging Effects Striking	Master Release Output

FIG. 1.1 – Depending on the requirements of the individual production, the size of the crew, and the length of the production, some of the functions and operations of each of the three steps may be combined or completed simultaneously.

The Production Process

Importance of Goals-Audience Analysis

Before you commit yourself to a project, you ought to seriously consider what you have decided your goals must be to achieve your objective. You must work toward illustrating your concept accurately and as you have envisioned it in your own mind. Your project has little chance of success unless you have developed a story that will attract and hold an audience. As much as you may want to produce a project for your own enjoyment, there is no value in such a project unless someone else is interested in viewing it and understanding your message and unless it stands as an example of your ability to create a professional quality production (see Figure 1.2).

PRODUCTION GOALS-OBJECTIVES

GOALS	OBJECTIVES
Fulfill Personal Vision	Attract a Funding Source
Tell a Compelling Story	Attract an Audience
Create a Professional Production	Establish Professional Qualifications

FIG. 1.2 – Among the six key characteristics of a professional production are fulfilling a vision and telling a story that will establish your professional qualifications by attracting funding and an audience.

You may be able to produce a short using the equipment made available to you by your employer or school, but as a professional you must learn to create a concept that organizations or individuals will believe in enough to provide the funds that will allow you to complete the project. One aspect of what determines a funding source's decision is your convincing the organization that a large enough audience would be interested in the project to make the investment worthwhile. As producer, you must understand how to analyze audiences and how to create a production that will maximize the size of that audience.

Importance of Goals-Audience Analysis

Importance of Workflow

The process of moving video and audio signals in digital formats from one stage to another is now called *workflow*. As your production moves away from tape and even disc recording systems, solid-state devices allow digital audio and video signals to be handled as a data-digital, ones and zeros, not actual audio or video signals. Because the media signals are in the form of data signals, you may more easily move, manipulate, store, and transfer the data quickly from one location to another and to do it simultaneously. This allows you and others to edit, review, and manage a production at the same time. Such a workflow process makes broadcast news and multieditor postproduction facilities efficient operations (see Figure 1.3).

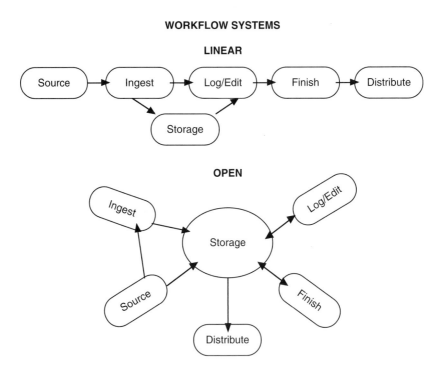

FIG. 1.3 – As workflow becomes a practical and widespread concept, different methods of using the system have developed. The two most common are the original linear, straight-through system and the more flexible system used in news operations, the open system.

Difference between Studio and Field Production

One of the first choices you will need to make once you have developed, researched, and found funding for your project is to decide whether to produce it in a studio or in the field. You will face advantages and disadvantages in either location (see Figure 1.4).

A studio production offers you the protection and control over all aspects of sound, lighting, personnel, and equipment. Once you design and construct the set, it is a known factor for which lighting can be designed to work for you. A soundproof studio guarantees you the best possible sound while shooting. The entire production, cast, you, and crew will have a set and a known location to begin each day's shooting. All equipment and other facilities will be secured and present when you need them on schedule without interference from any outside crowds or uncontrolled weather. A studio may restrict your actions and scenes to what can be constructed or is available between the studio walls and facilities. Your budget must include the daily cost of the studio and facilities.

Shooting in the field offers you creative flexibility in choosing a precise, realistic setting that cannot be reproduced easily in the studio, such as shooting on the side

LOCATION CHOICES

STUDIO	FIELD
Control Light	Realistic Environment
Control Sound	Unrestricted Movement
Control Environment	Subjects Unavailable in Studio
Single Location	Flexibility of Movement
Secure Equipment	Difficult to Reproduce Environment
Protected Cast and Crew	Impossible to Reproduce Environment

FIG. 1.4 – In many cases, the advantage of working in a studio may be the disadvantage of working in the field: controlled sound in the studio, less control of sound in the field. But advantages in one location may be offset by advantages in another location.

of the Grand Canyon. You may not be able to move some subjects or objects to a studio setting, and these are best shot in their natural environments. Obviously you can only shoot news and many documentary subjects in the field, and the disadvantages of field shooting must be overcome by your careful and creative production planning. Despite the wide-ranging ability of digital postproduction techniques to allow you to duplicate settings and situations not available in the studio, shooting on location adds a touch of empathy that cannot be created digitally.

Difference between Studio and Field Production

Importance of Technology

If you were to suddenly pick up a brush and start to dab paint on a canvas or any other handy surface, the chances of achieving an immediate masterpiece would be minimal. The same holds true if you tried to be a sculptor. You cannot attack a piece of marble with a chisel without first learning the skills necessary to properly mold the form without damaging the original material or exceeding the capabilities of the medium (see Figure 1.5).

Likewise, running through the woods with an out-of-focus camera may seem creative, but it is neither good art nor good video. You must understand the basic technology of any art form in order to utilize properly the artistic characteristics of that medium and to avoid the pitfalls of its technical limitations. Video is highly technical; the medium requires some basic knowledge of optics, electronics, electricity, physics, and mathematics. Of course, you could complete a video production without any knowledge of the subjects just listed, but the possibility of it being a top-quality production is limited.

Unplanned   Planned

FIG. 1.5 – Art or creativity in digital formats can occur in both unplanned and planned situations. But unplanned productions rely on the happenstance of the desired creativity surfacing without control or a goal. Planned productions create an environment to carry out the vision of the creator in a logical, controlled, and professional fashion.

With the development of lighter, smaller, and more powerful equipment that operates using digital technology, you can create higher-quality video productions at a lower cost than was possible a few years ago. But the advances in digital technology that make for better productions also require you to acquire some knowledge of the digital domain and how it can and should be used in video production. You may be able to operate digital equipment easily and with a minimum of knowledge of the media production process, but the ease of operation does not replace your thinking and your creativity, which are necessary for a quality production.

Importance of Technology

Chapter Two
The Technology

Connecting the Real World to the Digital World

To utilize video cameras and associated audio equipment effectively, you must be aware of the capabilities and limitations of each piece of equipment. In addition, you must know how each piece of equipment operates in relation to other equipment used in the same production. This awareness does not necessarily mean you have a broad range of knowledge of the technology involved in media production, but rather that you appreciate and understand why the equipment is designed to operate as it does and what it can accomplish.

Most important, it is necessary you understand what the equipment cannot be expected to accomplish. Digital equipment does not replace your knowledge of composition, shot sequencing, or the construction of characters and storylines necessary to assemble a professional production. In fact, the basics of production are even more important in your digital production because of the high level of resolution and clarity made possible in the digital formats. This clarity reveals poor lighting, bad framing, incorrect exposure, and all other gaffes that would barely show in analog production.

Limitations of Equipment

The human eye and ear are two extraordinary instruments for sensing light and sound. No human invention has ever come close to matching the capabilities of those two sensory organs. It is easy to forget how limited the electronic aural and visual equipment are until you compare them to your human counterparts (see Figure 2.1).

Your eye can focus from nearly the end of the nose to infinity instantaneously. Your eye can adjust to light variations quickly and can pick out images in light varying over a thousand times from the lightest to the darkest. Your ear can hear sounds varying in loudness from 0 decibels to more than 160 decibels and can respond to frequency changes from 15 hertz to more than 20,000 hertz. The best microphone is limited to less than 60 decibels in loudness range. Most audio equipment cannot reproduce frequencies without inconsistent variations beyond a range of 15,000 hertz.

The best professional digital camera cannot reveal detail in light variations greater than 300 to 1. The best lenses have limited focus range, and the depth of field depends on the amount of light present and focal length and f-stop settings. Digital equipment allows repeated duplication of signals without degradation, but it does little to extend the dynamic range of either sound or video.

COMPARISON OF HUMAN TO EQUIPMENT LIMITATIONS

HUMAN			EQUIPMENT		
EYE	Focus	$0-\infty$	10–30x	LENS
EYE	Field of View	Up to 140°	Up to 100°	LENS
EYE	Sensitivity	1:10,000	1:500	CHIP
EAR	Range	0 dB–+160 dB	10 dB–80 dB	MICROPHONE
EAR	Sensitivity	15 Hz–20 kHz	30–15 kHz	PROCESSOR

FIG. 2.1 – No electronic equipment—analog or digital—can sense or reproduce the equivalent of human senses of hearing and seeing.

Connecting the Real World to the Digital World

Audio Signals

Frequency

The audio signal has two basic characteristics: frequency (tone) and amplitude (loudness). In order to create with and record sound, you must understand these two characteristics. All sounds start as an analog signal, because the vibration in air that creates sound is an analog motion. Digital sound is created only within equipment and must be converted back to analog for you to hear it.

Frequency is measured in *hertz* or cycles per second and is abbreviated Hz. Because most of the sounds you can hear are above 1,000 hertz, the abbreviation kHz, or kilohertz, is often used (k is the abbreviation for kilo, the metric equivalent of 1,000) (see Figure 2.2).

A *cycle* is the time or distance between peaks of a single sound vibration. A single continuous frequency is called a *tone* and is often used for testing. Humans perceive frequency as *pitch*, the highness and lowness of tones. *Timbre* is a musical term often used in media production; it refers to the special feeling a sound may have as a result of its source. For example, a note struck on the piano may be the same frequency as that of the same note played on a trumpet, but the timbre is very different and will sound different to your ear (see Figure 2.3).

THE FREQUENCY SPECTRUM

Frequency	Frequency Uses	Type of Wave
0-10kH	Audio	Sound
10kH-100kH	Experimental, Maritime Navigation & Comm.	Very Low Freq.
100kH-1MH	Maritime & Aviation Navigation & Comm. & Ham	Low Freq.
1 MH-10MH	AM B-cast, Ham, Radio Navigation, Industrial	Medium Freq.
10MH-100MH	Int'l Shortwave, Ham, Citizens, Medical, LORAN	High Freq.
100MH-1GH	Aviation, TV B-cast, FM B-cast, FAX, Ham, Wx	Very High Freq.
1GH-10GH	Aviation, STL Microwave, Gov., TV B-cast, Ham	Ultra High Freq.
10GH-100GH	Gov., Radio Nav., Ham, Fixed & Mobile	Super High Freq.
100GH-1TH	Experimental, Government, Ham	Extremely Hi. Freq.
1TH-10TH	Industrial Photo, Research	Infrared
10TH-100TH	Heat Waves	Infrared
100TH-1PH	Heat Waves	Infrared
1PH-10PH	Light-Heat Waves	Light-Ultraviolet
10PH-100PH	Ionizing Radiation, Medical Research	Ultraviolet
100PH-1EH	Ionizing Radiation, Medical Research	Soft X-rays
1EH-10EH	Ionizing Radiation, Scientific Research	X-rays
10EH-100EH	Gamma Rays	Hard X-rays
100EH-1 ZH	Gamma Rays	Hard X-rays

The Higher Metric Classifications

KILO	1,000	Thousand
MEGA	1,000,000	Million
GIGA	1,000,000,000	Billion
TERA	1,000,000,000.000	Trillion
PETA	1,000,000,000,000,000	Quadrillion
EXA	1,000,000,000,000,000,000	Quintillion
ZETTA	1,000,000,000,000,000,000,000,	Sextillion
YOTTA	1,000,000,000,000,000,000,000,000,	Septillion

Frequency Spectrum Chart

FIG. 2.2 – The energy spectrum ranges from 0 Hz to above a *yottahertz*—a septillion hertz (a billion, billion, million hertz). The frequency range most humans can hear falls between 15 Hz and 20 kHz. Frequencies above the audible human range include radio frequencies (RFs) used as broadcast carrier waves, microwaves, X-rays, and light, or the visible spectrum.

Audio Signals

Digital recorders are capable of recording audio frequencies from 15 to 20 kHz, but because your hearing is limited, so is digital recording. You do not generally miss the frequencies excluded in recordings unless the production requires a wide range of frequency response, such as a music session.

Altering of the frequency response is called *equalization*. When you adjust the tone controls, treble or bass, on a stereo, you are equalizing the signal by modifying the frequency response. Although most video recorders do not have equalization controls, some audio mixers and microphones do.

Amplitude

Amplitude is the energy level of the audio signal. You perceive amplitude as loudness. Relative amplitude is referred to as level and is measured in *decibels,* abbreviated as dB. *Deci-* is one-tenth on the metric scale, and the *bel* is the measure of audio amplitude created by Alexander Graham Bell. Because the bel is a very large unit of measure, dB is more commonly used. The decibel may seem to be confusing unit of measurement because it is a reference measurement of the change of the power of the signal. It is not an absolute measurement and is logarithmic, not linear; it can be expressed in either volts or watts. A change of at least 3 dB is necessary in order for your ear to perceive a change in level.

Volume is the term used when referring to the measurable energy that translates into loudness and may be measured in either volume units (VUs) or dBs. You are sensitive to a change in volume, but your hearing is not linear. At some frequencies and at some volume levels, your ear senses a change but the actual measure of change is not registered accurately within your brain. Because digital recording equipment can handle a dynamic range of approximately 80 dB, accurate level readings must be available during recording to avoid distorted sound in digital systems.

There are two *aberrations* of audio to watch for: distortion and noise. *Distortion* is an unwanted change in the audio signal. The most common distortion is caused by your attempting to record the audio at a level that is too high for the equipment. In digital audio systems, high levels may cause the audio to skip or cease entirely. *Noise* is unwanted sound added to the audio. Digital systems are very sensitive to all sounds, so noise may be added to a recording if not adequately monitored.

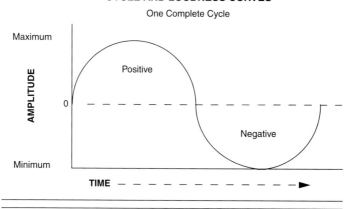

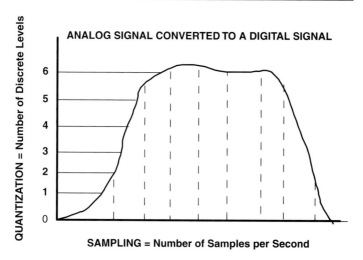

FIG. 2.3 – Both sound and video are measured in amplitude and time. Measuring time determines frequency, and amplitude determines loudness or level. Converting an original analog signal to a recorded digital signal requires both quantization and sampling.

Audio Signals

Measuring Audio Signals

You can measure the audio level as it is being recorded using a VU meter, a peak-to-peak meter, or light-emitting diodes (LEDs). Each of these gives you a comparable indication of the level of the audio. When the level is too high, the meters read above the 0 dB indicator, and with LEDs, the changing color of the flashing diodes indicates the audio level. When the level is too low, the meter needle barely moves, and few, if any, diodes flash (see Figure 2.4).

You need to keep dynamic levels within the specified range of the equipment, whether digital or analog, by attenuating the level (bringing it down) when the audio source is too loud and boosting the level (bringing it up) when the audio source level is too low. This is called *riding gain* and may be done either manually or automatically via circuits built into the equipment called *automatic gain controls* (AGCs) or *automatic level controls* (ALCs). AGCs and ALCs will maintain certain maximum and minimum levels, but they may add noise by boosting levels during a soft or quiet passage or by overdriving if there is a sudden, very loud increase in the input.

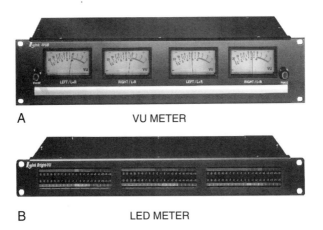

A   VU METER

B   LED METER

FIG. 2.4 – Audio level may be monitored by using one of three systems: VU meters, peak meters, or LEDs. VU meters *(top)* indicate average voltage, LED *(bottom)* and peak meters indicate peak voltage. Each one indicates potential under- and overmodulation levels as well as acceptable levels. (Courtesy Logitech,)

Dynamics refers to the difference between the loudest and the quietest passage you can perceive. Most analog equipment is limited to a range of approximately 60 dB; newer digital equipment features dynamic ranges greater than 100 dB. Crickets at night might be heard at 3 dB, a normal conversation at 100 dB, and a rock concert at 160 dB or greater (over the threshold of pain and damaging to hearing).

To achieve the highest possible audio quality, you should record and reproduce sound as close to the original as possible. Even though it is not possible to record all frequencies at the exact same level as the original sound was recorded, you should make the effort to exclude all noise and avoid distorting the audio signal. It is better for you to record digital audio at a lower level than at too high a level, because a lower-level digital sound can be boosted with minimal distortion or added noise, whereas over-modulated digital audio may disappear or be distorted.

Two additional measurements are required for you to record digital audio: *sampling* and *quantization.* Sampling is the number of times per second analog sound is measured as it is converted to digital. To transfer the maximum quality, samplings needs to be done at twice the highest expected frequency to be converted; 48 Hz is now the standard sampling rate. *Quantization* is the number of discrete levels at which analog sound is measured as it is converted. The greater the bit rate of quantization, the higher the quality of the conversion; 32- to 64-bit quantization presently is considered the professional rate. Increasing both the sampling and quantization rates increases the demand for memory and bandwidth for storing and moving digital files. (see Figure 2.3).

Measuring Audio Signals

Compression

The term *compression* in audio refers to two different manipulations of the audio signal. (1) Traditionally in both analog and digital audio, compression is a process of decreasing the dynamic range (loudest to quietest) of a signal. This allows you to record both the quietest and softest sound to be heard within one recording. (2) In the digital world, compression refers to a reduction in the amount of bandwidth required to record or transmit a digital signal. A compression system omits certain sounds unimportant or redundant in the overall signal so that the human ear does not recognize the loss. The amount of compression is stated as a ratio such as 2:1, which means the bandwidth has been cut in half. The higher the compression ratio, the greater the possibility that so much of the signal will be lost that you will detect a loss in quality. But all compression systems are based on duplicating a digital signal so that you are not aware of the compression. MP3 recordings are compressed to reproduce a signal lower in quality than a CD that is also compressed, but not as high a ratio.

The term *codec* (COmpression-DECompression) refers to a process or equipment that encodes or decodes data. To save storage space and time in moving files with high bytes of data, you may delete repetitious amounts of data. You may use two basic common systems: lossy and lossless. In lossy systems, you do not transmit or record unneeded data. Tests indicate you do not miss the deleted data. With lossless systems, either you do not compress the files or you do so in such a manner that the deleted data are replaced or substituted for when decompressed. Lossy systems use far less space than lossless systems but offer a lower-quality signal on reproduction.

Some Examples of Codecs Now in Use

CD	Compact disc uncompressed audio files on optical disc
MP3	MPEG-1 Layer III Lossy compressed 11:1, lowest quality, bit rate can be chosen before recording
AAC	acc Advanced Audio Coding Lossy compressed file system, higher quality than MP3
AC-3	Adaptive Transformer Code 3 Lossy compression file. Dolby 6 channel
AIFF	.aiff Lossless interchange file format for storing audio files
FLAC	Open source lossless audio format 2:1 compression
RealAudio:	.ra Compression codec for Real/Video, uses variable bit rate depending on application: mobile, streaming, Internet
Shorten	.SHN Losslessy compressing file format CD quality, replaced by FLAC, Wav
WaveForm	.wav Audio storing file format used on Windows PCs. Can store either compressed or uncompressed files

Compression

Video Signals

The video signal, like the audio signal, is made up of voltages varying in frequency and level. Even though the video electronic signal is complex, you should consider it in much the same manner as the audio signal. The camera cannot record all that you can see, nor can a video recorder process all the information fed into it. Avoid both video distortion and noise as vehemently as you avoid audio distortion and noise.

Video distortion and noise are defined in much the same way as audio distortion and noise, except that you can see video distortion as flare in brightly lit areas, as tearing, or as color shifts in the picture. Video noise can be seen as a grainy or "crawly" texture to the picture.

Changing Light into Electrons

Changing light into electrons is a *transducing* process involving two major changes in energy. The first change is the collection and concentration of light reflected from the subject onto the surface of the instrument that changes the light to electrons. The second change in energy is the transformation of that light to an electronic signal. A video camera lens has three primary functions:

- To collect as much light reflected from the subject as possible
- To control how much light passes through the lens
- To focus the image on the photosensitive surface of the camera

When you concentrate light through the lens onto the surface of the transducer, light is transformed into electronics by solid-state image sensors called *chips*. The chips form a light-sensitive, solid-state device known as a *metal oxide semiconductor*, also known as a *complementary metal oxide semiconductor* (CMOS) or a *charge-coupled device* (CCD) chip. The chip may vary in size from $1/3$ inch to 35-mm square and less than $1/8$ inch thick. It operates on much lower voltages and does not burn, streak, or lag as camera tubes did. As the light strikes the surfaces of the chips, an electronic scan beam is altered in proportion to the intensity of the light falling on that specific part of the light-sensitive surface. The brighter the light, the greater the reaction. The lower the light, the lesser the reaction.

Although light is an analog system, once the signal leaves the transducer, you can convert it to either an analog or a digital electronic signal. Both processes are complex, but the basic knowledge you need to properly operate a video camera is easy to acquire.

Video Signals

Synchronization

For you to reproduce the picture on the home receiver exactly as you shoot it in the camera, the signal must contain a component that keeps the lines and frames in synchronization. The scan line in the receiver must start at precisely the same time as the picture is scanned in the camera, and a new frame must start exactly at the same time as the new frame started in the camera. This timing sequence is critical and involves very small fractions of time. Each National Television Standards Committee (NTSC) frame lasts $\frac{1}{30}$ of a second; each field lasts $\frac{1}{60}$ of a second; and a new line starts every 1/15,700 of a second in the 525 system (see Figure 2.5). In the many other scan and line rates systems, the rates are different, but all must match the receiver. A Phase Alternative Line (PAL British system) receiver or tape deck will not synchronize with an NTSC signal, or vice versa. The same is true of the French Sequential Color with Memory (SECAM) system. The three systems are not compatible. The question of synchronization has been made more complex with the Advanced TV Systems Committee (ATSC) offering 18 different combinations of scan rate and aspect ratios. (See the next section.)

ELECTRONIC SIGNAL OF TWO FIELDS

AS SEEN ON THE FACE OF A

WAVEFORM MONITOR (OSCILLOSCOPE)

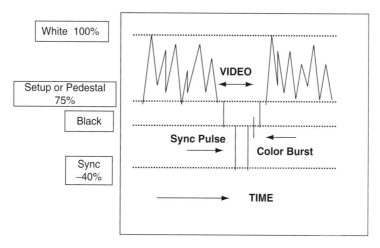

FIG. 2.5 – A video signal is made up of a series of pulses designed to keep the entire system synchronized and at proper levels for accurate reproduction.

The system you used to create a color image actually separates the light entering the camera into the three primary additive colors—red, green, and blue—by using filters and three camera sensors. That process created three signals: a red signal, a green signal, and a blue signal. These three signals were then combined into one signal, but each of the separate color components was placed out of phase so they could be separated later at the receiver. Out-of-phase signals are related signals on a common path that are shifted slightly in time so they may be kept separate in processing.

The color receiver has only one monitor or screen but three streams of electrons that strike the face of screen, which is coated with groupings of dots of the three colors. When the three separate signals from the camera are fed to the three separate guns in the monitor, the original color is reproduced by the relative brightness of the three different colors of dots. Tubeless monitors now are replacing cathode ray tubes (CRTs). Liquid crystal displays (LCDs), light emitting diodes (LEDs), and plasma display panels (PDPs) are manufactured in large sizes for monitors and receivers, and miniature units are manufactured for camera monitors.

Originally, color cameras and all color equipment were larger, bulkier, and much more expensive to manufacture and operate than existing black-and-white equipment. However, with the appearance of solid-state electronics, especially the chips that replaced camera tubes, and now with digital signal processing and recording, color equipment is smaller, higher in quality, less expensive, and easier to operate than the black-and-white equipment of 15 years ago.

One of the goals of developing an international high-definition television (HDTV) standard was to create a standard that all countries would follow, but that has not happened, partially because of different power line rates in each country. American power is on a 60-cycle system, whereas power in much of the rest of the world is on a variation of a 50-cycle system.

For this complex system to stay in synchronization, pulses are added between the fields and between the lines. These are called sync pulses, and they must be created either in the camera or in a sync generator. The sync pulses are part of the recorded signal, and the receiver or tape deck locks onto those pulses when the tape is played back or the signal is broadcast.

Scan Systems

The line-scanning system you use must match that of the receiver and operates in the same manner so that the picture can be duplicated exactly as you originally shot it in the camera. Knowledge about the scanning system is not crucial to video production except that you as the camera operator must be aware that the reproduction system is not based on complete coverage of the field. Instead, the reproduction system is based on a series of horizontal lines that make reproducing fine horizontal lines in a picture difficult. The scan system also limits the vertical resolution power of the video system.

Completely scanning the frame, called a raster, in the original National Television Standards Committee (NTSC) system requires 525 lines, 262.5 at a time, in a pattern called a *field*. The second 262.5 lines scanned are slightly offset from the first set in a pattern called *interlaced scanning*. The total scanning of the two 262.5-line fields is one 525-line frame that occurs once every $\frac{1}{30}$ of a second.

There now exist three international transmission digital systems: Terrestrial Integrated Digital Broadcasting (ISDB-T) developed in Japan; Digital Video Broadcast-TV (DVB-T) developed in Europe; and ATSC-DTV, developed in the United States. In addition the U.S. ATSC standard actually offers 18 different formats. The Federal Communications Commission (FCC) refused to set specific technical standards, leaving the industry to decide among the available formats. The FCC decreed that by June 12, 2009, all broadcasts in the United States will be in a digital format and all analog television transmitters will switch to digital or shut off (see Figure 2.6).

The line rate varies from 360 to 1080. The scan system may be NTSC interlace (that is, two fields making up one frame) or progressive scan that scans the entire frame from top to bottom. The frame rate may vary from 24 frames per second (fps) to 60 fps. In between, one can find 30, 29.94, 50, and 59.94 fps. The aspect ratio may be 4:3 (NTSC), or 16:9 (digital wide screen). Each person involved in the production process needs to be aware of which system the producer expects in order to release the production. The signals can be converted, but the highest quality and fewest problems occur when the team agrees on the standard before the first frame is shot.

DIGITAL VIDEO STANDARDS

INTERNATIONAL STANDARDS

SYSTEM/ COUNTRY	FRAME RATE	ASPECT RATIO	SCAN LINES	SCANNING
ISDB-T JAPAN	30, 60 fps	4:3, 16:9	480, 720, 1080	Progressive/ Interlace
DVB-T Europe	24, 30, 50 fps	4:3, 16:9, 9:4	480, 576, 720, 1080, 1152	Progressive/ Interlace
ATSC-DT No. Amer.	24, 39, 60 fps	4:3, 16:9	480, 720, 1080	Progressive/ Interlace

US ADVANCED TELEVISION SYSTEMS COMMITTEE (ATSC) DTV FORMATs

FORMAT	SCAN LINES	ASPECT RATIO	FRAME RATE	US ADAPTER
HDTV	1080	16:9	24P, 30P, 60I	CBS & NBC (60I)
HDTV	720	16:9	24P, 30P, 60P	ABC (30P)
SDTV	480	16:9 or 4:3	24P, 30P, 60P, 60I	Fox (30P)
SDTV	480	4:3	24P. 30P. 60P. 60I	None
LDTV	480	4:30	60I	None

DIGITAL MEASUREMENTS

1 Bit = 1/8 Byte
1 Byte = 1/1000 Kilobyte (KB)
1 KB = 1/1000 Megabyte (MB)
1 MB = 1/1000 Gigabyte (GB)

Pixel = smallest element of a picture
1 Video frame = 640 horizontal pixels x 480 vertical pixels = 307,2000 pixels
1 Color video frame = 307,200 pixels x 24 bits of color = 7,372,800 bits of 921 KB
1 Second of video = 30 frames = 28 MB of memory
1 Minute of video = 1680 MB of 1.68 GB of memory
60 Minutes of video = 100 GB of memory
Most consumer computer hard drives are limite to 1 GB or less of memory
Professional nonlinear editing systems require increased amounts of memory and use some form of compression to reduce the amount of memory required for processing and editing.

FIG. 2.6 – The FCC-recommended standards include 18 different combinations of line rates, frame rates, and aspect ratios.

Synchronization

Measuring Video Signals

To determine exactly how the camera is reacting to the light reflected from the sub-ject, you need a precise means of looking at the electronic signal. The equivalent of an audio VU meter, a test instrument called an *oscilloscope* or *waveform monitor*, is used to monitor a black-and-white video signal. It converts the electronic signal into a visual equivalent that is calibrated for precise measurement. Your scope can be set to look at one or two lines or at one or two fields at a time.

This electronic picture shows the sync pulses, their amplitude, their width, and their position in relation to other parts of the signal. It also shows the strength or level of the signal to indicate if the signal is too high (too much video amplifier gain or too much light coming into the lens) or too low (too little gain or not enough light). It also shows the relationship between the two major components of the signal: *gain* (white level) and setup (black level), sometimes called *pedestal*. You must keep these two signals in the proper relative strength to each other to provide an acceptable picture (see Figure 2.7).

In most newer cameras, the white level and black level are set automatically but may need to be adjusted periodically by a technician. The iris setting in the lens also con-trols white level. You only need to read and understand an oscilloscope during a multiple-camera shoot and in the editing room.

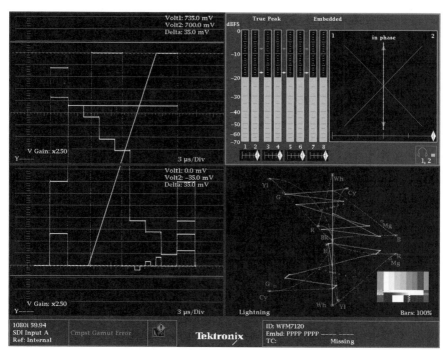

FIG. 2.7 – Oscilloscopes and vectorscopes are the two primary tools used to measure analog video signals. (Courtesy Tektronix.)

The second type of video-signal monitor is a *vectorscope*. It shows the relationship of the three color signals: red, green, and blue. These three signals are deliberately set out of phase with each other—that is, each of the three start at slightly different times (in fractions of microseconds). This out-of-phase condition is critical in converting the three black-and-white signals into one acceptable color signal. To make that adjustment, it is necessary to read a vectorscope, which visually displays the phase relationships of the three signals. Once again, this is an internal adjustment in most field cameras. Digital video signals are much more complex and require complex testing equipment and oscilloscopes, beyond the scope of this text.

Video Compression

The compression of digital video is the same as for digital audio, except that much higher ratios are necessary to handle the greater quantity of recorded material. Your original analog video signal is sampled and quantized, requiring up to 300 MB per second of recorded program, as compared with less than 100 K per second for digital audio. Higher tape speeds or compression of the signal before recording allows you to record sufficient video without consuming an impractical amount of tape stock.

The compression process removes redundant or repeated portions of the picture, such as the blue sky or white clouds. As long as there is no change in the hue, saturation, or luminance value, the digital program will "remember" the removed portions, and then it will decompress and restore them when the tape is played back. This process saves space on the tape, disc, or chip, depending on the recording method. Compression allows you to record a reasonable amount of programming material, but the price is a slight degradation of picture quality. If you compare the quality of a signal carried on an HDTV broadcast at a low compression ratio to the same signal on a cell telephone that must be highly compressed, the quality difference is obvious (see Figure 2.8).

You should be aware of two basic systems now in use: JPEG, developed by the Joint Photographic Experts Group and originally intended for compression of still images, and MPEG, developed by the Moving Picture Experts Group and intended for compression of moving images. Each system offers you advantages and disadvantages, and the possibility exists that new and better systems will be developed. Currently there are three MPEG systems: MPEG-1, MPEG-2, and MPEG-4. MPEG-4 originally was written for interactive media intended for consumer use, but later developments have made the system applicable to HDTV and other high-quality and bandwidth-demanding formats. Individual companies have developed additional MPEG standards for their own equipment, as technology continues to advance and develop.

VIDEO COMPRESSION STANDARDS

LABEL	FUNCTION	ORIGINATING ORGANIZATION
H.261 or P64	Compressed video over telephone wires	Int'l Tele/Tele Consultative Commission
H.264	Compressed Internet video	Int'l Tele/Tele Consultative Commission
JPEG	Compressed still images	Joint Photo Experts Group & ISO
Motion-JPEG	Edited moving video	Joint Photo Experts Group & ISO
MPEG-1	Compressed moving images-CD video	Moving Picture Experts Group & ISO
MPEG-2	Compressed moving images-DVD video	Moving Picture Experts Group & ISO
MPEG-3	Compressed audio for MP3 files	Moving Picture Experts Group & ISO
MPEG-4	Compressed Internet video	Moving Picture Experts Group & ISO

FIG. 2.8 – To record and manipulate high-frequency video signals within a digital format, some method of compressing the signals needed to be developed to avoid the need for tremendous amounts of computer memory. Two basic systems and variations on those systems have been established, JPEG and MPEG. Researchers constantly work at developing newer systems that require less memory yet maintain the highest quality possible.

Measuring Video Signals

Chapter Three
The Equipment

Equipment Development

The equipment presently used in single-camera video production has a relatively short history. In the early 1960s, a method of editing 2-inch *quadraplex* videotape was developed. It occurred to directors and journalists that some types of productions could be shot on one camera, recorded on videotape, even out of sequence, and then edited into a form suitable for airing. By 1969, amateur videotaping became possible with the invention and sale of a Sony black-and-white handheld camera combined with an open-reel $^1/_2$-inch videotape recorder.

In the mid-1970s, editing systems for both formats were developed, but the 2-inch format was difficult to edit, even with a computer controller, because it could not be still-framed for the precise location of edit points, and at that time the quality of $^1/_2$-inch tape was below the technical level for broadcasting, warranting the further development of editing systems.

The original small video field cameras were developed for broadcast news operations to replace the 16-mm film equipment used by most stations and networks. News operations wanted small, lightweight equipment that could deliver broadcast-quality picture and sound instantaneously. Because such a system would be entirely electronic, the picture and sound also could be transmitted over microwave or satellite links for live coverage. The equipment was bulky and heavy compared to film equipment, but it provided the live picture required by news (see Figure 3.1).

The development during the 1990s of smaller cameras using charge-coupled device (CCD) or complementary metal oxide semiconductor (CMOS) chips feeding $^1/_2$-inch high-quality digital videotape decks or recording directly onto computer memory, memory cards, or computer discs has moved the art and science of field recording to a new level of high quality and lower cost. Editing these new signals can now be accomplished with laptop and desktop nonlinear editors, providing shorter turnaround time between shooting and a completed news clip or making much more creative work possible on nonlinear editing equipment.

1970s "Creepie-Peepie" 2000s Camcorder

Field Cameras

Flatbed Film NLE Video

Visual Editing

FIG. 3.1 – Equipment designed for electronic field production (EFP) and electronic news gathering (ENG) together make up the field of single camera video production. Over the years, field equipment is smaller, lighter, of a higher quality, and HDTV capable. Visual editing moved from physically cutting to computer-based editing. (Courtesy JVC, Advanced Broadcast Solutions, and Grass Valley.)

Equipment Development

Cameras

When you first decide on which camera to use for your project, you are faced with five choices: standard-definition (SD) or high-definition (HD), either 4:3 or 16:9 frame ratio, interlace or progressive scan system, the frame resolution at 480, 720, or 1080 lines, and the type of camera.

Within each of these categories you will find a variation in terms of image quality and a distinction between handheld, professional, broadcast, and digital cinema cameras. Recorded images must be of high quality to be edited and duplicated for broadcast, and this usually requires more sophisticated and expensive equipment. Most modern cameras are capable of creating both 4:3 and 16:9 pictures with a flip of a switch. Because most of the circuits within the camera and camera control units now are digital, varying between SD and HD signals is easily accomplished. You may make a choice between frame and line rates also at a touch of a button, but you must make the choice carefully and be fully aware of the consequences.

You must match the image quality of a video camera with the format and quality of the recording media being used. It is as pointless to use an expensive three-chip studio camera to make a miniDV original videotape recording as it is to use a high-end digital recording system with an inexpensive single-chip consumer video camera (see Figure 3.2).

Camera Types

The proliferation of different SD, HD, and digital cinema recording formats makes any neat, clear, and simple classification of digital video cameras into mutually exclusive categories difficult. Today's digital cameras come in a wide range of quality and price categories, from acceptable SD cameras to the highest quality and expensive digital cinema cameras.

Within this range or continuum, you may separate cameras into four basic types by their recording systems: (1) HDV camcorders; (2) DV (including SD or DVSP, DVC Pro, and DVCAM) camcorders; (3) HD cameras (including HDCAM SR, DVC Pro HD, XDCam, and other full HD formats as well as broadcast HD); and (4) digital cinema cameras. Each category is vaguely separated by price, quality, and purpose. But there are no hard and fast divisions between camera types.

CAMERA TYPES

TYPE	DV	HDV	HD	BROADCAST	DIGITAL CINEMA
SENSOR	3-¼' -/13"	3-1/3"	3-1/2"	3-2/3"	2/3" TO 35MM
COST	LOW	LOW TO MEDIUM	MEDIUM TO HIGH	HIGH	EXPENSIVE
PURPOSE	CONSUMER TO SEMI-PROFESSIONAL	LOW TO MID-LEVEL PROFESSIONAL	MID TO HIGH-LEVEL PROFESSIONAL	HEAVY USE BROADCAST-FIELD/STUDIO	LONG FORM DRAMATIC PRODUCTIONS
RECORD MEDIUM	miniDV	miniDV or MEMORY MEDIA	P2, SxS, SD CARDS	P2, SxS, SD CARDS, EXTERNAL FEEDS	RAW DIGITAL, HARD DRIVE, EXTERNAL FEED
ASPECT/ LINES	4:3, some 16:9 720p	4:3, 16:9 720p, 1080p	4:3, 16:9 720p, 1080i and p	4:3, 16:9 720p, 1080i and p	16:9 all line rates
FOCAL LENGTH	3:1, 5:1	5:1	5:1-10:1	10:1-100:1	Fixed FL or 10:1

FIG. 3.2 – The characteristics of the various types of cameras cover a wide range of technical specifications and output quality.

Cameras

Handheld Cameras

Small, handheld single- and multiple-sensor cameras designed primarily for home and semiprofessional applications use $^1/_6$-inch to $^1/_2$-inch chips offering a 480 to 720 resolution and highly compressed SD signal, usually with interlaced rather than progressive scanning. These cameras generally are designed for you to record on miniDV tape, flash media, or DVD-R disc. You may easily operate the cameras in a basic point-and-shoot mode with almost all functions—focus, aperture, exposure rates—automatically set. They are designed for you to shoot quick, low-cost, fundamentally sound, but not the highest quality signal output (see Figure 3.3).

As the size of digital cameras decreased, it became apparent that a camera could be designed that you can hold it in one hand, much as a still camera is held. Such cameras have been designed primarily for the consumer market, but the quality of the output, especially if the camera uses three chips, makes the miniature camcorder useful for news, television sales, streaming, and some professional productions. They come equipped with lenses that zoom in a range from 10:1 to 20:1. Some models are designed to output directly to the Internet for video streaming.

FIG. 3.3 – A basic HDV camcorder may be as small as a consumer point-and-shoot or larger, with more professional controls and accessories. (Courtesy of Sony.)

HDV Professional Camera

The next most common digital cameras now available to the public and professionals are HDV cameras. HDV offers a compressed high-definition format as an inexpensive means of producing HD programs. The convenience and low cost of using standard miniDV tapes that are similar to or the same as those used in SD recordings will make HDV attractive to you as a low-budget producer. HDV cameras rely on greater flexibility in operation, higher quality of signal output, and a wider choice for you to determine how you want the camera to operate in frame rate, aperture, focus, and either progressive or interlaced scanning as well as choosing 720 or 1080 resolution in interlaced scan or progressive scan mode.

Sensors range from $\frac{1}{4}$ inch to $\frac{1}{2}$ inch and are either single with built-in color filters direct to lens or triple using a prism. Your output may be either SD or HD at any of the rates required for that particular production. Built-in storage may be a miniDV, a built-in or removable hard drive, an optical disc recorder, or any of several flash drives such as secure digital (SD), Personal Computer Memory Card International Association (PCMIA) P2, SxS, GFCam, or a compact memory flash card (see Figure 3.4).

Cameras

You may use these cameras in the field as a documentary maker, independent feature producer, news videographer, or freelancer working in industry or education. As digital circuits assume responsibility for many previous manual functions, as the size decreases, as battery life increases, and as flexibility of operation increases, the field camera takes on a new, higher level of creativity for you, the operator, and director. The increase in resolution and contrast range in field cameras moves them from handy production tools to truly high-quality creative tools. The smaller size and weight allows the camera to be held on a body mount, on the shoulder, or on any number of portable camera mounts. Increased battery life permits longer shooting sessions without the need to change batteries and also allows for the use of portable lighting fixtures powered by the camera battery.

FIG. 3.4 – HDV cameras usually use built-in miniDV tape decks or flash media. The optics are superior to basic HDV cameras but not as expensive or flexible as those used on DV or broadcast cameras. (Courtesy of JVC.)

Broadcast Camera

HD field cameras are designed for you to shoot HD sports, high-level documentaries, high- and low-budget television dramas, and live event coverage. Many of the technical specifications of HD cameras are similar but considerably higher than they are for HDV cameras. Special zoom lenses with long ranges of up to 100:1 are needed for some sporting events and live coverage (see Figure 3.5). Such cameras are capable of delivering high-quality signals that are superior to the highly compressed HD signals of HDV cameras, only they have greater flexibility to increase the quality level by taking advantage of higher-level technical specifications.

FIG. 3.5 – Broadcast camcorders record directly onto a built-in hard drive, removable disk drive, or large memory flash cards and may be equipped with long-range zoom lenses for sporting events. Broadcast news cameras must be small, lightweight, and offer as many flexible characteristics as possible. (Courtesy of Ikegami.)

Cameras

Digital Cinema Camera

Digital cinema (DC) cameras fall in the multipurpose category because you may use them both in the studio and in the field. But are designed specifically to produce the highest quality signal for conversion to motion picture film or projection as a digital signal on a large theater screen. DC cameras use much larger CCD/CMOS chips, from $^2/_3$ inch to 65-mm format, to create a data stream instead of a video/audio signal, or you may operate them totally in an uncompressed or minimally compressed mode. DC cameras generally are not camcorders, because they are designed to feed a large high-quality tape deck, a hard drive system, or a server rather than a portable media recording system (see Figure 3.6).

FIG. 3.6 – Cameras may now be equipped with all of the production accessories used in motion picture camera production. They are called (DC) digital cinematography cameras. (Courtesy of Panasonic.)

Specialized Digital Cameras

You may use microcameras, also called subminiature cameras, for security, law enforcement, surveillance, and special shots used to cover sports, documentaries, and dramas where you want to get shots from hard-to-reach or nearly impossible positions. Such cameras are small enough for you to mount them on helmets, on race-cars, on skiers, and on athletes who participate in other fast-moving sports. A micro-camera has no viewfinder, all automatic operations, and a remote-controlled zoom lens or a single fixed focal length lens (see Figure 3.7). Despite their small size (as small as 2 inches by 2 inches by 2 inches, plus a lens not much larger), these digital cameras create a reasonably acceptable output for professional productions. Few come equipped with attached recording media; instead, you must hardwire or connect the camera wirelessly to a recorder at a safe, secure location, or a small transmitter may be attached to the camera that is similar to a wireless mic transmitter.

FIG. 3.7 – Miniature HD cameras may be as small as 2 inches by 2 inches, but they still create a full HD color picture. Their small size allows them to be used in places a regular-sized camera would not fit or would be too dangerous or inconvenient to place. (Courtesy of IconixVideo.)

Cameras

Image Sources and Optics

Tubes

Until the late 1980s, all practical video cameras used an electronic tube to convert light to an electronic signal. Even though the quality and size of the smaller tube cameras made them applicable to both news operations and consumer use, the fact that they used tubes as light conversion transducers presented problems. The critical problem was their low level of light sensitivity compared to film, their sensitivity to burn and lag imaging, and the tendency to lose registration between tubes (see Figure 3.8).

Chips

In 1980s, the first video camera was produced that contained no tubes. The light conversion tubes were replaced with all-electronic charge-coupled devices (CCD). CCDs (also known as chips) are flat pieces of selenium and other light-sensitive metal crystal pixels. CMOS chips were developed shortly after. Instead of using a beam of electrons to scan the chip, the new technology uses a chip that is electronically read as light falling across its surface changes voltages. These changes become the electronic equivalent of the picture at the same frame and line rate as a picture tube. In addition, you can expose the signal from a chip at a variety of frame rates and equivalent shutter speeds to produce slow- or fast-motion video, depending on the design of the camera.

FIG. 3.8 – The evolution of the camera signal light source from tubes to chips was key to the ability of designers to create smaller, lighter, and more efficient cameras.

All chips require a very small amount of power and, because they are a flat piece of metal, they may be mounted directly to the surface of the light-splitting prisms inside the camera. This avoids any changes in registration between the chips, thus making the camera more rugged. Because the chips are solid-state components just like transistors, they last as long as any other component in the camera.

Today's chips vary in size from $^1/_3$ inch to 65 mm. The quality of the signal produced by the better chips intended for digital cinema (DC) approach that of 35-mm film for commercial and feature-length motion picture production.

Optics

For your camera to operate, it must be able to concentrate light reflected from the surface of subjects to the light-sensitive sensor. In today's cameras, this function is provided by the *lens*, a series of optical glass or plastic elements cemented together and mounted in such a way as to focus light on the surface of the light-conversion chips.

The lens is mounted permanently on the front of a consumer-quality camera. In equipment used at the professional level, interchangeable lenses may be employed. The three basic characteristics of a lens are its focal length, its focus range, and its aperture settings.

Image Sources and Optics

Focal Length

The *focal length* of a lens is a measurement of the ratio between the diameter of the lens and the distance from its optical center to the focal plane (the location of the chip faces), usually given in millimeters. The important factor to remember about focal length is that the longer the measurement, the greater the enlargement of your subject; the shorter the measurement, the smaller your subject will appear. Conversely, the longer focal length allows space for fewer subjects in your frame, and the shorter focal length allows more subjects to be included in your frame (see Figure 3.9).

In addition, the longer the focal length, the more compressed the distance appears going away from the camera (called the *Z axis*). Also, movement in front of the camera (the *X axis*) appears to be accelerated. The apparent distances on the Z axis using a short-focal-length lens appear to be increased, and movement on the X axis appears to be slowed down. The focal length of a lens also determines its ability to focus over a range from close to farther away from the camera, called *depth of field*. Other characteristics of lenses determined by the focal length are explained later in this section.

Long Focal Length   Short Focal Length

FIG. 3.9 – A long-focal-length shot (on the left) enlarges the subject and compresses the appearance of distance on the Z axis. A short-focal-length shot (on the right) decreases the size of the subject and increases the appearance of distance on the Z axis.

Focus

The ability of the lens to concentrate light reflected from a subject to create the sharpest image is called *focus*. Focus is a relative term, because a lens is in focus on an image when that image appears to you as sharply and clearly as possible on the surface of the chips. You may focus an image in two separate parts of the optic system: front focus and back focus, both of which must be accurately set in order to achieve that sharp image.

The most obvious way is called the *front focus*. You achieve front focus by adjusting (usually by turning the barrel of the lens) until the image is sharply focused at a point behind the lens called the *focal point*. The second way to focus is the *back focus*. Back focus involves adjusting either the lens body or the pickup surface until an image located an infinite distance from the camera is in focus on the surface of the chips. The back focus is a technician's adjustment and should not have to be readjusted unless the camera or lens is jarred or bumped out of adjustment.

Focusing your zoom lens is more complex than focusing a prime or fixed-focal-length lens. The lens must be zoomed to its maximum focal length, framed and focused on the intended subject, and then zoomed back to the desired framing. All subjects located the same distance from the camera as the original subject will be in focus. Shooting any subject closer or farther away from the camera requires resetting the focus.

Image Sources and Optics

Aperture

The third basic characteristic of your lens is its *aperture* or *iris* setting. To better control the amount of light that strikes the surface of the chips, an *iris* or variable opening is built into the lens. In the early days of photography, a numbering system was developed that is still in use today—not only in photography, but also in cinematography and videography (see Figure 3.10).

The carefully calibrated sizes of the opening in the aperture are labeled with numbers called *f-stops*. Although the numbering system may seem strange to you, each full f-stop doubles (if opening) or halves (if closing) the amount of light allowed to pass through the lens. The f-stop number is the ratio of the focal length to the diameter of the aperture opening. The common full f-stops used in videography are f 1.4, 2, 2.8, 4, 5.6, 8, 11, 16, and 22. One of the confusing aspects of f-stops is that as the number increases in size, the aperture opening decreases, allowing less light to pass through the lens. The converse is also true: the smaller the f-stop, the more light that passes through the lens. In addition, the term *stop down* means to close the aperture or increase the f-stop number; to *open up* means to increase the size of the aperture opening but lower the f-stop number. An easy way for you to remember the change is to think of f-stops as fractions: 1/22 is smaller than 1/1.4.

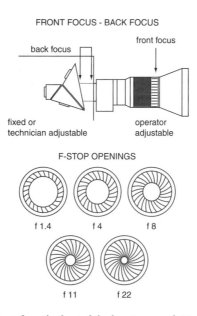

FIG. 3.10 – A lens cannot focus from the front of the lens to any point to infinity. Instead a range of distances that subjects are placed in front of a lens will allow a shot to be as clearly defined as possible—in focus. The amount of the light that strikes the chips must be controlled precisely using a numbering system called f-stops.

Depth of Field

A fourth characteristic of lenses, *depth of field* (DOF), is dependent on the three characteristics already described: focus, focal length, and aperture. Depth of field is the range from the camera that subjects appear in acceptable focus. This distance depends on the focal length of the lens, its focus setting, and the aperture opening. The longer the focal length, the closer the focus point; the more wide open the aperture setting, the shallower the depth of field. The converse is also true (see Figure 3.11).

Depth of field is critical when you try to focus on close-ups; on rapidly moving subjects, such as in sports; and when light levels are limited. You also may use DOF creatively to exclude some subjects by placing them out of focus but within the frame.

Deep Depth of Field   Shallow Depth of Field

FIG. 3.11 – Increased depth of field allows subjects to spread out closer and farther away from the camera to remain in focus (on left), and it allows the camera operator flexibility when covering action sports and news. Shallow depth of field (on right) concentrates the audience's attention to specific parts of the frame or specific subjects.

Image Sources and Optics

Viewfinder and Camera Controls

Viewfinder

For you to see subjects you have included in your picture frame, you need an accurate viewfinder designed to accompany the camera. The viewfinder is usually mounted to the camera body so that the camera may be either handheld or tripod mounted.

A viewfinder is simply a small video monitor with an attached eyepiece to protect your eye while viewing; it is similar to a home television receiver except that it is wired directly into the camera and does not contain radio frequency (RF) circuits to take signals from the air. Most cameras have small signal lights mounted inside the view-finder hood so that you can monitor the operational characteristics of the camera without taking your eye from the viewfinder. Signal lights may tell you if the light level is too low, if the tape is about to run out, or if the battery is running low. In addition, an indicator shows when you have achieved white balance during the white-balance action (see Figure 3.12).

Most viewfinders are mounted on the left side of your camera, making it difficult if you use your left eye to operate the camera. If you wear eyeglasses, you also may experience difficulties looking into the viewfinder. Some viewfinders on professional cameras can be rotated to the right side of the camera for operators who wish to use their left eye for viewing. Many viewfinders can be rotated into positions that are more comfortable for you if the camera is held under the arm or over the head. Most digital cameras include a flat screen viewfinder that swings out from the side of the camera, usually the left side, again designed so you may view your subject with either the right eye or both eyes.

The majority of viewfinders include contrast and brightness controls for adjusting the monitor in the viewfinder. You must not adjust these controls except when the camera is either focused on a well-lit test pattern or is generating an internal test pattern called *color bars*. If you attempt adjustments while shooting anything other than a test pattern, the viewfinder may be incorrectly adjusted in an attempt to compensate for a poorly lit subject. Most viewfinders provide only a black-and-white image for more accurate focusing, but the newer flat screen monitors are color monitors. Digital cameras provide a series of menus visible in the viewfinder or as a separate screen mounted on the side of the camera, enabling you to set camera and lens controls.

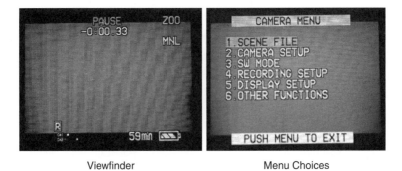

Viewfinder   Menu Choices

FIG. 3.12 – Depending on the camera manufacturer and model indicator lights viewed inside, a viewfinder may indicate if the tally light is on, if the light is too low to operate, battery level, audio level, and length of recording time. A menu may give the operator a choice of auto or manual iris, white balance, shutter speed, frame rate, aspect ratio, gamma settings, and other technical controls.

Viewfinder and Camera Controls

Camera Controls

You will find that each brand and model of camera and recorder may have different controls and, more than likely, different labels for the same controls. The description in this section uses the usual labels for the most common controls on digital cameras. The same controls described here, plus others specific to a particular model of camera, may be accessible through the menus. Always consult your operation manual before attempting to operate any piece of equipment as complex as a video camera.

Bars/Gain Selector

The first control you set is the *bars/gain selector*. Generally, the two functions are combined on one control, but on rare occasions they are separated. When the selector is set to "bars," color test bars appear in the viewfinder that originate internally in the camera. This test signal is necessary for you to set the controls on the monitor accurately. In addition, you should always record the bars for 30 seconds to 1 minute at the head of each tape, disc, and solid-state recording at the start of each shooting session. This signal will be invaluable later for troubleshooting if there are problems with either the camera or recording. The gain selector, which also may be labeled "sensitivity," provides a variety of increases in video gain in case you find light levels are too low for shooting at the normal gain position. The switch usually is marked with several steps: 6 dB, 9 dB, 18 dB, and so on. Each of these steps provides you with the equivalent of one more f-stop of amplification. The price paid for the use of this control is that video noise increases as higher gain is used. Video noise appears to your eye as a "crawling" on the surface of the picture (see Figure 3.13).

Color Temperature Control/Filter Selector

A color temperature control designed to change the filters placed between the lens and the pickup chips may be labeled "filter selector." It is a wheel that holds a variety of filters. You can access the color temperature control from the side or the front of the camera. Turn this wheel to select a particular filter or no filter. The no-filter position is intended for use indoors under incandescent lighting. For outdoor shooting, the filter you use is either an 85 (yellow), maybe labeled as a 5,600 K or 85 + ND (neutral density) filter designed to add the yellow that is missing from the blue daylight. The ND filter added to the 85 compensates for bright sunlight, which might provide too much light for the video camera. In addition to those two positions, you may have several other choices of different intensities of ND filters. There also may be an 80 (blue), maybe labeled 3,200 K for interior tungsten correction, or an FL-M filter (magenta) to help compensate for fluorescent lighting. You may find additional camera controls through menus visible either in the viewfinder or on a panel on the side of the camera.

Side Panels & Controls

FIG. 3.13 – The location of specific controls situated on the sides of cameras will vary depending on the model and brand of the camera. Check your operator's manual before working with any video equipment. (Courtesy Panasonic.)

Viewfinder and Camera Controls

White Balance

Once you have chosen the proper color temperature filter to match the lighting under which the shoot is to take place, you must white balance the camera. Focus the camera on a pure white source, generally a card or the back of a clean T-shirt, and then hold down the white balance or auto-white button for several seconds. Many cameras include a built-in automatic white balance that does not need setting except under extreme lighting conditions (see Figure 3.14).

On better cameras, the following controls will be found:

- You may use a *power selector switch* to indicate whether the camera has a battery mounted on it, is powered with its own separate AC power supply, or derives its power from the recorder's power supply or battery.

- A *record start switch* may be mounted on the camera body, but more than likely it is mounted on the lens handgrip close to the thumb for easy use. This switch allows you to start and stop the recording with your thumb without leaving the camera or taking your eye from the viewfinder.

The following controls are usually located on the lens or lens mount:

- The *iris mode* control allows you to choose between setting the iris manually or letting the camera's automatic iris circuits set the iris.

- The *iris inst. control* is designed so that you can zoom in on the surface that is reflecting the average amount of light for that scene, such as the face of the subject. Press the iris inst. control, which locks the iris at that setting, and then zoom back or pan to whatever framing is needed or to the beginning of that scene.

- The *zoom mode control* allows you the same option for the zoom lens. You can either zoom the lens manually or use the lens's motorized control to zoom the lens.

- The *zoom lens control* is usually a rocker switch that allows you to press one end to zoom in and the other end to zoom out. The harder you press, the faster the lens zooms. A gentle touch produces a slow, smooth zoom. On some cameras, an additional control allows you to set the speed range of the zoom control from very slow to very fast. One additional control may be mounted on either the lens or the camera body. The *return video control* is a button that, when pressed, feeds the picture being played back from the record deck into the viewfinder, allowing you, the videographer to observe the images already recorded.

Rear Panels & Controls

FIG. 3.14 – Most controls are located in logical positions so that the camera operator can manipulate them easily without taking his or her eye from the viewfinder during production. (Courtesy Panasonic.)

Viewfinder and Camera Controls

Camera Supports

One of the first visual characteristics separating novice and professional videographers is the stability of the picture. Although you may be able to handhold most cameras, some digital professional cameras are so small that a tripod seems redundant; a steady, controlled picture is essential for you to produce a quality video picture.

Tripods and Body Mounts

The standard method for you to support your video camera is on a *tripod,* also called sticks. A tripod has three legs that you may collapse and individually adjust in length to provide a solid, level support for the tripod head. The head of your tripod is designed to fasten to the tripod and allow you to move the camera back and forth on a horizontal plane, called a *pan*, and up and down, called a *tilt*. In addition, better tripod heads provide you a method for precisely leveling the head by viewing a leveling bubble built into the tripod. Most cameras are equipped with a plate that fastens to the bottom of the camera and allows you to easily snap the camera onto the top of the head or snap it off for easy removal (see Figure 3.15).

Depending on how expensive and how professional a piece of equipment you want on your tripod, you will find heads manufactured in a variety of designs. The critical factor in the design of heads is the method you use to provide enough back pressure or *drag* so that you can make smooth steady pans or tilts. The method for creating drag separates the amateur tripods from the professional tripods. The least expensive and most common heads for the consumer-model tripods are friction heads that develop drag by the friction of two metal-surfaced or fabric-surfaced plates rubbing against each other. It is difficult, if not impossible, for you to pan or tilt smoothly while recording with a friction head.

The next most expensive and higher quality head available to you develops its drag through a set of springs. In some designs with lighter weight cameras, this system works well. The most suitable and expensive is the fluid head. The movement of a thick fluid from one chamber to another creates drag in this type of head. This provides the basis for you to make the smoothest and most easily controlled pans and tilts.

Body mounts range from a simple shoulder hook and pistol grip to hold the camera to a complex gyroscope or spring-controlled full-body case that encloses your body. Such a mount allows you complete flexibility to walk, run, climb stairs, or turn in any direction without losing framing or disorienting the audience. As cameras became lighter and easier to handhold, the problem of developing methods and systems of accurately controlling the positioning and movement of the camera has brought about a variety of new and flexible mounts to fulfill the needs of whatever shot an operator is called upon to create.

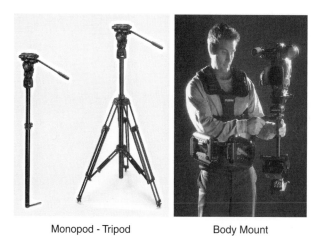

Monopod - Tripod   Body Mount

FIG. 3.15 – Camera mounts must perform two critical functions for the operator: provide a means for controlled, steady pans and tilts, and at the same time, if needed, give the operator the freedom to move the camera in space without being tied to the earth. (Courtesy Sachtler, GlideCam.)

Cranes, Dollies, and Pedestals

In the professional world, many other support systems are used for single-camera production. Some of them are *cranes, dollies, crab dollies,* and *pedestals.* Most of these systems are expensive, bulky, and physically large. However, they do contribute a wide variety of potential movements that the director in a production may use when needed. Some of the same camera movements may be created by exploiting simpler pieces of equipment such as a wheelchair or grocery cart (see Figure 3.16).

One way for you to move a camera while recording is to add wheels to the tripod, but this is not a stable or satisfactory method. You could sit in a van to shoot from a side or rear door as a means of getting movement into a sequence. It helps to let a little air out of the tires first. Handholding the camera in a moving vehicle—whether it is an automobile, airplane, helicopter, or boat—absorbs some of the shock and vibration, but the more you can isolate the camera from the movement of the vehicle, the better. You might try supporting the camera in a harness made of the heavy nylon or rubber bungee cords used by motorcyclists and truck drivers, which may provide a type of flexible but vibration-proof support.

It is possible for you to duplicate a 360-degree crane shot by placing the camera and tape deck on a slow-moving merry-go-round. A friendly electrician or telephone installer may allow you to ride in the bucket on the crane truck for a high-rising or lowering shot. A forklift with a platform large enough for a tripod and you produces a limited pedestal up or down shot. Even riding up or down in a glass-sided elevator can provide you with an opportunity to take a long vertical shot. You can use a low mount without tripod legs, called a *high hat,* to mount the head near the ground or on the hood of an automobile or boat. One method of duplicating this effect is to clamp the head to a heavy board, such as a short length of a 2-by-12. Then you either set the board on the ground or clamp it to the hood or deck. A safety rope is a necessity for this type of operation.

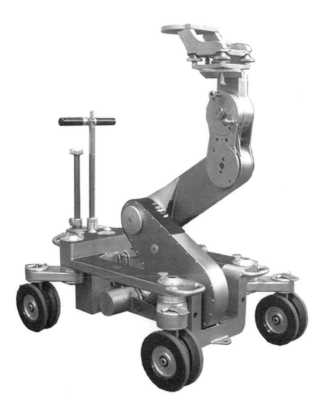

FIG. 3.16 – Dollies, cranes, and pedestals are manufactured in a variety of sizes and styles. (Courtesy Chapman).

Camera Supports

Handholding the Camera

You and amateur videographers may feel constrained by mounting the camera on a tripod or any other support. A much better production is possible with a stable support, but if you cannot or will not use a tripod, here are some helpful hints on handholding a camera.

You need to find a substitute for the third leg of the tripod. The first rule is to replace the tripod with your body, even though the body is only a bipod and a fairly unsteady one at that. By leaning against a third support to create a tripod, the unsteadiness of handholding can be minimized. Lean against a wall, a post, an automobile, a building, or any other stable support to steady yourself as a substitute for the third leg of the tripod.

Hold the camera firmly on your shoulder, with your elbows held tightly against your rib cage. For an even steadier platform than you can obtain from holding your camera on your shoulder, hold the camera under your right arm. This works only if the lower camera angle is proper for the shot, and it is only possible if the camera's viewfinder is swiveled up so that you can look down into it. An extended shoulder mount provides some stability (see Figure 3.17).

If you are attempting a "walking shot," remember that the professional body mounts are designed around springs and gyroscopes that keep the camera pointed in one direction and level at all times. You may partially duplicate this effect by using your body effectively. Hold the camera on your shoulder or under an arm, watch through the viewfinder, and move stiff-legged, swinging your body weight from one leg to the other. You must compensate the swinging motion by swinging the camera an equal amount in the opposite direction so that it is always pointed at the subject. If the shot is supposed to be the point of view (POV) of someone walking, then the slight weaving and bobbing is acceptable. If not, much practice will be necessary for you to make a smooth "dolly" while handholding the camera.

When panning with a handheld camera, place your feet in a comfortable position at the finish of the pan. Then twist your body into the starting position. This unwinding effect allows your body to relax as it approaches the end of the pan, instead of building tension and the shakes that go with such tension. This same technique works somewhat the same in a lengthy tilt. Position your body in a comfortable position at the end of the tilt, not at the beginning.

Remember, your body was never meant to handhold a camera, and only through much practice, some additional equipment, and physical conditioning can you reasonably achieve a satisfactory shot by handholding.

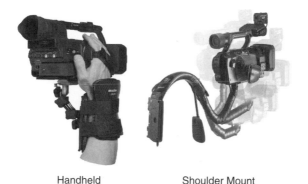

Handheld   Shoulder Mount

FIG. 3.17 – Handholding a camera is not only an art, but it requires a certain level of physical strength and body awareness. Breath control is critical when handholding a camera. Slow, steady breathing, rather than taking in large gulps of air, causes smaller changes in the position of the camera. (Courtesy WristShot and AntonBauer Stasis.)

Camera Supports

Digital Recording

Recording

The fourth segment of your camera body is the recording section. This may be a tape deck, a CD or DVD laser burner, a solid-state chip, various types of flash media, a variety of floppy discs, or a digital hard drive. Each of these drives may be either removable or permanently mounted within the body of your camera. The design of each camera is somewhat dependent on the recording medium, and this area of camera design is rapidly changing.

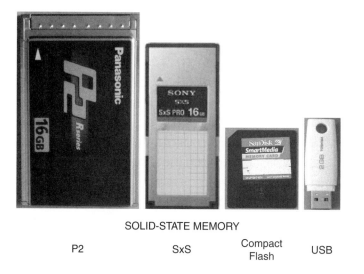

SOLID-STATE MEMORY

| P2 | SxS | Compact Flash | USB |

FIG. 3.18 – Many means of recording digital data may be used to record the output of a digital camera. The recorder may be built internally or an externally as a memory system using any of several different solid-state memory recording devices. (Courtesy Panasonic, Sony, SanDisk, and Toshiba.)

Digital Recording

Your digital recorder may record as a separate unit from the camera or attached to the camera, making a complete unit or camcorder. The function of the recorder is to store the digital pulses that represent the sound and picture created by your camera and microphone in the form of ones and zeros, rather than as a continuously varying stream of electrons. The storage for a digital signal is not that much different than storage for an analog signal, but in many ways it is a much simpler signal to record. Despite its simplicity, the digital signal must be recorded in such a manner that you may retrieve the digital impulses easily in as close to their original form as possible. Digital recorders, whether they are recording an audio or a video signal, produce checking and compensating signals designed to correct any errors that may inadvertently have been recorded.

The audio signal is fed either as a separate signal, or the signal is recorded with the video signal by embedding the audio within the video signal. The audio signal then becomes a segment of the video signal.

If your recorder is tape based, the tape is wrapped around a drum containing one or more video recording heads that rotate inside the drum in the opposite direction from that taken by the tape as it is moving around the drum. The video heads touch the tape just enough to record the video and audio signals in a series of segmented, slanted tracks across the tape. A digital tape in the pause mode shows you a single field of each frame.

If your recorder is disc based, the audio and video signals are recorded as impressions on the front or back side of the disc, depending on the individual system. The disc may be a standard DVD-R or CD-R, a Sony XDCAM optical disc, or a small 8-inch DVD-R disc. The signals must be encoded specifically for each type of disc.

If your camera records signals on solid-state flash media or specialized media such as Panasonic's P2 or Sony's 2x2, the cards must each be encoded for that particular media. The amount of programming allowed on each medium varies from a few minutes to hours, again depending on the specific medium (see Figure 3.18).

Hard drives are designed and operate the same as the hard drive on your computer, whether the drive is designed to be internal or external to the body of the camera.

Because a digital signal is more easily manipulated in both the editing and special effects operations, there may be a variety of built-in special effects in a digital camera that are not available on an analog camera. Some cameras allow editing dissolves and wipes within the camera, adding *pixilation* or other special effects while shooting. Most digital cameras are smaller, because the digital circuits are smaller and digital tape formats tend to be narrower, requiring smaller recorders.

Digital Recording

Recorder Operation

Today's digital recorders are relatively easy to operate because their controls parallel those of the universal audiocassette recorder. Once you insert the tape or disc correctly into the machine and you apply power, either from batteries or from an AC power adapter source, operations take place via the familiar functions of record, play, fast forward, rewind, and stop.

All decks contain some means of measuring the amount of programming that has been played or recorded. If you set the counter at zero when a new tape is loaded into the deck, it is possible to keep approximate track of where shots have been recorded on the cassette, thus enabling you or the editor to find that same shot at a later time. Professional and better consumer decks measure usage by reading time code (TC), a signal recorded on the media at the time of the original recording. TC indicates the amount of time in hours, minutes, seconds, and frames that has elapsed from the moment you zeroed it (see Figure 3.19).

Most recorders include a multipurpose meter and a switch that you can set to read the video level, audio level, or state of the battery charge. You can find a switch that allows manual or automatic gain control of the audio located near this meter. Several warning lamps may also be a part of the control panel of the deck. These indicate when the machine is recording or is paused, when the battery is running low, or when the stock is about to end. On more advanced machines, there may be lamps that indicate high humidity, lack of *servo lock*, or other malfunctions of your machine.

DVD and CD decks may offer additional controls: skip, program, repeat, or pause. Some DVD controls appear on screen, and you can access them by scrolling through menus and choosing an operation. Solid-state readers also provide indications of shot location, timing, TC, levels, and operational controls.

FIG. 3.19 – Although the simplest means of downloading digital signals from original recordings is directly to a computer, there are situations when a computer may not be available or when monitoring or logging without a computer is needed. In that case, a multiformat player/recorder may be used to play back any format for monitoring or for dubbing one format to another without losing quality in the signal. (Courtesy Panasonic.)

Digital Recording

Connecting Equipment

Before you consider connecting equipment, you need to understand the somewhat confusing world of cables and connectors. Unless a cable is permanently wired into a piece of equipment—such as a microphone, recorder, camera, monitor, or power source—the specific type of cable and specific cable connectors must be assembled and properly connected. The connector at either end of a cable is called a *plug*; the connector mounted on the wall or on the side of a piece of equipment is called a *jack*. There are both female and male plugs and jacks, and it takes one of each to make a connection. The contacts on a female plug are contained within the plug; the contacts project out of the male plug. There are four major types of plugs/jacks: power, audio, video, and specialized digital connectors.

Connecting Equipment

Cable Coiling

Before handling the cables with plugs on each end, you need to learn to coil a cable professionally after it is used. The professional method prevents damage to both the cable and the plugs on each end and provides an efficient means of quickly gathering a cable for proper storage and moving (see Figure 3.20).

Place one plug in your right hand with the cable strung out on the floor ahead of you. Slide your left hand down the cable for about 15 inches (depending on how large the loop in the coil will be), grasp that point on the cable, lift it, and lay the cable across your open right hand, handholding the plug and creating a loop that hangs straight without any snags or twists. Then slide your left hand down the cable, grasp the next section of cable and as you bring the length of cable up, and twist it so that the loop now runs in the opposite direction. Alternate creating what are called over and under loops. If you follow these directions properly, you will end up with cable coiled in a solid set of loops that when opened for the next use will lay out without kinks, twists, or tangles.

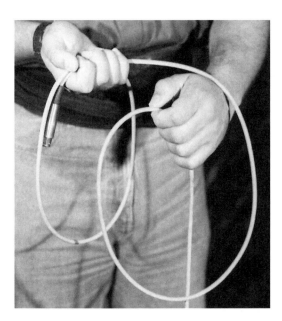

FIG. 3.20 – Professionally coiling a cable seems to be confusing and difficult, but once mastered flows easily and quickly. Just remember to alternate the coils of cable in the loops held in your hand. The size of the loops depends on the weight of the cable. Heavy power cables need larger loops; lighter audio cables need smaller loops.

Power Connectors and Plugs

Power connectors for your equipment carry either 110/220-volt AC or 12-volt DC power. Connectors for AC power are the same as the connectors on home appliances and are mounted on the walls of homes and offices. It is important for you to maintain polarity and proper grounding on all cables and plugs. Connect DC power using either *DIN* (a German connector), a special multipin *XLR* connector, or, for most digital equipment, a special microplug used only for 6-, 9-, 12-, or 15-volt DC. Each piece of equipment may require its own specific microplug, so check to make certain the correct voltage is applied to the equipment (see Figure 3.21).

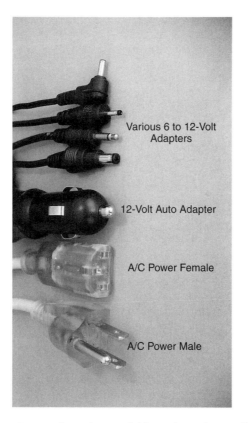

Various 6 to 12-Volt Adapters

12-Volt Auto Adapter

A/C Power Female

A/C Power Male

Connecting Equipment

FIG. 3.21 – **Power connectors vary from micro or mini low-voltage plugs, to DIN, BNC, or standard 110-volt or 220-volt connectors.**

Audio Connectors

As with video cables and connectors, you will find no universal standard for audio connectors. Some differences exist because of the origins of the equipment, the level of production professionalism, and the physical size of the equipment.

Professional microphone audio connectors are called XLRs. XLRs have a clip on the female plug or jack that either locks the plug to the jack or locks two plugs together. You must release the clip in order to separate the plug from the jack. XLRs are the best audio connectors to use because they cannot be unplugged accidentally and they contain three conductors, in addition to a shield for the best audio transmission.

Many manufacturers use a *miniplug* (sometimes called a $^1/_8$*-inch phone plug*) or an *RCA plug* (sometimes called a *phono plug*). You may use both of these connectors for microphone and high-level audio connectors, but they can be easily mistaken for each other. However, they are not compatible, and damage can occur if you force an RCA plug into a minijack or vice versa. You can easily accidentally disconnect either of these plugs, mini or RCA, because they are held in place only by friction (see Figure 3.22).

You will discover that some professional equipment utilizes RCA (phono) plugs for line-level input and output audio connectors. This implies that the cable is a single conductor with a shield and is designed to operate with an unbalanced circuit. With line-level signals, the higher signal is less affected by outside signals. You may find that an unbalanced line may pick up FM signals from nearby radio transmitters and noise generated by any equipment operating in either the audio or radio frequency (RF) ranges. You should not use an unbalanced mic line longer than 5 to 10 feet to minimize picking up such noise and interfering signals. Some other audio circuits, such as headphones, may use a miniplug as a connector.

An older audio plug is the $^1/_4$-*inch* (sometimes called *phone*) plug, probably because the early telephone companies commonly used it. Because it is easy to confuse the terms *phono* and *phone,* it is preferable to differentiate audio plugs by the alternate terms listed previously.

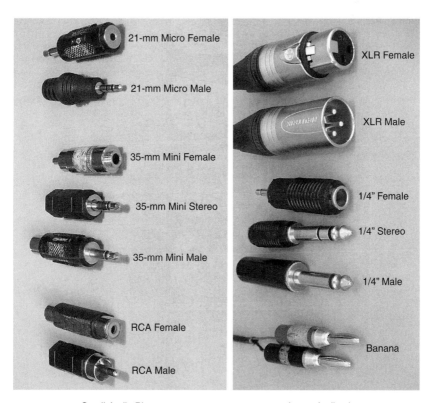

21-mm Micro Female

21-mm Micro Male

35-mm Mini Female

35-mm Mini Stereo

35-mm Mini Male

RCA Female

RCA Male

XLR Female

XLR Male

1/4" Female

1/4" Stereo

1/4" Male

Banana

Small Audio Plugs

Large Audio plugs

Connecting Equipment

FIG. 3.22 – Audio connectors may be RCA, mini, XLR, or, in older equipment, $^1/_4$-inch phone or a banana plug.

Video Connectors

There are six basic video plugs in common usage today. The RCA connector, unfortunately, has become standard for consumer and some small video equipment. Because it is a friction plug, you can unplug it unintentionally and easily, and because it is a common audio connector, you may misconnect cables by accident.

Professionals use a connector called a *BNC*, a name for which no two video specialists can agree upon the derivation. The BNC is designed so that it twists and locks into place, making a sure connection, but it is still easy to connect or disconnect with one hand.

BNC connectors are designed to carry only the video signal and are all male connectors. If BNC cables need to be connected together, you must use a female adapter called a *barrel* between the cables (see Figure 3.23).

You may use two methods of transmitting both audio and video information through the same cable. The first uses separate conductors inside the cable for audio and video. The multipin camera and 8-pin monitor cables and plugs are examples of multiconductor cables. You may use the second special cable and connectors called *RF* or *F*. To use an RF cable, you must combine the audio and video signals into one signal using a circuit called a *modulator*. On the other end of the line, you must use a *demodulator* to separate the audio and video signals again. Cable companies use the RF connector to connect their signal to a home receiver, and antennas are often connected with RF cables and plugs. The German DIN plug also is used on some European-manufactured equipment to carry both audio and video or only video or power voltage signals.

You may use an S-VHS cable to carry video signals; it is split into two separate signals, Y and C, for higher-quality transmission of video.

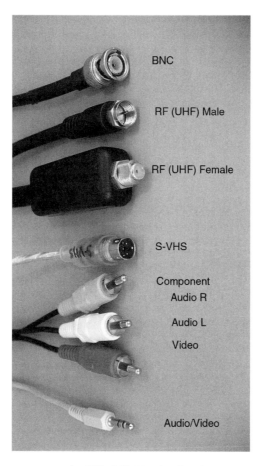

BNC

RF (UHF) Male

RF (UHF) Female

S-VHS

Component
Audio R

Audio L

Video

Audio/Video

FIG. 3.23 – Video connectors may be BNC, UHF, RF, RCA, SVH-S, or multipin camera or monitor connectors.

Digital Connectors

Because digital signals are different from analog signals, you will need to learn an entirely new set of plugs, jacks, and cables designed and accepted by the industry. Also, since the digital world is still in a state of constant flux, periodically new connectors and cables are designed and placed in use, usually for new and specific uses. The S-VHS plug listed previously also may be used for digital VHS (D-VHS) circuits. You use DIN plugs for connecting computer peripherals to the main *central processing unit* (CPU) of a computer (see Figure 3.24).

Ethernet systems were designed in the 1970s and are still in use for *local area networks* (LANs). The Ethernet plug looks much like a standard telephone plug but is wider and carries more signals. You will find it useful for connecting equipment at greater distances than other cables without loss of signals. The standard telephone plug in use today also is capable of carrying digital signals when used in a *digital subscriber line* (DSL) to feed broadband data down a telephone line. You may also use F and RF cables to carry digital signals if the modulators and demodulators are designed for digital transmission.

A leading standard digital connector is the *universal serial bus* (USB). Each end is shaped differently, even though both are modified female connectors. You connect the smaller end to the peripheral, the larger end to the computer. Extension cables and breakout boxes are designed to allow more than one cable to be connected to a single computer outlet for a flexible and faster means of moving data from printers or keyboards than you would attain from serial connectors and cables. You may use a faster system of cables and connectors labeled Institute of Electrical and Electronics Engineers, IEEE 1394 (its official name) but also known as iLink and FireWire. Firewire can support up to 63 devices at distances of up to 14 fed on one cable and has 30 times more bandwidth than USB. There are two types of FireWire connectors: a four-pin you use on camcorders and a six-pin you will find connected to computers and hard drives.

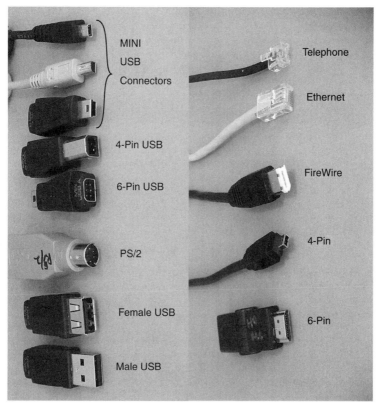

USB   Ethernet & FireWire

Digital Connectors

FIG. 3.24 – As new equipment and types of services are designed and placed into operation, there will be new connectors and cable systems. Pay close attention each time you connect or disconnect a cable to make certain you are matching the plugs and jacks properly. They are the weakest link in any system and most prone to damage at critical stages of a production.

Connecting Equipment

Audio

Audio, in the past, has been the forgotten half of the audio-video production world. With the arrival of digital audio and increased audience awareness of the value of quality sound, audio production now has become more important than in years past. Two developments in audio have contributed to your ability to improve the quality of your audio: digital audio and the condenser microphone. Both have reduced the size of audio equipment and measurably increased its sensitivity and frequency response. But with HD and other digital productions, audio now becomes that much more important. Audio provides the clean, clear sound to match digital video, but at the same time, any noise, poor equalization, or other deficiencies you create in the audio become that more obvious to the audience.

Microphone Types

Microphones are categorized in three ways: by their electronic impedance, by their element construction, and by their pickup pattern. Microphone choices are also made on the basis of their specific purpose or the type of audio pickup required.

Electronic Impedance

Microphones are classified as either *low impedance* or *high impedance*. *Impedance* is a complex measurement of resistance that also includes inductance and capacitance. All professional mics are low impedance. You need to connect a low-impedance mic to a two-conductor-plus-shield cable and XLR connector. This allows you to connect to a balanced circuit, which provides you the best audio pickup. You may connect high-impedance mics to a single-conductor cable and either an RCA or miniplug, but these mics should not be used more than 5 to 10 feet away from an amplifier.

Element Construction

The microphone element (transducer) types today are the *dynamic* (moving coil), the *ribbon*, or the *condenser*. The dynamic mic is the most common, most rugged, and, for fast-moving coverage such as news or documentaries, the best frequency response for the least cost. The pickup coil converts sound-wave energy to electric energy without an outside power source or amplification. These mics can be designed to be relatively small and are available in any pickup pattern (see Figure 3.25).

You should use the ribbon mic for studio or booth use only, as it is heavy, large, and sensitive to movement, shock, or wind. It creates a fine vocal quality, especially for the male voice. Its *transducing* element is a thin corrugated ribbon suspended between the two poles of a heavy magnet. You may use a ribbon mic on electronic field production (EFP) shoots if the environment is controlled and the mic is kept out of inclement weather. The condenser microphone is gradually replacing most other mics. Originally it was expensive, heavy, large, and required amplifiers and power supplies located adjacent to the mic. With solid-state circuits and mini-preamplifiers powered by small batteries or by current supplied from the amplifier (*phantom power*), the condenser mic has become more practical. With its built-in preamplifier, it is sensitive, has a fine frequency response, and is small and lightweight. The condenser mic can be designed in any pickup pattern and is manufactured in a variety of forms and price ranges.

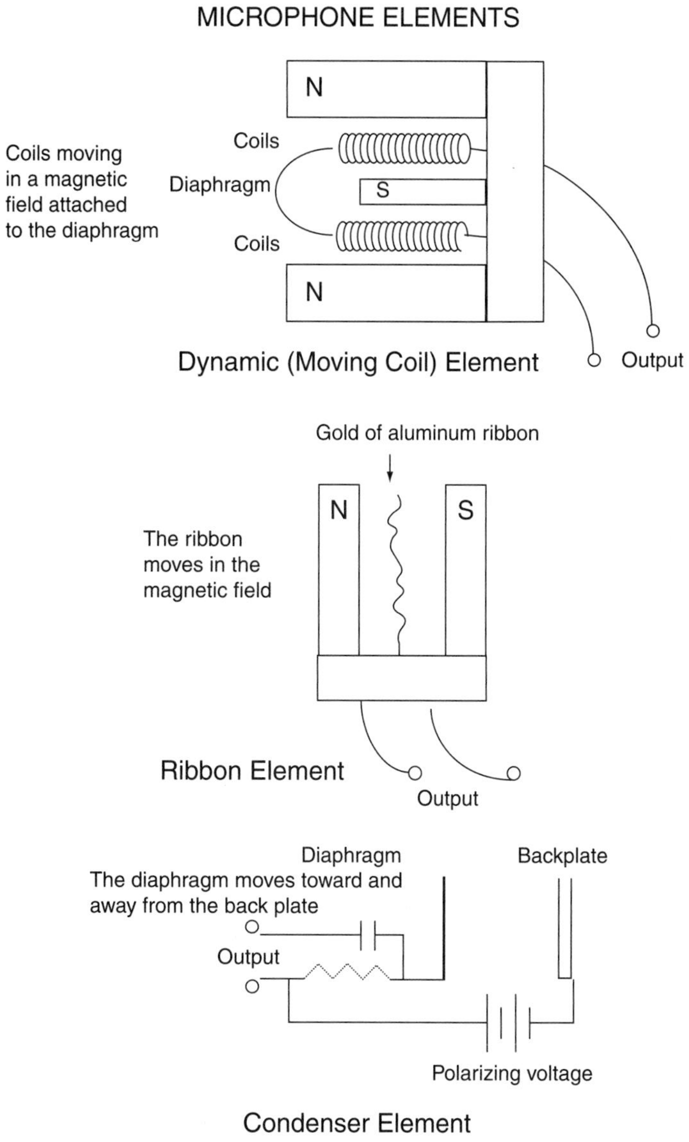

MICROPHONE ELEMENTS

Coils moving in a magnetic field attached to the diaphragm

Coils

Diaphragm

Coils

N

S

N

Output

Dynamic (Moving Coil) Element

Gold of aluminum ribbon

The ribbon moves in the magnetic field

N   S

Ribbon Element

Output

The diaphragm moves toward and away from the back plate

Diaphragm   Backplate

Output

Polarizing voltage

Condenser Element

FIG. 3.25 – Microphone elements are constructed of three types of transducers: dynamic (moving coil), ribbon, or condenser.

Audio

Pickup Pattern

There are three basic pickup patterns: *omnidirectional, unidirectional*, and *bidirectional*. You will find little use for bidirectional mics in field productions, and you should reserve them for studio productions. If you stage the shoot in a controlled environment or interior location, a bidirectional mic may be used for interviews. Its name is derived from its ability to pick up sound from two sides equally while suppressing sound from the other two sides (see Figure 3.26).

Omnidirectional mics pick up sound from all directions, 360 degrees around the mic, with nearly equal sensitivity in all directions. Your EFP audio kit should contain at least one good omnidirectional mic for crowd pickup and ambient noise recording.

The general background ambient noise of a location is called either *wild sound* or *nat* (short for "natural") *sound*. You will find wild or nat sound is valuable material to record for use in editing to provide an audio transition between scenes and to create the atmosphere of the original location for later voiceover narration.

The most useful mics are unidirectional mics. A true unidirectional mic picks up sound only from the end of the mic. An extreme example of a unidirectional mic is a *shotgun* mic. It is designed to have a narrow (as narrow as 5 degrees) pickup pattern. Its sensitive area is predominately straight out from the mic, but there are nodes or areas to the side and behind within which you also may pick up sound. This cannot be avoided, even with the best and most expensive shotgun mics. Your EFP audio kit should contain several shotgun mics of various lengths and pickup patterns.

The *cardioid* mic is a special type of unidirectional mic designed to combine the pickup pattern of the unidirectional and omnidirectional mics to create a heart-shaped pattern in front of the mic. This provides the ideal pattern for you or an interviewer to handhold a mic between two people, to describe an event without picking up too much background noise, and to use as a shotgun with a close mic. If you carry only a single mic, then a cardioid mic is your best choice.

Some professional microphones are designed with variable directional settings. There will be a switch on the case that you can use to change the pickup pattern from omnidirectional, to unidirectional, to cardioid, for example. As with all equipment, multipurpose electronic equipment seldom performs as satisfactorily as equipment designed to perform a specific function.

Remember, the output of all microphones is an analog signal. You will need to convert the analog audio signal to a digital signal either in the preamplifier or in a digital-to-analog (D-A) converter located later in your camera or signal stream.

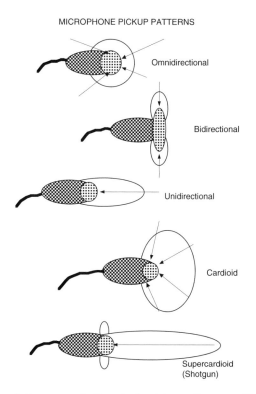

MICROPHONE PICKUP PATTERNS

Omnidirectional

Bidirectional

Unidirectional

Cardioid

Supercardioid
(Shotgun)

FIG. 3.26 – Even though there are only three basic pickup patterns, combining patterns create specialized patterns such as cardioid and supercardioid.

Mounting Devices

Besides the electronic design of a microphone, mics also are designed to fulfill a specific purpose. The purpose or how you mount the mic for a particular shot in a production may determine partially the shape of the body of the mic as well as how it is physically mounted. Four basic body styles and mounting methods fulfill most purposes: lavalier (lapel), handheld, stand mount, and shotgun (see Figure 3.27).

You place a lavalier unidirectional mic on the body of the subject. You may attach the mic in plain view, hanging from the neck as a lavalier, or as a smaller peanut mic attached under the talent's necktie, shirt, or blouse, or to a jacket lapel. A more specialized lavalier is worn on a headband, placing the mic near or to one side of the subject's mouth. You will use such a mic for vocalists and on-stage performers.

You may use a handheld mic on a table or as a stand mic. You may mount a microphone at the end of a small handheld boom called a *fish pole* or on a small, movable, tripod-mounted boom called a *giraffe*, or, if space allows, on a large-wheeled boom that the operator rides called a *perambulator*. You usually use a cardioid or short shotgun mic mounted on booms. You can hang the same type of mic from a gaffer hook from the ceiling; from a hanging light fixture, door, or window frame; or from any other stable piece of tall furniture in the room. Another method of mic placement is to hide it behind objects between the talent and the camera: floral arrangements on a table, books, telephones, or any other set piece large enough to hide the mic and its stand. You may handhold a shotgun mic, but more often you should mount it on a stable stand mount to avoid inducing unwanted noise from handling (see Figure 3.28).

You may wire your mic directly to the camera, or it may be a wireless mic feeding a small transmitter hidden on the talent's body and picked up by a small receiver wired to the camera. Wireless mics are becoming more popular as the price and their sensitivity to other RF signals in the area are reduced. Today's transmitters are designed to be smaller and more powerful, correcting many of the past problems of interference.

For some field productions—sporting events, game shows, and live coverage of non-video events—you do not need to hide the microphone. Those situations allow you to place the mic or mics in the best position for maximum quality or sensitivity of audio pickup. Make certain you place the mic in direct line with the performer's mouth, below the face, and depending on the type of microphone, approximately 12 to 15 inches from the mouth. The microphone should be close enough for clear pickup and the exclusion of unwanted sounds, but it should be far enough away to avoid picking up the popping of Ps and other plosive sounds.

In addition, you should place the mic so that its pickup matches the approximate perspective of the picture. If it is an extremely wide shot, then the audio should sound off mic; if it is a tight close-up, then the pickup should be intimate and the mic should be close. Often the type of environment—closed-in small room; out in the open; or a large, echo-filled auditorium—partially determines the best choice of microphone.

Audio

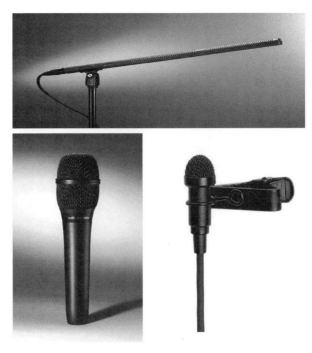

Top - Shotgun
Bottom - Handheld & Lavalier

FIG. 3.27 – Microphones are designed for specific purposes or frequency requirements and may include lavalier, handheld, or shotgun types. (Courtesy Sennheiser, and AudioTechnica.)

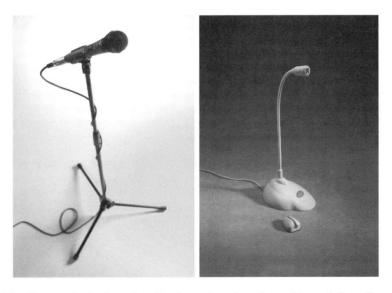

FIG. 3.28 – The mounting hardware for microphones depends on the need to reach the audio source and may include boom, stand, or desk mounting. (Courtesy AudioTechnica.)

Nonmicrophone Audio Sources

In addition to recording audio from microphones, you may find it necessary to record nonmicrophone audio sources without using any mics. Such sources may be the output of amplifiers, public address systems, or tape or disc decks. Each of these produces high-level output, and you must feed the signal into a high-level, high-impedance input on the recorder. You must match impedance and level for a satisfactory recording. Check the output specifications of the high-level source and match it to the specifications of the recorder being used. If they do not match, then you must insert a matching transformer or amplifier into the circuit to guarantee a proper match. If not closely matched, either the audio will be badly distorted or the level will be too low for any practical use (see Figure 3.29).

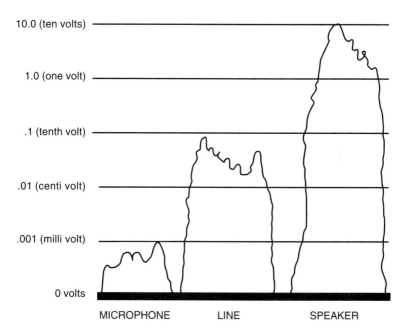

COMPARISON BETWEEN AUDIO LEVELS

10.0 (ten volts)

1.0 (one volt)

.1 (tenth volt)

.01 (centi volt)

.001 (milli volt)

0 volts

MICROPHONE   LINE   SPEAKER

FIG. 3.29 – The three primary audio levels vary in voltage, from the very weak signal directly from a microphone, pickup head of turntable, disc, or tape deck, to the middle level of the output of a preamplifier signal called line level, and finally to the high level of the output of an amplifier intended to power a speaker or speaker system.

Which Audio Track to Use

Another consideration is your choice of which audio channel to feed to a camera or record deck. All professional cameras and record decks offer at least two tracks for audio recording.

Midlevel cameras using such formats DVCam also have audio tracks recorded in different positions on the tape stock. These formats record the audio digitally within the video signal as a pulse code modulation (PCM) integrated signal as well as longitudinal tracks. The digital tracks are stereo and are very high quality.

Audio pickup, whether it is analog or digital, is often ignored or thought of last, when in reality, audio often carries more than half the critical information in a story. It is important, then, for you to plan seriously for and spend time properly setting up microphones, mixers, and cables, and choosing audio channels for the best possible audio recording along with the video recording.

Lighting

The function of lighting at its simplest is to provide enough illumination so that the camera can reproduce an image. You draw the complexity of lighting and lighting techniques from the need for the instruments to serve the aesthetic needs of the medium: to set mood, time, and location, and to draw attention to the critical portions of the frame.

Lighting instruments have evolved from both the stage and motion picture industries, just as most audio equipment evolved from the radio and motion picture industries. Digital production has only increased the need for your careful and thoughtful consideration of lighting designs and techniques. The high quality of digital signals allows a greater creative range because of its increased sensitivity and dynamic contrast range, but the digital systems reveal errors in poorly designed and executed lighting plans.

Floodlights

You will use three basic types of field lighting instruments: *floodlights, focusing spotlights*, and *fixed-focus instruments*. Floodlights provide a broad, relatively uncontrolled, soft diffused light that you use to cover large areas and to fill in shadow areas. The most common field floods are *LED banks, softlights, broads*, and *umbrella lights*. LED banks are groups of LED instruments arranged in a frame for mounting on a gaffer stand. Softlights are the largest, but because they are now constructed of folding aluminum frames and cloth reflector covers, they are portable. Broads are smaller, boxlike instruments usually equipped with some type of barn door to control the coverage of light. They commonly contain only one lamp. Umbrella lighting is more of a technique than a specific type of instrument, because you can fit any spotlight with an umbrella. The concept of umbrella lighting is for you to focus light from a spotlight onto an umbrella-shaped reflector mounted on the instrument so that light strikes the inner concave surface of the umbrella and is reflected back in the opposite direction (see Figure 3.30).

Fluorescent lighting uses specially designed tubes that radiate light within a reasonable range to match the Kelvin temperature of either daylight or tungsten. Newer units are portable and can be equipped with dimmers for better lighting control in the field.

Top - Fluorescent
Bottom - Open-faced flood, LED, Softlight

FIG. 3.30 – Floodlights are designed to provide a soft, smooth, shadow-free source of light to act as fill or supplemental light. (Courtesy Arriflex, Lowell Lights, and LitePanels.)

Focusing Spotlights

Focusing spotlights are either open faced without a lens or lensed with a *Fresnel* or *plano-convex* lens. Focusing spots are essential for your critical creative lighting. You use spotlights generally as the main or key source of light in a scene that requires the equivalent of sunlight as the apparent source. Spotlights come in a wide range of sizes from small handheld battery-powered spots to huge brute spots powered by generators or special power sources used on feature film and major television productions. You can use small LED and fluorescent spots as key lights for close-in shots (see Figure 3.31).

Top - PAR, Fresnel
Bottom - Open face, LED

FIG. 3.31 – Spotlights have been the workhorse fixtures of the production industry but are slowly being replaced by flexible and lightweight instruments to fit the subtle nature of digital productions. (Courtesy Arriflex and Lowell Lights.)

Fixed-Focus Instruments

Fixed-focus instruments are designed around a lamp similar to an auto headlight. A bank of these lamps is built into a cabinet that allows each lamp to be turned on and aimed individually. You use these lamps to light a wide area with an even but controlled field of light. The lamps are called *FAY* if the output is 5,400 degrees Kelvin (°K), and *PAR* if the output is 3,200K.

You may operate both of these instruments from portable floor stands, and they may be driven by 110- or 220-volt AC power. They also can be mounted from a variety of gaffer mounts on walls, doors, or other sturdy objects.

FIG. 3.32 – Even in the field, gaffe equipment designed to mount, hold, and position instruments, filters, flags, umbrellas, and scrims is important to properly place all of the lighting equipment required to create the professional setup. An EFP lighting kit should contain a set of gaffer's accessories: gobos, clamps, stands, weights, brackets, reflectors, and gaffer tools. A *gaffer* is a lighting technician. (Courtesy Lowell Lights.)

Lighting

Controlling Light

Because you seldom will have the opportunity to use a portable light dimmer board, control over the light output in the field becomes critical for creative shooting situations. You can use two simple, portable instruments: reflectors and tents. *Reflectors* are large foam boards covered on one side with a variety of surfaces: plain white, colored, or textured. You use these reflectors to throw a soft fill light into areas not easily reached with instruments or to provide light that will not cast an additional shadow. You use *tents* to diffuse light, allowing the lighting instruments mounted behind the fabric of the tents to create even light without creating unwanted shadows (see Figure 3.32).

Power Sources

In the field, you may use three sources of power: the alternating current present in most buildings, batteries, and portable generators.

Portable generators are expensive, noisy, and, for video cameras, an uncertain source of stable power. The instability presents no problem for lighting directors, but the noise and expense might present problems for you or the director. Batteries for electronic news gathering (ENG) crews are becoming more dependable and last long enough for most EFP production situations, but they require care in handling the charging and discharging functions. The most dependable source of power for lighting will be the AC circuits in most buildings. Because lighting instruments draw much more current than any other piece of equipment, you need some knowledge of wattage, current, and voltage. The standard power in the United States is delivered either at 110 or 120 volts. The lamps in lighting instruments are rated in watts, and the rating on power circuits in buildings is measured in amperage (amps). You can perform the simple translation of watts to amps or vice versa by using Ohm's law: wattage equals voltage times amperage. If voltage is treated as a constant of 100 (this provides a built-in 10 percent safety margin), then to find wattage, simply multiply amps by 100. To find amps from known wattage, simply divide wattage by 100. Both can be done easily without a calculator (see Figure 3.33).

A janitor or building engineer will control and know the location of the circuit breaker box that controls the AC circuits in the building. Find that person and the box before connecting more than two lighting instrument in one room. Most breaker circuits are limited to provide 20 amps or less. Each breaker is marked. Check before connecting your instruments, especially in any one room at a time.

APPLICATION OF OHM'S LAW TO TYPICAL LIGHTING SETUP

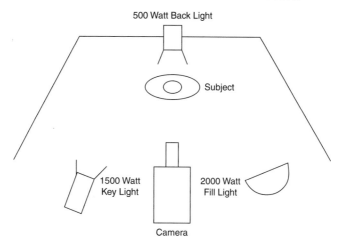

OHM'S LAW: WATTAGE = VOLTAGE × AMPERAGE
$$W = V \times A$$

Assume V = 100 V as a constant

To find Amperage: $A = \dfrac{W}{100}$

To find Wattage: $W = A \times 100$

In the example above: Back Light = 500 W
Key Light = 1500 W
Fill Light = <u>2000 W</u>

TOTAL = 4000 W

Amperage = $\dfrac{\text{Wattage}}{100}$

Amperage = $\dfrac{4000}{100}$

Amperage = 40 A

FIG. 3.33 – The total amount of amperage available in a typical room in a home or office might not exceed 20 amps, which means the amount of wattage available from all of the outlets on that one breaker cannot exceed 2,000 watts, or 1-1,000-watt and 2-500-watt lamps. If more power is needed, additional power cords must be run to other sources served by other breaker circuits.

Lighting

Color Temperature

The final consideration in lighting equipment actually is a part of the camera operation, but the problem starts with the source of light. All light sources are not equal in their actual color. Your eye and mind compensate for this variation by creating the illusion that light within a certain range appears white. Actual measurement of the color of light is in degrees Kelvin, based on the color of carbon heated and measured at certain temperatures. The lower the Kelvin temperature, the more reddish yellow and warmer the color of the light. The higher the Kelvin temperature, the bluer and cooler the light appears.

There is no actual "white light" on the Kelvin scale. Typical candlelight measures below 1,800°K. An ordinary incandescent lightbulb measures 2,800°K. Professional tungsten-halogen lamps measure 3,200°K. Daylight varies from approximately 4,000°K to over 12,000°K, but the standard is considered 5,400K. Today's film and digital cameras can be adjusted to operate accurately within a range of 3,200°K to above 5,400°K, but you must make proper adjustment to the camera to compensate for the color differences (see Figure 3.34).

The critical factor concerning the color temperature is that a camera sees and reproduces the actual color of the light source as it is reflected from the subjects. You are able to adjust an electronic camera to compensate for any variation in the color temperature by the process of white balancing. To light a scene properly, though, it should be lit with consistently color-balanced light sources.

Professional lamps are accurately rated for their color output, but when shooting in the field, you may be in an environment where you cannot control the light source. Home incandescent lighting is warmer than studio lighting; office fluorescent lighting is bluer and greener. Because fluorescent light does not emit a specific color temperature, you can either filter the light at the camera or place filters on the tubes themselves to correct the temperature to match the camera settings. Newer fluorescent tubes now are available that have been designed to match 5,400°K.

If you are shooting next to a window, the daylight does not match the color temperature of the production lamps. This situation is called mixed lighting. You should consider the color temperature of the available light sources by measuring them with a Kelvin temperature meter or by arranging to have all light sources be of the same color temperature. One method you may use to change the Kelvin temperature of a light source is to filter the source with large gels. You can cover complete office or home windows to balance the blue sunlight with the warmer incandescent production instruments.

COLOR TEMPERATURES OF LIGHT SOURCES

SOURCE	DEGREES KELVIN	MIREDS
Match flame	1700K	588
Candle flame	1850K	541
Sunrise or sunset	2000K	500
Consumer lamps	2650K-2990K	317-345
Standard tungsten/halogen	3200K	313
Photoflood	3400K	294
Early morning, late afternoon	4300K	233
Daylight photoflood	4800K	208
HMI	5600K	179
Typical noon	5400K-5800K	185
Carbon arc	5800K	172
Overcast sky	6000K	167
Summer shade	8000K	125
Full summer sun	10,000K-30,000K	100

Comparable Degrees Kelvin for Fluorescent Sources

Warm white	3050
White	3500
Natural white	3700
Cool white	4300
Daylight	6500

FIG. 3.34 – The differences in the actual color of light sources range from the full summer sun to the candle flame. Fluorescent sources also vary over a wide range, but not as widely as incandescent and natural light sources.

Measuring Light Intensity

In addition to measuring the Kelvin temperature of the light sources for the best lighting, you must measure the intensity of the light sources and the light reflected from the subjects.

You measure the light from the light sources (*incident light*) by pointing an incident light meter at the light source. You measure the light from the subject (*reflected light*) with a reflected light meter pointed at specific areas of the subject (see Figure 3.35).

Some light meters are designed to permit both types of meter readings, but professional-quality meters are designed specifically to read either reflected or incident light levels. You need to use the two methods of taking light-level readings in order to determine the two types of lighting ratios necessary for quality lighting.

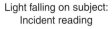

Light falling on subject:	Light reflected from subject:
Incident reading	Reflected reading

FIG. 3.35 – To take an incident light reading, your meter must be placed near the subject so that the key light falls on the meter (on left). To take a reflected reading, your meter should be placed between the camera and the subject with the meter aimed at the subjects (on right).

Lighting Ratio

Regardless of the cost of your digital camera, some minimum amount of light is required to produce an acceptable picture; this is called a base light. An incident light reading of the amount of light falling on the subject gives you or the lighting director two pieces of information: the base light level necessary to produce an acceptable picture and the ratio of fill light to key light. When you point the meter at the lights from the subject's position with just the fill light turned on and then take another reading with fill and key lights on from the same position, a numerical ratio, called the lighting ratio, is determined. The standard starting lighting ratio is 2:1, twice as much light from the key and fill as from the fill alone. A backlight ratio may also be taken, and it should be close to 1:1; the backlight should approximately equal the key light.

Contrast Ratio

The measurement for *contrast ratio* is a little more complex. You use a reflected spot-light meter to measure accurately the amount of light reflected from the brightest object in the picture and then compare the light reflected from the darkest object. The difficult part is that when there are either highly reflective or very dark objects in the frame, it is not necessary to include these areas in the readings if you do not need to reproduce detail in either of those areas (see Figure 3.36).

If the amount of light reflected from the brightest portion of the frame in which detail is necessary reflects more than 30 times more light than the darkest areas needed for detail, then more fill light will be needed on the dark areas or some light will have to be taken off the lightest areas. If you carefully light for the contrast range of the video camera, you avoid having areas "blooming" or "flaring" into a white mass or important areas appearing so dark that they look muddy.

Top - Reading reflected light from lightest object
Bottom - Reading reflected light from darkest object

FIG. 3.36 – To determine the contrast ratio of a scene, take a meter reading of reflected light from the brightest portion of the set and compare it to a meter reading from the light reflected from the darkest portion of the set.

Digital cameras can accept a slightly broader range of contrast than analog cameras, but because a digital image will show much more fine detail, you must accomplish a fine level of lighting. Lighting for digital productions simply requires more attention to small details that might not appear in images taken with an analog camera but will become obvious in images taken with a digital camera. Digital cameras may operate with less light, but the light must be well balanced within the contrast range of the camera.

Regardless of the changes in technology and advances in electronic signal processing, basic media production equipment operation varies little from the analog to digital. The care and understanding of your equipment will mean more in the quality of your final production than the expense and advancement of your equipment. Remember, it isn't the paintbrush; it's the artist that makes the difference.

Lighting

Chapter Four
The Production Process: Preproduction

You can easily understand the organization of the production process by its three steps: preproduction, production, and postproduction. Each step involves specific functions and operations that are interdependent and critical to the final production. Before either the production or the postproduction tasks can be accomplished, preproduction must take place, and the foundation of any media project lies in the time and effort spent during preproduction.

Preliminary Forms

Before any serious work can begin on a video project, you must find a source of funding. You need to locate an interested party who will commit money for staff, crew, cast, research, facilities, equipment, and expendable materials. Sources of funds may be clients who have contracted for the specific project, such as television stations, networks, or cable networks. You should not overlook other funding agencies such as government agencies, the Public Broadcasting System, money-lending agencies, banks and savings and loan companies, or insurance companies as funding sources.

The Proposal

Regardless of the source, there is common information that must be supplied in order to gain access to funding. The first document you will create in your preproduction process is called a *proposal*. A proposal generally is your responsibility as the producer, but it is better written with the assistance of the writer(s) and director. You must possess considerable knowledge of the subject to avoid mistakes, misinformation, or serious inaccuracy. You need to complete a site survey, interviews, and library and other research before the proposal can be written.

Once you have completed your research, you will organize all of the information into a concise, meaningful package that briefly explains the objectives of the production, the target audience, and the distribution methods. You need to clearly explain key production factors, basic style and genre, unusual production techniques, and special casting and location considerations—along with the length, recording, and release formats—in easily understandable lay terms. You must be acutely aware of how you plan to distribute the completed project: the Internet, podcasting, streaming, broadcasting or cable-casting, or by converting it to a digital format on tape, disc, hard drive, or memory media. You must understand that a nonmedia person may be reading the proposal and reaching a funding judgment. You must write the proposal so that all aspects of the production are presented clearly and avoid the use of production jargon (see Figure 4.1).

You must complete the proposal package with an approximate timeline and budget. You need to prepare both of these carefully and realistically. Too much or too little of either can discourage a client or funding source. Worse yet, either miscalculation can place you in a position in which it is impossible for you to complete the project because of insufficient funds or time.

SAMPLE PROPOSAL FORMAT

TITLE: Safety Training   PAGE: 1
WRITER: T. Bartlett   LENGTH: 10 min
CLIENT: Mountain Industries   DATE: 10-10-09

Rivers and Streams Productions, Inc. will produce a ten minute, color program, to be used as a training medium for new and present employees of Mountain Industries. The program will target specific safety procedures necessary to be followed in the unique operation of logging in the mountains of Montana. The program will emphasize personal safety actions and procedures required by the Occupational Safety and Health Administration.

The shooting schedule will last for ten days, weather and other acts of nature notwithstanding. Postproduction will last for four weeks following the completion of principal videography. Shooting will start within two weeks of final script approval. Research and preparing of the treatment will last three weeks following the acceptance of the proposal. The final script will be prepared within three weeks of acceptance of the proposed treatment.

The program will be budgeted at approximately $35,000.00, depending on specific technical requirements of the script. Because the script calls for a series of dangerous actions requiring stunt actors and technicians, some allowances for costs and shooting overruns may be required.

The format will be semi-documentary/instructional with the program narrated and techniques explained by an actor representing a skilled and knowledgeable logger. Both incorrect and correct operational procedures will be illustrated. Employees, equipment, and facilities of Mountain Industries logging operation will be required for the production of this tape.

Preliminary Forms

FIG. 4.1 – The proposal must be written succinctly and accurately, yet as a sales tool to convince a potential funder of the value of the project, the possibility of its completion, and the capability of the producer to create and complete a professional and viable production.

Treatment

Once the proposal has been written, you must prepare a *treatment*. A treatment is a narrative description of the production. Like the proposal, you intend the treatment to be read by the potential financial backers to assist them in making a decision as to whether they are willing to entrust their money to you.

In the first paragraph of the treatment, you repeat key information from the proposal: title, length, format, and objective of the production. You can assume that the proposal and treatment will be presented and read at the same time.

You should write the treatment as if you are describing what the audience will see when watching a playback of the completed production. Dialogue is not used, but indications of the types of conversations or narration should be included. Also, you should avoid technical terminology such as *dissolve, medium close-up,* and *voiceover*. Remember, the person reading the document is not a media professional. Any person who controls money should be able to make sense of the proposal and the treatment, which are, in essence, sales tools designed to sell your ability to successfully complete your production within budget and on time, while accomplishing the stated objective.

The potential financial backers should be able to read these two documents, proposal and treatment, easily. They should be able to imagine exactly what the production will sound and look like without any other explanation or verbal description from you (see Figure 4.2).

In reality, you may write both the proposal and treatment after the script has been finalized, because the proposal and treatment must accurately reflect the script. From a practical point of view, you may prepare the three preproduction writing functions simultaneously.

SAMPLE TREATMENT FORMAT

TITLE:	Safety Training	PAGE:	1
WRITER:	T. Bartlett	LENGTH:	10 min
CLIENT:	Mountain Industries	DATE:	10-10-09

The ten-minute training program will open with a montage of incorrect logging operations followed in each case by the possible disastrous and life-threatening results of such actions. Examples of such scenes are:

A logger without a safety belt steps back and falls from a tree stand.

A chainsaw jams and flips back into the logger.

A tractor tips over on the driver because it exceeded its tilt limit.

A logging truck driven too fast forces an on-coming car from the road.

A log falls from a truck being loaded and strikes a logger who was standing too close to the truck.

A logger refuels his saw improperly, causing a fire.

A truck or tractor becomes a runaway when left improperly locked down.

A logger dumped into the river and crushed by logs.

A log avalanche occurs because of careless blocking of a log stack.

This series of accidents will be enhanced with sound effects and dramatic music as well as the actual sound of each accident.

Following this montage, the narrator will walk into the scene and describe in general the dangers and reasons for following OSHA safety requirements for those working in dangerous occupations such as the

(continued)

FIG. 4.2 – The treatment must support the proposal by filing in more details of the production without appearing to be a script, but rather as a narrative short story of what the script will reveal when produced. It should read as an exciting description of action, characters, and plotlines, and it should sell the value of the production to the possible funder. The treatment also may become an outline for the script-writing process.

Preliminary Forms

Your next step in preparing a production is gathering the information needed to create an accurate budget. Your budget form must include every conceivable value in materials, labor, equipment, travel, graphics, distribution, and legal costs. Budgeting is a science that combines economics and production knowledge. You need to do a thorough study of the price of each item in the budget before any proposal is presented to a funding entity. To ensure accuracy while creating the budget, you need to check the costs of leasing equipment, renting facilities, labor agreements, and the prices of expendable items such as recording stock, makeup, and gaffer tape (see Figure 4.3).

Your budget must be as accurate as possible, indicating you have carefully considered every aspect of the production and the best method of creating each aspect at a reasonable cost. You need to include enough flexibility in your budget to cover a certain number of uncontrolled activities that occur during any production, but you must keep within as tight a range as possible to avoid overbudgeting and thereby frightening away a funding source. You should include a contingency item at the bottom to cover unexpected items, but you may include it in the final billing if the funds are not used during the production. Overhead is your profit value that covers normal business expenses such as office operation and noncrew staff costs.

PRODUCTION BUDGET

TITLE: DATE:
PRODUCER: DIRECTOR:
CLIENT: PHONE:
ADDRESS: MEDIUM: FORMAT:
CONTACT: PHONE:
ALTERNATE: PHONE:

1. SCRIPT (Rights, research, writing, duplication) _____ 0

2. STAGING (Sets, costumes, location fees, props) _____ 0

3. EQUIPMENT (Rental, lease, use fees) _____ 0

4. SPECIAL EQUIPMENT (Mounts, aerials, submarine) _____ 0

5. RAWSTOCK _____ 0

6. DUPING (Time code copies, off-line copies) _____ 0

7. AUDIO (Effects, fees, rights, sweetening, looping, etc.) _____ 0

8. MUSIC (Fees, rights, performance) _____ 0

9. GRAPHICS (Titles, animation, art) _____ 0

10. EDITING _____ 0

11. PERSONNEL: Staff   _____ 0
                  Crew   _____ 0
                  Talent   ____#REF!____   ___#REF!___

12. TRAVEL (Transportation, lodging, per diem) _____ 0

13. DISTRIBUTION (Dubs, promotion) _____ 0

14. POSTAGE/INSURANCE _____ 0

15. OTHER _____ 0

                                SUB-TOTAL _____ 0

OVERHEAD _____ 0

CONTINGENCY _____ 0

                                GRAND TOTAL _____ 0

PRODUCTION BUDGET WORKSHEET

PRODUCTION:XXXXXXXXXXXXXXXXXXXXXXXXX   DATE:XX/XX/XX

FIG. 4.3 – The summary page of a budget indicates the total of each category summarized from one or more pages of the full budget.

Preliminary Forms

Legal Considerations

You are responsible for obtaining permissions and releases. Permission to use personal property and copyrighted works, such as specific locations and music, require negotiations with the property owners. For example, if you wish to use a piece of popular music in your production, you need to obtain permission from both the owner of the musical recording or CD, such as Sony Music, *and* the publisher of the music, such as ASCAP, BMI, or SESAC. By obtaining personal releases signed by people appearing in the film or video, you can avoid subsequent legal suits brought by them against you, especially when they are dissatisfied with the final product or outcome.

Script Formats

Preparing a script for a production may take you several steps before reaching the shape of the script containing all of the information needed for both the cast and crew. The first script is the scene script, followed by the shooting script. Each script may be rewritten several times depending on your demands and those of the client (see Figure 4.4).

Scene Script

The first completed draft of a script is called a *scene script*. You include in the scene script a detailed description of each scene and the action occurring during that scene, but not specific shots. Each scene description should indicate whether the scene is set during the day or at night and in an interior or exterior setting. You must describe the characters, key furniture or objects present, character movements, and all dialogue and narration in the scene script.

FADE IN:

1.   INT   CLUB CAR OF MOVING TRAIN   DAY   1.

The desert landscape of central Arizona flashes by outside the window.
A drunken MAN staggers up the aisle holding a cocktail glass. He notices
ROBIN BALLARD, a delicate, thirty year old woman, who stares blankly
out the window. He holds the glass out to her.

MAN
(slurred)
Buy you a drink pretty lady?

Robin continues to stare out the window.

ROBIN
(coldly)
No.

The Man pulls back the drink.

MAN
Well, pardon me.

He turns and walks away. Robin's reflection in the window returns her gaze.

(DISS)

2.   EXT   UNION STATION, LOS ANGELES   DAY   2

Robin, surrounded by other disembarking passengers, frantically searches
the crowded platform. She brightens as she recognized LAUREN CHANDLER,
a beautiful, fifty year old, self-possessed woman, walking through the crowd and
waves at her.

ROBIN
Mom!
(calling louder)
Mom!

Lauren spots Robin, waves and hurries toward her. The women embrace.
Robin starts to cry.

LAUREN
(concerned)
Baby, baby....What's the matter?

ROBIN
I. . .I left Tom.

FIG. 4.4 – Scene scripts are summaries of all of the information needed to shoot a scene or sequence.

Script Formats

Shooting Script

The *shooting script* is a more detailed version of the scene script. You describe each shot specifically and numbered in order. You indicate the framing—WS, MCU, CU—but you allow some leeway for the director's creativity. Your descriptions should be complete enough so that the director is able to interpret accurately what you had intended in each sequence, scene, or shot. You should include in a shooting script much more detail to guide the work of the lighting director, art director, sound director, technical director, and editor (see Figure 4.5).

Script Formats

Professional scripts will be instantly recognized by the format used. Every studio, station, or other production facility may design and mandate its own specific script formats, but the basic formats indicated in this text will be accepted in the field if they are professionally prepared.

FADE IN:
1.   INT   CLUB CAR OF MOVING TRAIN   DAY   1.

WS: Through window
The desert landscape of central Arizona flashes by outside the window.
MCU: Down aisle of train car a drunken MAN staggers up the aisle holding
a cocktail glass. He notices
MS: drunk/Robin

ROBIN BALLARD, a delicate, thirty year old woman, who stares blankly
out the window.
2-shot drunk/Robin: He holds the glass out to her.

MAN
(slurred)
Buy you a drink pretty lady?

Robin continues to stare out the window.

ROBIN
(coldly)
No.

CU: Drunk: The Man pulls back the drink.

MAN
Well, pardon me.

MCU up aisle: He turns and walks away.
2-shot Robin & her reflection in window
Robin's reflection in the window returns her gaze.

(DISS)

**FIG. 4.5 – A shooting script also may indicate overlapping shots, special effects, graphics, or any
other details needed to complete the scene.**

Script Formats

Single-Column Format

You may use two basic script formats in preparing scripts for electronic field production (EFP): the traditional film single-column format and the traditional television dual-column format. The *single-column format* evolved from stage script format to motion picture format to radio before it was adapted again for video productions. The format defines various aspects of the scripts by varying the width of the margins and by capitalizing certain portions of the copy. The rules at first seem complex, but can be summarized as follows (see Figure 4.6):

- Each shot starts with the shot number at the extremes of the right-hand and left-hand margins. In uppercase type, either the word DAY or NIGHT indicates lighting conditions, followed by either INT or EXT, to indicate location.

- Camera directions, scene descriptions, and stage directions are typed next, within slightly narrower margins. How the line is to be delivered is typed in still narrower margins within parentheses, and dialogue is typed within even narrower margins.

- The name of the speaking character is centered above his or her line in uppercase letters.

- Single-spacing is used for dialogue, camera angles and movements, stage directions, scene descriptions, sound effects, or cues.

- Double-spacing is used to separate a camera shot or scene from the next camera shot or scene, a scene from an interceding transition (FADE IN/FADE OUT, DISSOLVE), the speech of one character from the heading of the next character, and a speech from camera or stage directions.

- Uppercase type is used for INT or EXT in heading line, to indicate the location, to indicate day or night, for the name of a character when first introduced in the stage directions and to indicate the character's dialogue, for camera angles and movements, for scene transitions, and (CONTINUED) to indicate that a scene is split between pages (avoid if at all possible).

MASTER SCENE SCRIPT FORMAT

(Margins and tabs set as indicated below, assuming 80 space wide paper)

5   15 20   40 45   55 60

FADE IN:

1. INT./EXT.   BRIEF SCENE OR SHOT DESCRIPTION   DAY/NIGHT 1.

In upper and lower case, a more detailed description of the scene giving setting, props, and CHARACTERS position if needed with margins set at 5/60.

CHARACTER

(Mode of delivery, upper and lower case, margins at 20/40)

[NO ACTION]

The dialog is typed in upper and lower case centered within 15/45 margins.

Any other descriptions of shot framing, movement of CAMERA or CHARACTER is at margins set at 5/60.

[If needed]   (TRANSITION) or

(CONTINUED)

FIG. 4.6 – The single-column format evolved from stage, film, and radio formats and remains popular in feature motion pictures, soap operas, and in some commercial, animation, game, and music video scripts.

Dual-Column Format

The *dual-column television script format* evolved from audiovisual format and instructional film format. This format is based on separating audio instructions and information from visual instructions. Two columns are set up on the page. The video is located on the left side of the page, the audio on the right. This is not an absolute rule; some operations prefer the opposite, and some include a storyboard on the left, right, or down the middle of the page.

Each shot number is identified in both the video and audio columns, matching the appropriate audio with its video. All video instructions are typed in uppercase letters, as are all audio instructions. Copy to be read by the performers is typed in uppercase and lowercase letters. Many performers, especially news anchors, prefer all uppercase letters in the misguided belief that uppercase copy is easier to read. However, all readability studies indicate the opposite, and today most computerized prompter systems display copy in both uppercase and lowercase letters (see Figure 4.7).

Video instructions should be arranged in single-spaced blocks; audio copy, in double-spaced blocks. Triple-spacing between shots helps both the talent and the director follow the flow of the script. The name of the talent is typed in uppercase letters to the left of the right-hand column. If the same audio source continues through several shots, it is not necessary to repeat the source's name unless another source intervenes.

You should avoid hyphenating words at the end of a line and avoid splitting shots at the bottom of the page. Spreading copy out allows for notes and additional instructions to be added during actual production.

You repeat information concerning the production at the top of each page; this will include the title, your name, and other pertinent information. You must number each page in sequence. If pages are added, you add letters or other indicators to keep the pages in order (for example, page 25a falls between pages 25 and 26).

Some production types, such as documentaries and interview segments, use an outline format, rather than either the specific dual- or single-column format.

Computer programs have been designed to facilitate the preparation of scripts by allowing you to concentrate on the creative part of writing and not the formatting. These computer applications are specifically designed for both single-column and double-column scripts in a variety of formats: television, audio/video, multimedia, motion pictures, and radio.

DUAL-COLUMN SCRIPT FORMAT

TITLE: PAGE:
WRITER: LENGTH:
CLIENT: DATE:

VIDEO	AUDIO
1. SINGLE SPACE VIDEO INSTRUCTIONS	1. ANNCR: Audio copy is lined up directly across the page from its matching video.
2. TRIPLE SPACE BETWEEN EACH SHOT	2. Double space between each line of copy.
3. EACH SHOT MUST BE NUMBERED ON THE SCRIPT	3. The audio column's number must match that of its video.
4. EVERYTHING THE VIEWER IS TO SEE; ALL VISUALS, VIDEO TAPES, CG, CAMERA SHOTS, ARE INCLUDED IN THE LEFT-HAND COLUMN.	4. Everything the viewer hears; narration, music, voices, sound effects, all audio cues are in this column.
5. EVERYTHING ON THE VIDEO SIDE IS TYPED IN UPPER CASE,	5. Everything spoken by the talent is typed in upper and lower case letters. All instructions in the audio column are typed in UPPER CASE. (FADE IN NAT SOUND)
6. THE TALENT'S NAME STARTS EACH NEW LINE, BUT DOES NOT HAVE TO BE REPEATED IF THE SAME PERSON OR SOUND SOURCE CONTINUES.	6. SAM: Note--the name is in caps, what Sam says is in upper and lower case.
7. DO NOT SPLIT SHOTS AT BOTTOM OF THE PAGE.	7. Don't split words or thoughts at the end of the line or page. If the story continues to the next page, let the talent know by writing-- (MORE)

Script Formats

FIG. 4.7 – The dual-column format clearly separates visual and aural aspects of the script. This makes it easier for audio operators to concentrate on their responsibilities and for graphics and camera operators to do the same. The most common use of the dual-column format is in live-action television productions, commercials, sports, and game shows.

Organizing Forms

Once you prepare scripts, the next line of paperwork begins. You give all members of the production team storyboards, location scouting information, site surveys, and plots as handy tools to maintain consistency and to help others understand what you are trying to accomplish with this production and how it will be accomplished.

Storyboards

Storyboards are paper visualizations of the production. You provide a flexible means of working out sequences, framing, and shot relationships before bringing an expensive cast and crew together for the actual production. Storyboards are usually organized in three parts: picture, copy/instructions, and shot number (see Figure 4.8).

Generally, a storyboard form displays a 4:3 or 16:9 area, with rounded corners; it contains the video frame, with a small space above the frame for writing in the shot number. Below the frame is an area, usually slightly smaller than the frame, designed to contain the audio or other specific instructions for that shot. Storyboard forms are available in preprinted packets or as a computer program template. Such templates allow you to draw and redraw until the design is satisfactory without creating stacks of printed boards. Such templates may be passed among creative staff for alterations and feedback before the final script is created.

You sketch the key objects in the shot into the frame block. These visual representations can be as simple as stick figures or as accurate as color photographs. The more accurate the drawings, the more serviceable the storyboard will be in solving problems during preproduction and production. The matching space for instructions may contain "pan," "dolly," or other camera movement or composition concepts. The shot number must match the shot number on your script. If you make additions or deletions, then you must change the shot number on both the script and storyboard. You should represent each shot by at least one storyboard frame. In some cases, additional frames may be necessary to show beginning and ending frame positions if a pan, dolly, or zoom is indicated.

Once completed, you can place storyboard frames on a wall or flannel board so they can be rearranged easily. Standing back and looking at all of the storyboard frames gives everyone involved in the production a better overall view of the production and can provide the means to spot problem areas or solutions to problems.

Because the storyboard frame, description, and shot number can be separated from other storyboard frames, you can manipulate them until you reach the best possible shot sequence. This process may prevent continuity problems by avoiding jump cuts and may create a more organized method of shooting the production. Once you have arranged the complete storyboard order, then you can write the final shooting script.

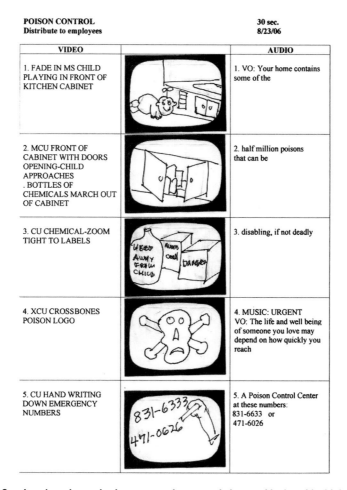

Organizing Forms

FIG. 4.8 – Storyboard can be as simple or as complex as needed to provide the critical information to all crew members. The images in a storyboard can be as sophisticated as photographs or simple line drawings as long as they accurately depict what is to be shown and heard.

Location Scouting

You should visualize of the type of shooting location you require early on in the production conceptualization process. Specific locations can be chosen after the scene script has been written, but you must finalize the location before the shooting script has been completed.

Besides the obvious characteristics you should look for in a location—accessibility and having the right setting or appearance—some are less than obvious. You want a cost-free location near parking, power, and sanitary facilities and convenient storage space for equipment and materials. The availability of temperature-controlled areas for cast and crew to use between takes is also important. Once you choose a location, arrange a meeting with the site authority.

At this meeting, you must gather and document the following information: the names, phone numbers, and exact locations or addresses of the authorities who control the areas and locations to be used. This person may be the resident, building engineer, building manager, janitor, department head, or a civil employee in charge of public areas. Make certain that the person who has given permission to use the location actually has the authority to do so, and then get it in writing, along with a location release (see Figure 4.9).

While meeting with the site authority, the producer should explain fully how the site will be used, what changes may be necessary, how restoration will be handled, and what access the production crew will have to the location. Discuss every contingency that could occur during the production so that no unresolved differences crop up during actual production.

Put into writing all agreements, have the site authority sign them, keep copies, give the site authority copies, and send copies to the ultimate authority of the location. Perform this act well before the shoot is scheduled so that any problems can be resolved before the cast and crew arrive for the shoot.

MOUNTAIN PRODUCTIONS
LOCATION RELEASE

    I hereby irrevocably grant to <u>Mountain Productions</u> the right to use the property described below which is owned and/or controlled by me at

_____
(full legal description of property)

in connection with the production, duplication, and/or distribution of the video, film, or sound recording program, segment, or shots recorded on:

_____ , by <u>Mountain Productions</u>.
    (Date)

    I hereby assign to <u>Mountain Productions</u> all rights, title, and interest in the materials as they are integrated into the final master film, videotape, or audio recording, granting full and unrestricted permission and authority to <u>Mountain Productions</u> to record, reproduce, and use in any manner, media, or form whatsoever including securing copyrights for the final master and subsequent copies of all media materials produced which includes the image of my property, warranting that I have unrestricted right to make this grant an assignment and hereby release and agree to indemnify and save harmless <u>Mountain Productions</u>, its staff and agents for any and all liability, claims, actions, and damages arising in an manner from the material which contains the image of my property.

    For the use of the above described property and the right described in this clearance, <u>Mountain Productions</u> agrees to compensate me as follows:

    I express my intention to be firmly and legally bound this_____ day of

_____, 20___ .

_____   _____
(Signature)   (Witness)

_____   _____
(Print Name)   (Print Name)

_____   _____
(Street Address)   (Street Address)

_____   _____
(City-State-Zip)   (City-State-Zip)

FIG. 4.9 – A location release is a legal document and should be treated as such. Make certain it is accurately filled out and properly signed and dated, and keep a copy in a safe location for future reference. The purpose of the release is to provide written proof that you have permission to shoot in the indicated location in case police or other authorities question your presence.

Organizing Forms

Site Survey

Be sure to visit the location at the time of day, day of the week, and, if possible, day of the month that the production will be shot. This precautionary act may help you to avoid unplanned traffic, noise, lighting, and ambient sound problems. You need to measure each room or space to be used accurately, and you need to plot a scale drawing indicating the location and sizes of windows and doors, the furniture placement, and placement of walls and power sources. In addition, you need to determine the location of power outlet and the location of the fuse or circuit-breaker box. Discuss with the site authority whether you may tap into the fuse box or if it can be left open in case a fuse or breaker blows. If the box is left open, the crew can correct the problems without waiting for the box to be unlocked or handled by an assigned person. While checking the location of the fuse box, check and make a note of the power rating of each circuit and determine which circuits control specific outlets that you may use.

Once all of the measurements have been taken and the plot is drawn, then you should identify possible locations for performers and cameras. Note the movements of the performers as well as camera movements. If furniture needs to be moved or extra furniture or set pieces are required, this should be indicated on the plot. The plot is a scale diagram drawn as if you are looking straight down on the location. Do not draw it in perspective, as it is useless if not drawn to an accurate scale (see Figure 4.10).

Before leaving the site meeting, determine from the site authority where production vehicles may be safely and legally parked and the location of a loading area. When possible, choose a loading/parking location that is well lit and under some security. If the location does not provide security for vehicles, it may be necessary to hire or provide your own security personnel. If permits for parking or loading are required, determine the process and authority for getting such permits. Keep in mind that not even public property can be used for any production purpose without permission, a permit, and often a fee.

Before leaving the site during the survey, recheck all of the information gathered and make certain you have all the facts, permits, measurements, and telephone numbers. Make sure that there are no conflicts or contradictions in your lists.

SITE SURVEY PLOT

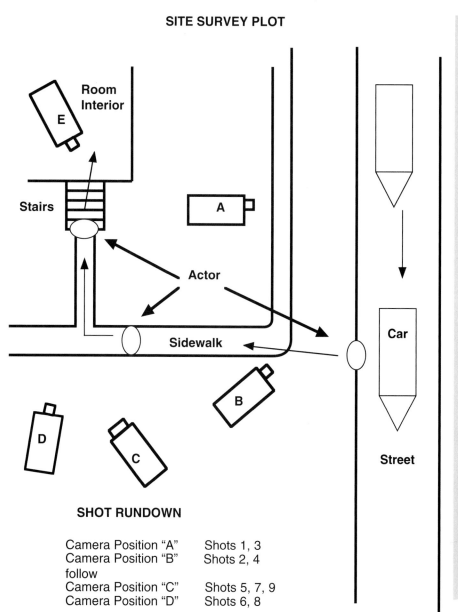

SHOT RUNDOWN

Camera Position "A"	Shots 1, 3
Camera Position "B"	Shots 2, 4
follow	
Camera Position "C"	Shots 5, 7, 9
Camera Position "D"	Shots 6, 8

FIG. 4.10 – A plot must be drawn accurately and to scale. Measure accurately while on site survey and then with plotting tools accurately draw the plan to reveal exactly the relationship between camera and subject positions as well as physical objects such as buildings, stairs, and sidewalks.

Organizing Equipment and Crew

With the completed shooting script and plot in hand, you can sit down at the site later and determine which shots are to be made from each camera location. You should indicate on a *shooting list, shot rundown* (shot sheet), which shots are to be taken at each camera location and the order in which they are to be shot. The most efficient use of cast, crew, and equipment should be the key factor in this determination. Make certain all possible shots are planned from each location before the camera and lights are moved to the next location.

Once the site survey has been completed, meet with your camera operator, gaffer, and audio operator to list the equipment required for the shoot. These three key crew members should accompany the director on the site survey if at all possible. Each crew chief is responsible for the equipment needed to fulfill his or her responsibilities, but a production meeting should be held to double-check all aspects of the production and to exchange ideas, generate solutions to problems, and resolve unanswered concerns.

Making a list of equipment helps ensure that everything has been thought of that will be needed. It can also be used as a checklist when packing up the equipment to make certain that nothing has been left behind at the end of the shoot. You confer with the crew chiefs on the number and skills of crew members required. Most EFP shoots are organized to use a minimum number of people, but the complexity of the production determines the size of the crew.

Once all the lists are completed, you and your producer work out a detailed schedule that starts with that day and ends with the delivery of the finished product. You need to organize each stage of the production on a *timeline* so each stage can proceed unaffected by delays in other stages, if at all possible. The interdependency of media production makes a timeline critical in the efficient completion of any project (see Figure 4.11).

Once all of the preproduction planning has been completed, you can move the cast and crew into the production stages toward completion of the project.

TIMELINE PLOT

DATE	RESEARCH WRITING	PRE-PROD. SURVEYS	PRODUCTION	POST-PROD.
Jan. 1	Begin research			
Jan. 15	Develop concept			
Feb. 1	Deliver proposal			
Feb. 15	Deliver treatment			
March 1	Compete research			
March 15	Treatment approved			
April 1		Location scouting		
April 15	Scene script approved	Sign location contracts		
May 1	Shooting script approved	Cast-crew equipment contracts		
May 15		Begin rehearsals	Set up for shooting	
June 1				Begin editing
June 15			Complete major videography	
July 30			Pick-up shots	Review rough cut
Aug. 1				
Aug. 15				Deliver answer print
Aug. 30				Deliver completed master

99

Organizing Forms

FIG. 4.11 – A timeline provides a general guide for planning on when cast, crew, and equipment must be ready to work. It also gives the producer a schedule to refer to while preparing the writing aspects of the production. A copy of the timeline often accompanies the proposal/treatment/budget package presented to the funding source.

Chapter Five
The Production Process: Production

Production Stages and Setup

In the production process, you will follow four standard stages in the actual shooting of an electronic field production (EFP): setting up, rehearsing, shooting, and striking.

Setting Up

Assuming you followed the preproduction steps, the first step of the production stage is to unload the equipment and move it to the first shooting location. A word about security: Professional video equipment is expensive and looks attractive to thieves. You must never leave equipment unguarded, and never leave the production vehicle unlocked. You and the crew move the equipment from the vehicle efficiently to the first camera setup, unless you use the vehicle as a field control room.

Field Equipment Considerations

You will find field equipment much more susceptible than studio equipment to damage and technical problems from the environment. Because the majority of the operating parts are electronic, at a certain level of humidity your equipment becomes inoperative. This is particularly true of tape and disc decks. In addition, keep all liquids away from all electronic equipment. Severely cold weather slows mechanical works, such as the motors that drive decks and zoom lenses. Extreme heat affects circuits inside the camera and decks and may damage tape stock. In most cases you can compensate for these factors, but they must be taken into consideration when planning a field production. If your camera records directly onto a computer hard disk, memory card, or disc medium, you need to take this into consideration to prevent moisture or dust from entering the medium case. If your signal is recorded onto a chip, that process does not require any moving mechanical operations, making your camcorder much more rugged and impervious to temperature and humidity changes.

Setting Up

Camera Setup

Once you determine the camera's position, set up your tripod. Its legs need to be set in a wide enough stance to provide a stable base, but not spread so far apart that they are in the way of traffic or the operator. The height of the tripod should be adjusted to the eye level of the subject, unless you require a special angle.

You should level the head of the tripod with the bubble level, and then you can mount the camera on the head. Make certain the pan and tilt locks are tight, or if the tripod head does not have locks, tighten the drag controls so the camera will not tilt out of control. Set the drag controls tight enough so that there is enough back pressure to allow for a smooth, even pan or tilt, not so tight as to cause a jerk when you try to pan or tilt. You should set the legs of the tripod so you can stand between two legs and do not need to straddle a leg (see Figure 5.1).

If you mount the camera on a body mount, a second person should help balance the camera and rig until all of the controls are balanced and set. If you handhold the camera, you need to adjust all of the controls ahead of time instead, before placing your camera on your shoulder. It is difficult to look at the menu in order to set all of the variables—such as aspect ratio, frame rate, white balance (automatic or manual), and the choice of scan rates—and balance the camera at the same time.

Depending on your choice of power source for the camera, check to make certain the battery is fully charged or make certain the power cord is long enough to allow for whatever movement is required. Also, all power cords should be protected from accidental disconnect; have a gaffer tape the cable both at the end where it is plugged into the source and to the tripod, not the camera.

FIG. 5.1 – Solid, stable, yet flexible camera mounting equipment gives the camera operator the maximum freedom to operate the camera according to the needs of the director and production. (Courtesy JVC.)

Setting Up

Audio Preparation

While the camera operator and gaffer set up their equipment, the audio operator strings mic cables or sets up the receivers for wireless mics. If a mixer is used, then the operator needs to string cables to the mixer and the output of the mixer to the recorder or camcorder. Make certain levels are checked to determine if the entire audio system is operating and is balanced.

If you use a boom mic, then its position needs to be checked with the camera operator, lighting director, and director. If you use body mics, the operator needs to place them on the performers, check batteries, show the performers how to turn the mics on, and check to be sure a signal at the proper level is being received at the mixer or recorder (see Figure 5.2).

The audio operator is responsible for all sound. If playback audio is required, then the audio operator must set up the speakers, cables, and audio source, such as a tape deck, CD, or iPod player. If the production involves live music, then the audio operator has the responsibility of placing mics on the band, soloists, or other music sources. In some cases, you will require that the audio be recorded on a separate recorder, usually a digital deck. This arrangement is also the responsibility of the audio operator. Headphones, audio monitor circuits, and any other source or control of sound belongs to the audio operator.

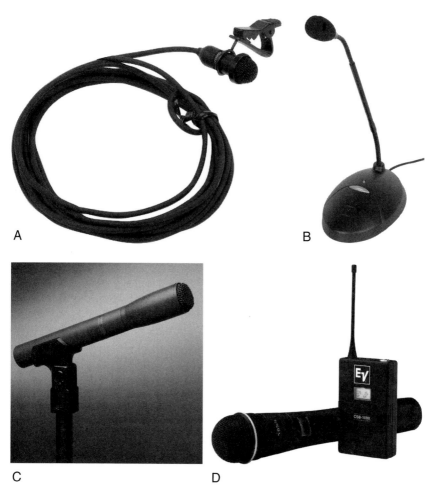

A

B

C

D

FIG. 5.2 – Stable and security mounting equipment and secure cable connections are key responsibilities of the audio operator. The decision about what type of mic works best for each shot or sequence should be made by the audio operator and the director. (Courtesy Electro Voice and AudioTechna.)

Prompting Devices

Often you will require some type of *prompting device*, especially for commercial shoots. There are three basic types of prompters: handheld, camera-mounted, and in-ear devices.

Handheld prompters are pieces of poster board bearing either the entire copy lettered in large bold type or an outline of keywords that the performer ad-libs around. These cards have been called *idiot cards* in deference to the talent.

The most common prompting device today is a monitor mounted above or below the camera lens with two angled mirrors reflecting the monitor image directly in front of the camera lens. This gives the members of the audience the impression that the talent is looking directly at them, but in reality, the performer is looking at the image of the copy reflected from a mirror mounted in front of the camera lens. The source of the copy can be scripts that are taped together in a continuous sheet and passed under a black-and-white camera or from a dedicated prompter computer or character generator (see Figure 5.3).

The third method requires a special skill on the part of the performer. A small headset is placed in the performer's ear, and a recording of the copy (which the talent previously made) is played back in the performer's ear. Skilled announcers can repeat vast amounts of their own words slightly delayed from the original as if they were speaking from memory. Of course, the best option is for the performer to take the time and trouble to memorize all of his or her lines.

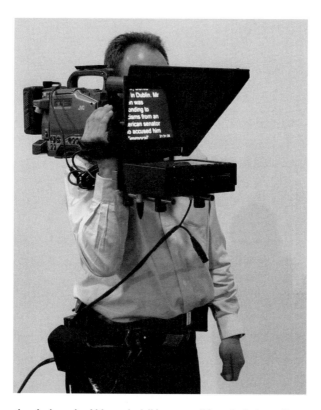

FIG. 5.3 – Prompting devices should be as invisible as possible to both the audience and the rest of the production process. As cameras decrease in size, a large set of monitors and reflectors mounted on the front of the camera can become a problem. In that case, the prompter can be mounted on a gaffer stand close to the side of the camera or immediately below the lens. (Courtesy Autocue-QTV.)

Setting Up

Sets and Properties

For most field productions, sets and properties (props) exist at the chosen location but need to be carefully checked before or during setup. The convenience of using already existing rooms, furniture, and other props may be one of the main reasons you choose to shoot a production in the field. At the same time, a careful choice of a location is critical in the field production process.

There are three levels of items in this category: sets, set pieces, and hand props. *Sets* are backgrounds. They may be actual walls, trees, construction made of cloth or wood, or simply the actual location suitable for the particular production. *Set pieces* are items attached to or placed within a set. Generally, set pieces include paintings on walls, furniture, automobiles, or bookcases. *Props* are items small enough to be picked up and handled, but for the most part, they are items that the talent needs to handle during the production (see Figure 5.4).

You make choices in each of the categories with the art director. These items should match the tone, time period, quality, and attitude of the production. A beautiful painting should not hang in a set that is supposed to be a dingy office. At the same time, a cheap, poorly done painting should not be seen hanging in a room that is supposed to be the office of a Fortune 500 CEO. You make these choices on the basis of your and your team's knowledge of art, architecture, and interior design.

Designing for high definition (HD) is more critical than designing and executing for standard definition (SD). The increased detail of HD shows every small defect in appearance, every sloppy paint job, and every poorly matched or worn and outdated set piece. Design for HD needs to be examined with a magnifying glass to check each detail in the completed design before cameras start looking.

As in lighting design, your set design sends a clearly defined message and must match the rest of the production details to avoid confusing and misleading the audience. You need to make set design decisions during preproduction planning, but often you cannot finalize the plans until the setup period with the crew on location. This is when you should rearrange furniture, rehang paintings, and remove unnecessary or conflicting items from a room being used as a location site.

FIG. 5.4 – A set and its decoration should match the time and mode of the production. Everything on the set should have a purpose, including balancing the frame. The arrangement must fit the action of the scene and the movement of the performers.

Lighting Preparation

As soon as you and the crew arrive at the location, the lighting director or gaffer should run the power cable to your camcorder or recorder and then string power cables to the lighting instrument locations. Once you place your camera in position, the gaffer can start placing the instruments. The crew should run power cables where there is the least amount of foot traffic, out of sight of the camera, yet with as short a run as possible. As mentioned earlier, you must give close consideration to the amount of amperage drawn by the lighting instruments to avoid blowing breakers or fuses.

Proper lighting is an artistic endeavor. While there is much science and practicality to lighting design, lighting is probably the most artistic portion of video production. There are no hard and fast rules, only guidelines. There are typical and traditional setups, but every lighting situation is unique and must be approached from an individualistic direction. The lighting depends partly on you and the writer's concept of the production and partly on the requirements set by the location, budget, availability of equipment, and time to create the lighting ambiance desired.

You might use one of three types of basic EFP lighting: *realistic, abstract*, or *neutral*. Dramatic productions and some types of commercials require as realistic a lighting setting as possible. You may require abstract lighting that goes beyond realism for music videos, some commercials, and science fiction dramas. You may use neutral lighting for game shows, newscasts, situation comedies, and some commercials. Hard and fast rules defining each of these types of lighting do not exist, but the end result must match the director's requirements.

Lighting for a high-definition production requires greater attention to detail and the needs of the highly critical cameras. It is not a matter of more light, rather a better placement of lighting instruments and the shadows and light patterns that follow.

In addition to your requirements for the lighting—that it set the mood, time, and type of production—the lighting must provide enough base illumination for the camera to create a usable image. As mentioned early in this text, the camera or chips reproduce what is presented to them. The light must be of the correct color and intensity and be within the contrast range of the particular type of camera in use. These three factors—*color, intensity*, and *contrast*—control the basic lighting setup. Once they have been satisfied, you may use creative and innovative lighting techniques.

Lighting Preparation

Controlling Color Temperature

You control color temperature in studio productions by installing lamps with the same color temperature output in all lighting fixtures. In the field, controlling color temperature is not that simple. Even though all of the instruments may be lamped with the same Kelvin temperature bulbs, windows, fluorescent lighting fixtures, and even standard incandescent fixtures create variations in color temperature. If possible, you should light a set only with lighting instruments lamped with the proper bulbs. Cover windows with drapes, blinds, or a large sheet of Wratten 85 (yellow-orange) filter material.

A second method you may use if daylight is entering a room is to convert the field lighting fixtures to approximate daylight by covering them with Wratten 82 (blue) filter material or a dichroic filter. This helps match the mixed lighting, but it does not help you to balance the difference in light intensity between the daylight and the lighting instruments. This is because the blue filter reduces the lighting instrument output by about half, requiring more powerful or a greater number of lamps.

If many incandescent fixtures are present and you cannot cover or turn them off, the white balance circuits on most digital cameras will reach white balance without a filter in place.

If you must shoot in a location lit by existing office fluorescent lamps, you may consider several possible solutions. First, the process you use to white balance when only fluorescent lamps are present is determined by the type of fluorescent tube. Newer tubes designed specifically for media production are intended to match either daylight or tungsten lighting Kelvin temperature. New portable fluorescent, halogen metal iodide (HMI), and light-emitting diode (LED) lighting fixtures balanced close to daylight are now available, providing another method of field flat lighting (see Figure 5.5).

You may set white balance automatically with built-in circuits in some digital cameras, or you may shoot a white board within the light source of that shot and press the white balance button on the camera. You can correct white balance using color filters mounted between the lens or mounted on the lens.

A   B

C

Lighting Preparation

FIG. 5.5 – Color temperature can be controlled with filters and digital circuits within the camera, on light instruments, and by a choice of specifically design light instruments such as LED, HMI, and fluorescent. (Courtesy Arriflex, Lowell Lights, and Lite.)

Controlling Light Intensity

You may control light intensity in a studio setting in a variety of ways: by varying the voltage to each instrument through a dimmer board, by adding *filters* or *scrims* to the instruments, or by mounting or moving instruments closer or farther away from the subject.

In the field, you are limited with light intensity controls by the types of portable equipment available. For the average EFP production, simpler means of light control than those used in the studio are necessary. Generally, the lighting instruments you use in the field are open-faced instruments, which means that the light is harsher and more difficult for you to control. You can use scrims and filters and bouncing the light to soften, diffuse, and lower the light level to that required for fill lights. Small portable dimmers are available for field use, but lowering the voltage of a tungsten lamp changes the color temperature approximately 100 degrees for each 10-volt variation.

The most practical way to control light intensity in the field is your placement of the lighting instruments. Because light levels follow the inverse square law, a relatively small movement of a lamp makes a major difference in the light level falling on the subject. If a lamp provides 100 foot-candles of light at a distance of 10 feet from the subject, moving the lamp to 5 feet boosts the light level to 400 foot-candles (the inverse square of $1/2$ equals 4 times the original light level; therefore, 100 becomes 400). If you move the lamp back to 20 feet, the light level falls to 25 foot-candles (the inverse square of 2 is $1/4$ times the original light level of 100, resulting in 25 foot-candles) (see Figure 5.6).

INVERSE SQUARE LAW

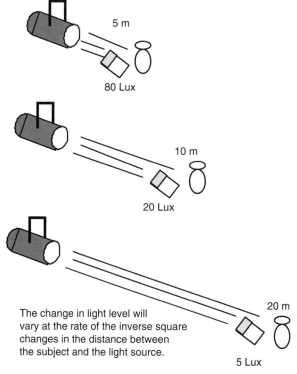

The change in light level will vary at the rate of the inverse square changes in the distance between the subject and the light source.

Cut the distance in half will quadruple the light intensity = 4 x Lux (4 x 20 Lux = 20 Lux)
Double the distance will cut the light intensity by 1/4 = 1/4 x Lux (1/4 x 20 Lux = 5 Lux)

FIG. 5.6 – Most EFP lighting directors find they can achieve the light levels and effects required by the director with a combination of lighting instrument placement and the judicious use of scrims, filters, barn doors, and flags.

Lighting Preparation

Contrast Range

The control for contrast is a little more complex. You need a reflected spotlight meter to measure the amount of light reflected from the brightest and darkest objects in the picture. These light measurements are called *reflectance values*. If you measure the amount of light reflected from the brightest portion of the frame in which detail is required more than 30 to 40 times the light in the darkest area needed for detail, then you need to add full light to the dark areas or you need to remove some light from the lighter areas. By carefully lighting for the contrast range of the video camera, you can avoid having important areas "bloom" or "flare" into a white mass or having large areas appear so dark and black that they look muddy.

You will find the most difficult situations for maintaining proper contrast range are those shots taken in the bright sunlight or at night with available light. During a cloudless bright day, it is nearly impossible to balance the bright sun with any other light source to maintain contrast range. The best method to balance the lighting is to use the sun as the backlight and reflect the sunlight back toward the subject.

Night lighting is more difficult. Some source of fill is needed to overcome the bright, harsh light from streetlights, automobile headlights, advertising signs, and other lights. The easiest method is for you to shoot at dawn or dusk, except that the time period when there is enough light to shoot and still have it look like night is very short.

Basic Three-Point Lighting

Lighting practice is based on two suppositions: that there will be enough light for the camera to create a reasonably useful picture and that the appearance will fulfill the look that you desire. *Basic three-point* lighting is designed to satisfy both of these requirements. Three-point lighting derives its name from the three lighting instruments used to achieve satisfactory levels and appearance: key lights, fill lights, and back-lights. The *key light* duplicates the major light source in our lives, the sun, and, sec-ondarily, the overhead lighting present in most homes and work spaces. The *fill light* balances the key light, reducing the contrast ratio and softening the harsh look of a one-light source. The *backlight* adds a rim of light around the subject to separate it from the background and adds a third dimension to the two-dimensional video field (see Figure 5.7).

Backlight

The backlight is the first instrument set in place, because once performers, set pieces, and props are in place, it is difficult to reach the proper position for a backlight. You set the key light next; then the fill, kickers, set, and extra lights are set. The backlight instrument is mounted above and slightly behind the major subject and directly oppo-site the camera position. Because this lamp is focused toward the camera, you must use barn doors or flags to avoid having the backlight shine directly into the lens of the camera.

Key Light

You use the key light as the main source of light. It should always have motivation—that is, there should be a reason for its angle and position. If there is no apparent motivation, then set the key about 45 degrees above the camera and from 60 to 40 degrees to one side of the camera. The key should be the brightest light under normal circumstances. It can create shadows, adding depth to the picture, and should set the major color temperature for that shot or scene.

Fill Light

The fill light represents the reflected light from clouds, the sky, buildings, and multiple light sources found in buildings. In some ways, it is like the backlight, an artificial light, but it is very important in video production to bring the contrast ratio down to a level that a video camera can handle. You mount the fill light on the opposite side of the camera from the key; this is of a lower intensity, softer and more diffused, and should not create any visible shadows.

Lighting Preparation

Kicker and Set Lights

You may require a variety of other lighting instruments to create either realistic light or the effect desired in the scene. The two most common are the kicker and the set light. You mount the *kicker* light to one side of the subject so that it throws its light along the side of the subject. This light acts much like the backlight, helping to separate the subject from the background, thus adding depth to the frame.

The *set light* is designed to highlight specific areas of the set. Sometimes it also separates the subject from the set, but more often it is designed to draw attention to particular areas of the set, such as a logo, important set piece, or a lit area of an otherwise dark background.

BASIC LIGHTING PLOT

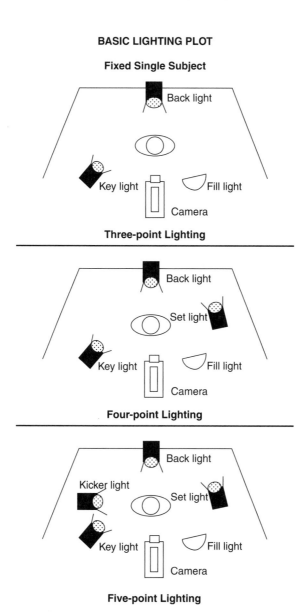

FIG. 5.7 – Basic three-point lighting must be approached as a starting point for establishing the appearance needed for a particular shot or sequence. Three-point also is the starting point for adding instruments as needed for four- or five-point lighting.

Lighting Preparation

Multiple or Moving Subjects

Lighting a single subject that does not move during the recording is relatively simple. The lighting process becomes complicated when there is more than one subject in the frame and those subjects begin to move about on camera.

You may light multiple subjects by spreading the light wider to take in more than one subject, but this method is usually unsatisfactory. Unless both subjects are facing the same direction and are an equal distance from the light source, they will be lit unevenly. Another solution is to *cross-key* light—that is, use the key light for the subject on one side and as the fill for the subject on the other side, and vice versa. If you are shooting more than two subjects, you may require key lights for each subject and a widespread series of fill lights covering the entire area. You can avoid multiple shadows by washing out some of the shadows with fill and set lights or by focusing the keys so that the shadows fall outside of the area covered by the camera frame (see Figure 5.8).

If subjects move, lighting becomes even more complex. One solution is to arrange key lights and backlights so that they throw a relatively even pattern of light over the area of movement at an equal distance from the light source. Fill is easily flooded out to cover the entire area. Another solution is to break the movement down into several shots. Each shot will cover only a small portion of the movement area and can be more easily lit because the subject can be lit in roughly the same intensity for each shot.

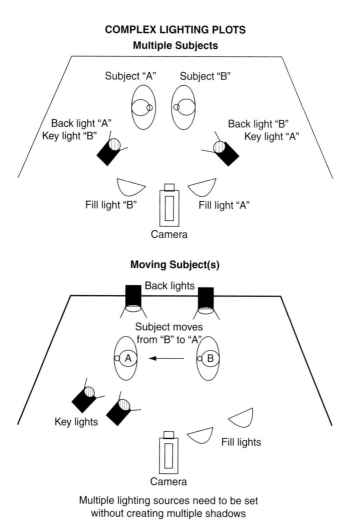

COMPLEX LIGHTING PLOTS
Multiple Subjects

Subject "A"   Subject "B"

Back light "A"   Back light "B"
Key light "B"   Key light "A"

Fill light "B"   Fill light "A"

Camera

Moving Subject(s)

Back lights

Subject moves
from "B" to "A"

A   B

Key lights

Fill lights

Camera

Multiple lighting sources need to be set
without creating multiple shadows

FIG. 5.8 – One advantage of lighting for digital cameras is their ability to provide well-balanced images with a minimum of harsh key lights. Using fill lights for key light often will provide the needed amount of light as well as the contrast ratio required.

Creative Lighting

Beyond providing enough light for the camera to produce a usable picture, lighting is also a key creative visual element. Light sets the mood and may be used to indicate the time, the date, and the location of a production.

Mood Lighting

From the first moment an audience sees the opening shots of a situation comedy, the viewers are made aware that they are in for some light-hearted entertainment. Much of that realization comes from the high-key, low-contrast, nearly shadowless lighting used, known as *Notan* lighting. This term came from Japanese artists who painted brightly lit scenes without any shadows. The brightly lit set without any dark areas lets the viewers know the mood the director wants them to experience.

On the other hand, if you light the first shot of a scene with low-key, high-contrast, heavy, dark shadows, the audience is made aware that this is a heavy drama. This type of lighting is called *chiaroscuro*, borrowed from the Italian painters who used the same high contrast to set the mood of their paintings. Of course, you may use all creative techniques in contrast; a comedy scene may be lit in low key to make it funnier because that visual approach is unexpected.

Lighting for Time, Date, and Location

You may use lighting to indicate time, date, and location as a more subtle but important consideration when designing a scene. Early morning and late afternoon light is different from that at high noon. The colors are different (early and late in the day, the light is warmer, redder), and the angle of the light is lower. Winter sun is bluer and colder; the lights of summer, fall, and spring each have their own colors and contrast levels.

You also may use light simply as an abstract creative object in and of itself. Light slashes across the background create a feeling of prison bars, window slats, venetian blinds, or other settings not actually present. *Cukaloris* patterns on a plain background tell the audience an infinite number of characteristics about a scene. A cukaloris (also know as a cookie or gobo) is a metal disc inserted into an ellipsoidal spotlight that creates a light pattern or mottled design on the background (see Figure 5.9).

Top - Ellipsoidal Spotlight
Bottom - Cukaloris (Gobo, Cookies)

FIG. 5.9 – An ellipsoidal spot with "cookies" installed may created a variety of patterns on a background. (Courtesy ETC and Apollo Design Technology.)

Lighting Preparation

Directing and Rehearsing

Directing Talent

Once all of the physical setup procedures have begun, you then concentrate on the human values that make up a production. Direction of actors is the most complex part of your job. The performance of an actor depends on many variables beyond your control. An actor's training, background, experience (both in acting and in life), and mental state during the shoot all affect a performance. You must then blend this knowledge with the results of an in-depth study of the script and the plan the director has for how to accomplish his or her interpretation of that script.

Interpersonal communication is the key to working with actors, who are in a vulnerable position. It is their faces and voices that the audience will view. If the production comes off poorly, it is actors that the audience will remember. You must clearly communicate to the actor exactly what you need, how it fits into the overall production, and how the actor will look and sound. The more precise the direction, for most actors, the better the performance. Without delving into various acting schools and methods, actors perform better if they are aware of why they are doing what they have been asked to do. Supplying this motivation makes their job easier and their acting generally more realistic.

Rehearsal

While the crew is setting up equipment, you work with the talent and supervise all of the other operations. You also check on all sets, props, prompting devices, and other materials to be used in the first sequence. The setup period blends into the rehearsal period, but actual rehearsal cannot take place until cameras, lights, and microphones are in place and the crew has received preliminary production instructions. You must include a written instructions sheet for each crew member or crew section. The lighting director and key grip receive the instructions if a full crew is used; the gaffer and grip receive the instructions if there is one crew member for each position.

LIGHTING PLOT AND SHOT RUNDOWN

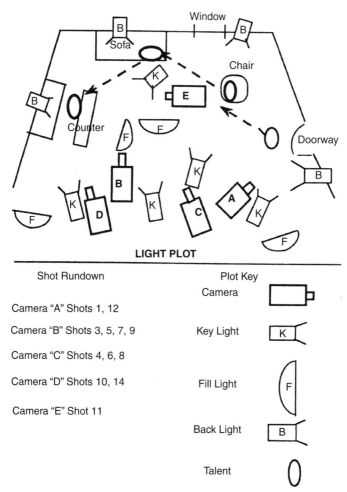

Shot Rundown	Plot Key
	Camera
Camera "A" Shots 1, 12	
Camera "B" Shots 3, 5, 7, 9	Key Light
Camera "C" Shots 4, 6, 8	
Camera "D" Shots 10, 14	Fill Light
Camera "E" Shot 11	
	Back Light
	Talent

FIG. 5.10 – An accurate plot of the set helps the rehearsal to run more efficiently by mapping out the camera positions, lighting instruments, set piece placement, and, as important, the planned movement of the performers.

Directing and Rehearsing

For the lighting and stage crew, a plot shows the position of the camera for each setup, talent positions and movements, key furniture, and backgrounds or other set pieces. The camera operator receives a shot sheet listing the camera positions in the order of setup and shots to be completed at each camera position in the order they will be shot. A plot also is helpful for the camera operator (see Figure 5.10).

During setup, you make certain that all performers are present, in makeup and costume, and prepared to shoot their scenes. You lead general discussions about movements, line delivery, motivation, and relationships between actors and other objects while the crew is completing the setup process.

Once the location is ready, you walk the actors through their starting locations, blocking, and movements, if there are any. You have the camera operator watch the blocking rehearsal so that she or he can visualize the camera movements needed for each shot. At this time the actors should deliver their lines with mics properly placed so the audio operator can set levels and determine if any audio problems exist.

You play the role of a benevolent dictator to the cast and crew. You must have absolute control, but at the same time, you must respect and listen to the members of the crew for the benefit of their knowledge and expertise. No crew or cast member should argue with you, but a professional difference of opinion leading to a discussion is permissible if there is time. At the end of the discussion, your decision is final and must be accepted by all of the cast and crew as such without rancor or spite. Your decision should be based on your knowledge of the entire production, not on the relatively narrow view each cast and crew member might hold.

Once you have completed a successful walk-through rehearsal, you should run several camera rehearsals. This involves everyone on the cast and crew completing their roles as if the shot is being taped. Once you are satisfied with the performance of both cast and crew, then you order a take.

Directing and Rehearsing

Shooting

The actual process for shooting a take is as follows: You call for quiet on the set by calling out, "Quiet" or "Stand by." At that command, complete silence is expected from all cast and crew members. If the shoot is at a public location, a crew member may have to circulate and quiet the adjacent crowd unless the noise of the crowd is part of the audio ambiance. At the "Stand by" cue, all cast and crew assume their starting positions and prepare physically and mentally for the beginning of the shot.

When you feel everyone is ready, you call, "Roll tape," "Roll it," or maybe even "Roll 'em." As soon as the deck is up to speed, either the camera operator (if a camcorder is used) or the tape operator (if a separate recorder is being used) calls out, "Speed," or "Locked in," or "Framed." You perform a 5-second count, either silently or out loud, and then call, "Action." This 5-second delay is necessary to make certain the deck has recorded at least 5 seconds of clean sync and control track or time code, which is needed for editing purposes. Professional actors will pause a beat and then start their movement or lines. The crew will follow the action as directed during rehearsals (see Figure 5.11).

During a take, there are three people who may shout, "Cut." The major responsibility lies with you, but either the camera operator or the audio operator also may cut a shot. If the camera operator sees in the viewfinder a visual error bad enough to make the take unusable, he or she may yell, "Cut." It is best if the camera operator quickly consults with you before doing so in case the audio portion of that take is usable even though the video is not. The audio operator has the same responsibility in monitoring the recorded audio. If a noise is present that makes the take unusable, the audio operator also may call "Cut," but once again, because there is always a chance the video is usable, the audio operator seldom cuts a take without a quick conference with you. In fact, an audio operator seldom cuts a take because most audio can be looped or rerecorded in a *Foley* session during postproduction if necessary. Any crew member may shout "Cut" if a situation occurs that may hurt either a cast or crew member. During both rehearsals and actual recording, standardized electronic media communication hand cues and signals should be used.

HAND CUES

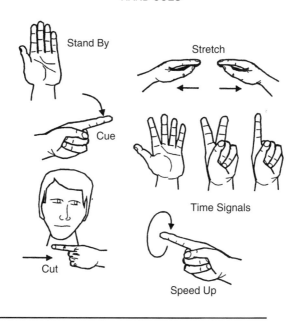

Stand By

Stretch

Cue

Time Signals

Cut

Speed Up

DIRECTOR'S VERBAL CUES

STAND BY   This is a call for quiet on the set or location, especially from
            the cast and crew. It means they must give the director their
            undivided attention and wait for the next cue.

ROLL TAPE   This is the cue to the tape or camera operator to start tape
            rolling and recording, and must be followed by--

SPEED   (By the tape or camera operator)
            This cue indicates to the director that the tape is rolling
            and recording, up to speed and locked in, ready for the
            call for action.

ACTION   This indicates to both the cast and crew to start their
            rehearsed action, speech, movement, etc.

CUT   This cue means to stop recording, acting, or any other action.
            It is an indication from the director that either the required
            material has been recorded or that something has gone
            wrong and to continue would be a waste of time.

FIG. 5.11 – Silent hand cues are a necessity to communicate quickly and accurately without disturbing the performers, adding unwanted noise to the sound track, or interfering in any way with the efficient operation of a scene. Most hand cues are understood universally within the media production industry, but as with any language, variations do exist.

Shooting

Shooting and Framing

A relationship of trust and communication must also exist between you and the camera operator, only this time, the trust runs in the opposite direction. You must trust the camera operator to frame, focus, and expose the shot as the director wants. Detailed communication from you to the camera operator provides the best first step toward accomplishing that relationship. If the camera operator understands what you want and need in a shot, sequence, or scene, she or he is better equipped to provide it.

Standard Shot Names

Over the years, starting with motion pictures, the different placements of objects in the field of the camera, called *framing*, have acquired specific names. As in every aspect of media production, there are some variations in these names; nevertheless, the following definitions are accepted and understood by all professionals.

When the angle of view varies from the narrowest angle (tightest shot), it is called an *extreme* or *extra close-up*, abbreviated ECU or XCU. A wider angle is a *close-up* (CU); continuing wider are the *medium close-up* (MCU), *medium shot* (MS), *wide shot* (WS), and *extreme* or *extra-wide shot* (EWS or XWS), the widest shot. You can call shots by specific framing: a head-to-toe shot is always an MCU. Others prefer to make their shot variations in reference to the widest or narrowest shot. For example, in a football game, a shot of the entire field from a blimp is obviously an XWS, while a shot of the quarterback from the waist up is an XCU. However, in a television commercial where a football player holds a product in his hand, the XWS is a head-to-toe shot, and the XCU is the shot of the label of the product (see Figure 5.12).

Other names of shots are derived from the objects included in the field of view. A *two-shot* contains two objects, usually two people; a *three-shot*, three objects. An *over-the-shoulder* (OS) is a typical news interview shot in which part of the inter-viewer's shoulder appears in the foreground and the person being interviewed faces the camera. A *point-of-view* (POV) shot appears to be what persons in the scene are actually seeing from their position in the set (see Figure 5.13).

Shooting

XWS

WS

MS

MCU

CU

XCU

FIG. 5.12 – Shot nomenclature describes how a shot is framed from XCU to XWS.

OS

POV

FIG. 5.13 – Specific types of shots carry their own titles such as OS or POV.

An entire set of shots is called for by each shot's relative framing on the human body: *head shot, bust shot,* or *waist shot.* One caution on this type of nomenclature: no shot should cut objects off at logical cutoff points. If a human head is framed so that the bottom of the frame cuts off the head at the neck, it appears in the shot that the person has been decapitated. It is better to include just a small portion of the shoulders to indicate that the body continues. The theory of closure also applies to objects other than body parts. A series of houses may appear to be just the two visible, or if parts of others on each side are visible the appearance is of an entire chain of houses, not just the three visible (see Figure 5.14).

FIG 5.14 – Closure allows a shot to tell more than the obvious. If three objects are shot with empty space between the objects on the end and the side of the frame, then the audience's perception is that the three objects are all that exist. On the other hand, if a portion of the objects on the outside edge of the frame is cut off, then the audience's perception is that there may be more than the three visible objects.

Shooting

Framing Principles

Aspect Ratio

The original video standard (SD) frame ratio was 4 units wide by 3 units high. This means that to fill the video frame without exceeding its boundaries, you must fit subjects into a horizontal rectangle 75 percent wider than it is high. This is an absolute. If you turn the camera on its side to frame a predominantly tall, slender subject, it will result in an image that is lying on its side.

On the surface this does not seem to offer much of a problem to you or the camera operator, but in reality there are very few objects that fit neatly into 4:3 space. Either you will cut off some of the object or you will need to add items to the picture to create an acceptable composition. The 4:3 ratio becomes especially critical when you shoot images of people. Unless one lies down, the human body does not fit into a 4:3 horizontal rectangle; neither do automobiles, most tall buildings, ships, airplanes, or any number of everyday objects.

The new digital (HD) standard frame ratio is 16:9—that is, 16 units wide by 9 units high. This ratio is a compromise between several motion picture wide-screen frame ratios. Translation circuits are included in digital cameras to enable the equipment to be switched between ratios. As always with a major change in technology within an existing system, there will be a period of time for transition during which both ratios will be used. Digital cinema is shot in 16:9, as are many commercials and music videos. You should plan all productions with both ratios in mind, as it will be several years before all receivers and consumer recording media will be able to view in both formats; you should allow for conversion when necessary or required (see Figure 5.15).

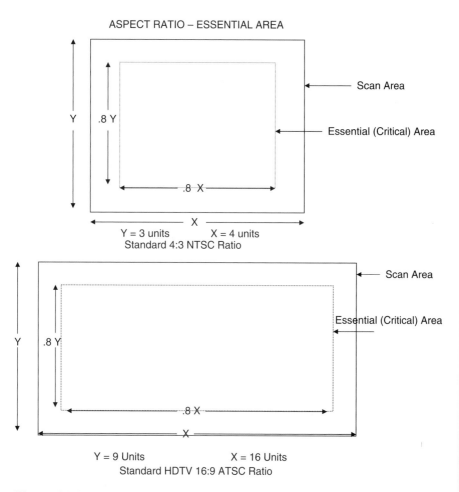

ASPECT RATIO – ESSENTIAL AREA

Scan Area

Essential (Critical) Area

Y = 3 units   X = 4 units
Standard 4:3 NTSC Ratio

Scan Area

Essential (Critical) Area

Y = 9 Units   X = 16 Units
Standard HDTV 16:9 ATSC Ratio

FIG. 5.15 – It is important for camera operators as well as directors and designers to keep in mind that nearly all productions may soon be reproduced in both 4:3 and 16:9 ratios. Placement within the frame of critical objects must neither be lost in the transition between formats nor look awkward with unnecessary empty space.

Framing Principles

Critical Area

Besides the 4:3 or 16:9 horizontal aspect ratio, you must deal with an additional framing problem in video. Not all of the video signal created by the camera reaches the television receiver or monitor. In addition, the scanning sweeps of most receivers have increased because of age or misalignment. This means that the audience cannot see as much as 5 to 10 percent of the picture. The 80 percent of the center portion of the frame is considered the critical or essential area. The industry accepts this 80 percent (allowing a 10 percent border on all four sides) as the critical area standard. You should frame all important information—names, addresses, phone numbers, and prices—well within the critical area to make certain that all viewers receive it.

Any objects framed in the 10 percent border may be seen by some viewers, so unwanted objects should not be framed in this area, which is called *edge bleed area*. For sports or other action-oriented coverage, the acceptable framing limitations are a little broader than the critical area, allowing approximately a 5 percent border. The difference in philosophy is that in an action sequence, closure fills in any portions of objects that momentarily appear beyond the critical area (see Figure 5.15).

Lead Room or Edge Attraction

Psychological studies indicate that objects in the area near the edge of the frame create a different perception than those in the center of the frame. A major factor is what is called *edge attraction theory*, in which an object appears to move toward the edge, even if it remains stationary in the frame. This effect increases when the object near the edge is a person's face. This lack of *nose room* makes the audience uncomfortable and should be avoided. The attraction of the edge is compounded when you move the subject toward the edge. That is why you should give moving objects plenty of space ahead of them as the camera follows them on a pan or tilt.

Framing Principles

The Rule of Thirds

Related to the edge attraction theory is the artist's *rule of thirds*, which states that the most aesthetic location for a predominantly vertical form is one third of the way in from either the left or right side of the frame. Conversely, a predominantly horizontal figure's most aesthetic position is either one third of the way up from the bottom or down from the top of the frame (see Figure 5.16).

FIG. 5.16 – Framing rules may seem arbitrary, but years of experience and study of visual response shows that the rules work when properly applied. Like all rules, they may be broken when the need arises and there is valid reason to do so. Placing critical objects or information on the one-third lines in the frame helps the audience understand what is most important. Also it is important to leave extra space in front of any moving object.

Framing Principles

Creating Movement

Even though video is a moving art form, the individual frame is essentially a still photograph. The manner in which you frame each picture can add to or subtract from its perceived movement. You can create movement in either video or film three basic ways: by moving the subject, by moving the camera, and by editing. Within each of these three basic movements are ancillary movements.

Subject Movement

You can move subjects in three directions within the frame: on the horizontal (X-axis) and vertical (Y-axis) planes in front of the camera or moving toward or away (Z-axis) from the camera. The Z-axis is the most powerful, and you should use it judiciously. In Western culture, moving from left to right suggests moving ahead; conversely, moving to the left signifies returning or backing up.

The Y-axis movements are more complex and less universally accepted, except when you move from the upper left to the lower right, which implies the most powerful movement forward, except for straight toward the camera on the Z-axis (see Figure 5.17).

Interestingly, the cultural values attributed to these movements also affect the relative value of positions within the frame. If you divide the frame into nine areas—upper left, upper center, upper right, middle left, center, middle right, lower left, lower center, and lower right—the position considered the most beneficial for passing information to the audience is the lower right. That conclusion is based on the philosophy that in Western culture, the eye starts at the upper left and proceeds to the lower right and comes to rest there. For that reason, better newscasts place the visuals on the right, and, almost universally, you should frame prices, addresses, and other critical commercial information on the right.

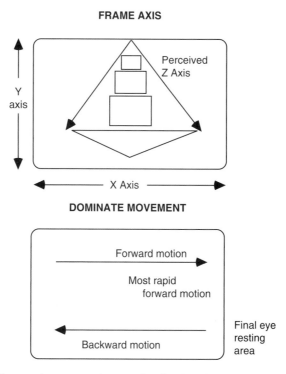

FRAME AXIS

Perceived
Z Axis

Y
axis

X Axis

DOMINATE MOVEMENT

Forward motion

Most rapid
forward motion

Backward motion

Final eye
resting
area

Creating Movement

FIG. 5.17 – Some frame and movement rules are culturally oriented. For that reason, a producer should consider the culture or nationality of the intended audience.

Camera Movement

The second means of creating movement is by moving the camera: on its pan head, panning left or right, or tilting up or down. If you have the means to raise and lower the camera on a center shaft, this movement is called *pedestaling* up or down. Depending on whether the camera base is a tripod on dolly wheels, a pedestal mount with wheels, a wheeled dolly, crab, or crane mount, the movements may be a *dolly* in or out, a *truck* left or right, or a combination of both to move in an *arc*. The crane mount also permits additional combinations of movement up, down, in, out, left, and right (see Figure 5.18).

Movement through Zooms

Supplementary movement created within the lens is the zoom. You create a zoom movement by varying the focal length of the lens, increasing or decreasing the angle of view. The zoom movement does not change the perspective of a shot, so that as the angle narrows and the picture appears to become larger, the camera's angle is not closer. Instead, it shows a smaller portion of the picture. You can achieve the same movement with a dolly, and it is more realistic because as the camera moves closer to the subject, the perspective also changes. The zoom, especially with a motorized control, is an easy and flexible movement. But it is an unrealistic movement, so you should use it with great caution. Amateur videographers use the zoom instead of advance planning. You can zoom digital cameras "digitally" by enlarging the pixels. At a certain point in the zoom, the quality of the picture degenerates as the pixels increase in size.

Although even the most professional film and video camera operators now use zoom lenses, they do not use them during a shot. Instead, they use the zoom lens as it was intended to be used, as a means of varying the focal length of the lens without changing lenses.

You may use a zoom on a flat, two-dimensional object, because there is no perspective involved, or as a special effect. But like all special effects, you should use a zoom sparingly and with specifically planned intent other than just tightening or loosening a shot.

CAMERA MOVEMENTS

TRUCK RIGHT OR LEFT
Camera points at subject, but moves parallel to the subject

PAN RIGHT
Handle moves to the left

PAN LEFT
Handle moves to the right

TILT UP
Handle moves down

TILT DOWN
Handle moves up

PEDESTAL UP
Camera moves straight up

PEDESTAL DOWN
Camera moves straight down

DOLLY IN
Camera moves toward subject

DOLLY BACK
Camera moves away from subject

Creating Movement

FIG. 5.18 – Camera movements provide the second most powerful tool of creating interest in a moving picture (editing is more powerful). All camera moves should be made purposeful with full intent, not just random for the sake of moving the camera and creating movement in the frame.

Z-Axis Movement

Video—like painting, photography, and cinematography—is a two-dimensional art form. The picture has only a height and width as received on a receiver/monitor or shown on a screen. The depth, or third "Z" dimension, of the picture is perceived; it does not actually exist as a third dimension, but it appears to exist. This three-dimensional appearance is important to any visual medium. Video particularly depends on the Z-axis to compensate for its smaller screen and lower resolution as compared to photography or motion picture film. The development of both film and digital 3-D productions moves forward slowly, but the techniques and philosophies of productions are the same as for 2-D, only more complex.

Therefore, it is imperative that the camera operator and you specifically think about and design the shots so that the Z-axis is exploited to its maximum. You should move subjects in the frame or move the camera around the subjects, arrange the objects in patterns that appear to be in perspective, and use as short a focal length lens as possible Next, arrange objects and subjects in the frame to create a background, middle ground, and foreground to help create a usable Z-axis. If you line up objects in front of the camera in neat rows, at an equal distance from the camera, and place all objects on surfaces of the same height, size, or color, you decrease the appearance of the Z-axis (see Figure 5.19).

If you arrange objects in the frame so that, even at rest, there appears to be movement—by utilizing the object's graphic forces—this composition also improves the three-dimensional perception. Do not shoot a person or object straight on. Not only is this boring, but it adds pounds and width to that person. Instead, you should rotate the actor so the camera is getting a three-quarter view, but always keep both eyes visible. Avoid having two people stand next to each other talking to the camera or each other; place them so they are facing each other, with the camera shooting past first one and then the other.

Straight - In line

Angled

FIG. 5.19 – Because the Z-axis is the most powerful of the three axes, and the one that does not actually exist in two-dimensional media, using techniques to develop the appearance of such an axis may be critical to creating interesting and informative productions. Avoid framing objects on the X-axis only; instead stagger the objects.

Creating Movement

Graphic Force Movement

Another aesthetic theory you should consider when framing a shot is the graphic weight of the objects within the frame. Each discernible object has some graphic weight or value. A large, dark object has a greater value than a small, light-colored object. An object with jagged, irregular edges has more weight than an object with smooth, rounded edges. Two small objects may equal the weight of one large one, even though their actual square measurement might be slightly smaller.

In addition to the perceived graphic weight of an object is its *graphic force*. The graphic force is derived partially from its graphic weight, but also from its movement. An object at rest has less graphic force than an object moving across the frame. Objects shaped like an arrow, a row of objects arranged to lead the eye in a specific direction, or a series of shots that show an object in a position of potential movement all carry more graphic force than an object the same size without the same graphic forces present (see Figure 5.20).

Color also becomes a factor in determining the weight of an object. "Hot" colors like red, yellow, orange, and light versions of other colors tend to extend toward the viewer. These colors appear to be heavier in graphic weight. The "cool" colors like blue, violet, green, and darker versions of other colors tend to recede from the viewer. These colors tend to appear lighter in graphic weight.

In the midst of all these "rules," don't forget that there are no absolutes in any aesthetic field. All of the suggestions made in this section are intended to be used only as guidelines. Each individual production situation determines to what extent you follow or ignore these suggestions. The final production will chronicle whether the best choices were made.

GRAPHIC FORCES

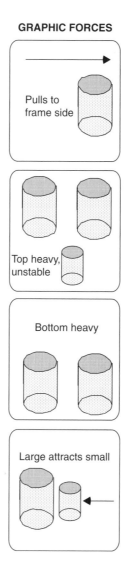

FIG. 5.20 – Of all of the framing rules, graphic forces are the most difficult to tie to absolute criteria. Part of the value of graphic force is that the observer feels movement without any existing. The arrangement of objects in a frame may create a feeling of movement or a sense of movement by their relative position to each other or their relative relationship to the edge of the frame.

Creating Movement

The Third Movement: Editing

Shoot to Edit

Regardless of the skill of both you and the camera operator in planning and framing shots, unless the shots have been recorded to be edited together, the aesthetic values will be lost. In EFP, each shot is recorded separately, often out of order. To be able to assemble the shots in a meaningful manner close to the original intent of the production, you must shoot them with editing in mind.

First, consider the *electronic aspect.* For nonlinear editing, any editor will always appreciate extra head and tail footage, regardless of the editing method. This makes certain each frame you expected to be recorded is usable, and the extra footage also assists in matching continuity.

Second, consider the *practical aspect.* Each shot should be recorded so that its action overlaps both the preceding and following shot. This allows the editor greater protection in case a shot did not start or end exactly as intended. This overlap also gives you a wider range of choices as to the best segment of an action to cut (see Figure 5.21).

The third aspect to consider is the *aesthetic aspect.* To edit in a seamless fashion, you must maintain continuity. The action from one shot must flow into the action of the next, unless there is a transition or change of scene There are three basic types of continuity that generally must be matched in each edit: continuity of action, direction, and location.

The Third Movement: Editing

Continuity of Action

As the actor picks up the pencil in the wide shot (WS), you must shoot the close-up so that the rate of picking up the pencil is the same and the same hand and pencil are used. This seems like a logical action, but even the best directors and camera operators make action continuity mistakes. For that reason, a *continuity assistant,* also known as a *script supervisor,* is an essential member of any major production crew. The continuity assistant watches every shot carefully and records the information on a script, or even takes digital still photos of the beginning and ending of each shot to check continuity.

Continuity of Direction

If the WS shows the actor facing to the left and the actor's right hand reaches across the frame to the left, then you must show in the close-up the hand moving to the left. If a shot shows an actor moving to the right, then the next shot must show the same actor still moving to the right, unless there is a change of direction shown on camera in the shot or a cutaway is inserted between the two shots. A cutaway can even confuse the audience, however, if viewers remember that the actor was moving in one direction and the next time he or she is seen moving in the opposite direction. You can use a straight-on shot from directly in front or from the rear of the actor as a transition. This same rule applies to all movement whether it involves automobiles, airplanes, people walking, running, or falling, or objects being thrown, dropped, or moving on their own. Psychologically, movement from the left to right is moving forward, from right to left is a returning movement.

Continuity of Location

Continuity of location includes lighting, background, and audio. If you light the establishing shot in low key with heavy shadows, then all of the close-ups must also be lit the same way. If one shot shows the ocean in the background, then unless a change of direction is shown on camera, all shots should indicate the ocean is the background. Audio continuity becomes an aesthetic tool as well as a continuity rule. If the scene is in a large, empty hall, all of the audio must sound as if it were recorded in the same ambiance. However, the ambiance of a wide shot in the same location sounds different from that of a tight close-up of two people talking and standing close to each other.

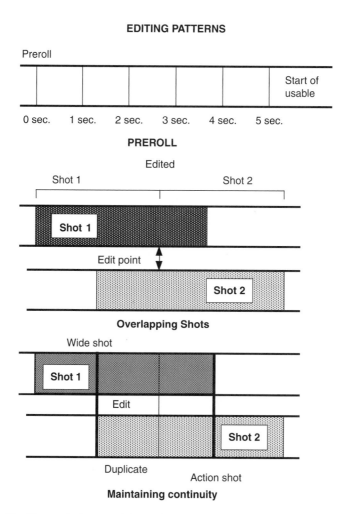

EDITING PATTERNS

Preroll

| | | | | | Start of usable |

0 sec.　1 sec.　2 sec.　3 sec.　4 sec.　5 sec.

PREROLL

Edited

Shot 1　　　　　　　Shot 2

Shot 1

Edit point

Shot 2

Overlapping Shots

Wide shot

Shot 1

Edit

Shot 2

Duplicate　　Action shot

Maintaining continuity

FIG. 5.21 – Matching continuity can only be achieved if the camera operator makes certain that every shot has footage overlapping the shot preceding and following, especially if there is specific action.

The Third Movement: Editing

Cover Shots

There are three types of cover shots that are the friends and saviors of the editor: *cover, cutaway*, and *cut-in shots*. Any capable director will call for them to be recorded, and any professional camera operator will shoot them even if you forget to do so.

A cover shot is an illustration of what is being talked about or referred to. If an announcer speaks of the use of a product, then a shot of the product being used in that manner is a cover shot. The announcer does not need to and probably should not appear in the shot. Instead of a single shot, a series of shots or a sequence would better illustrate what the announcer is talking about.

Cutaway and cut-in shots are similar, except that a cutaway is a shot of items that are not included in the previous or following shots—for example, when two people are sitting talking in a railway station and there is a shot of the train arriving. The two people in the scene do not refer to it (if they did, it would be a cover shot), and, most important, they must be sitting so they are not included in the shot of the train. But the audience realizes this train has something to do with the action. Generally, cutaway shots provide two important characteristics of a sequence. First, the shot gives the audience information that the main action does not reveal. Second, it can be used to cover an edit that would be a jump cut unless an intervening shot can be inserted.

A cut-in is a close-up of some object that is visible in the preceding or following frame. If a woman's purse is visible in a close-up as the two characters sit in the train station, it is a cut-in shot if the purse is also visible in the WS.

These three types of shots afford the editor the chance to correct mistakes made in the shooting continuity, or they can be used to speed up or slow down a sequence or to correct a continuity problem in the production (see Figure 5.22).

(A) Cover

(B) Cut-in

(C) Cut-away

The Third Movement: Editing

FIG. 5.22 – Three types of shots that editors depend on are valid cover (A), cut-in (B), and cutaway (C) shots. Each provides the editor a means of maintaining continuity and best telling the story visually.

In-Camera Effects

Technology exists that allows you to produce a series of special effects simply by utilizing the controls necessary for the normal operation of a camera. As technology advances, newer cameras have many digital special effects capabilities built into them. Several effects may be produced with digital camcorders: iris fades, rack focus, swish pans/zooms, reverse polarity, and manipulation of pedestal and gain, including electronic fades (see Figure 5.23).

Iris Fades

You create an *iris fade-in* or *fade-out* by placing the iris control on manual and setting the iris opening stopped all the way down. While shooting, you may slowly open the iris up and bring it to the proper setting. This creates a fade-in. A fade-out is created by reversing the procedure: you start a scene with the camera rolling and the iris set properly; at the right moment, you stop the iris down until the picture fades to black. Neither of these effects works well unless the light level is low enough that the iris is nearly wide open at the proper setting.

Roll or Rack Focus

To *roll* or *rack focus* simply means to start a scene in focus and rapidly turn the focus control until the picture is totally out of focus. The shot to be edited next should start totally out of focus and, on cue, you turn the lens into proper focus. Once again, this effect only works well when the light level is low enough so that the depth of field is quite shallow and the focus change should be rapid enough to appear intentional, not an error in shooting.

Swish Pans and Zooms

You may accomplish a *swish pan* by starting on a scene and at the end of the shot, quickly panning the camera at a high enough rate so that the image is blurred. The next shot starts with a fast pan and ends properly framed. The first of these is easy to accomplish, but for the second, it is difficult to stop at the exact framing without jerking or missing the mark.

A *swish zoom* is a little easier, especially if the zoom is motorized. The process is the same as a swish pan in that you start the shot at a normal focal length and, on cue, you operate the zoom control at its maximum speed, usually zooming in rather than out. The second shot starts with a zoom out and ends properly framed.

In-Camera Effects

Reversing Polarity

Reversing polarity is achieved by your throwing a switch, on some cameras internally and on others externally. This cannot be done while you are recording because there is a momentary loss of sync. The picture areas that were red become cyan, those that were green become magenta, and blue areas become yellow, and vice versa. Light areas become dark, and dark areas become light. The effect is the same as looking at a color film negative.

Digital In-Camera Effects

If the camera has built-in digital circuits, it may be possible for you to *solarize*, *freeze frame*, or *pixilate* the picture, among many other effects, depending on the individual camera. The solarized effect appears as if the picture is melting or reversing in polarity. A freeze frame effect locks a single frame of the picture as if it were a still photo. Pixilation is the process of removing a certain number of frames of the picture so that objects and subjects appear to move about in an irregular, jerky fashion. Each of these effects requires a separate control on the camera. You also can accomplish pixilation if the deck can record a single frame at a time. A control sets the number of frames per second at which the recorder will operate. This compresses the action in any time elapsed required for the production. You can better accomplish in-camera effects through the camera's camera control unit or, in some cases, during postproduction.

IN-CAMERA EFFECTS

- ❖ Iris Fades
- ❖ Rack Focus
- ❖ Digital zoom
- ❖ Polarity Reversal
- ❖ Solarization
- ❖ Pixilation
- ❖ Color Modification
- ❖ Level/Pedestal Modification

FIG. 5.23 – The number of in-camera effects depends on the design of the camera and related equipment. Check the owner's operation manual for instructions on how to manipulate the controls to achieve the effect you want or need.

In-Camera Effects

Logging and Striking

A manual operation often overlooked in the concentration on electronic operations in a video production is the manual continuity record keeping or logging process. A written record of each shot is kept on a log sheet in a form that supplies you and the editor with the information you need to accomplish your tasks. The log registers, in the order of shooting, the shot and take number, the location on the medium (counter or Society of Motion Picture and Television Engineers [SMPTE] time code number), comments on whether the audio or video take was good or bad and why, and any other comments you want noted (see Figure 5.24).

The log is invaluable to the editor. If not accurately logged during the shot, the recordings have to be previewed and logged in the postproduction process, which is a slow and painstaking procedure. One person should keep the logs, and logging should be her or his main responsibility. The person's title in a large crew is *continuity assistant* (CA) or script supervisor. In a smaller crew, the director or an assigned production assistant is in charge of logging. The importance of this function cannot be ignored. The person keeping the log must be familiar with the critical aspects of continuity and well versed in that particular production.

As each shot is set up and rehearsed, the logger notes positions of props, set pieces, lighting, or anything else that may be moved or changed. Because the production will be shot out of sequence, there may be hours or days separating the actual shooting of some shots in the same sequence, and every aspect of each shot must match in order to maintain continuity. As each shot is completed, the CA logs any deviations from the script and minute details, such as with which hand an actor handled which prop. A digital still camera is invaluable to a CA. After each shot, you, the camera operator, and the audio operator dictate comments to be added to the log.

If the editing is on a nonlinear digital editor, the logs become even more important. The tedious and time-consuming activity of dubbing in real time all of the footage shot into a digital format before editing can begin can be reduced by converting only those shots that are good enough to be used in the final production. All other shots are left in their original form to be dubbed later if they are needed in an emergency.

RECORDER LOG

RECORDER LOG PAGE _____ DATE _____

LOCATION _____ PRODUCTION _____

CAMERA/MEDIA _____ REEL/DISC # _____

PRODUCER _____ OPERATOR _____

DIRECTOR _____ D/V _____

TIME CODE	TAKE	DESCRIPTION	REMARKS

Logging and Striking

FIG. 5.24 – Logging can become a critical stage in the editing process if not completed accurately as shooting continues. The logs help the director, production manager, and editor once final shooting is completed and the project moves to the postproduction stage.

Striking

Once the excitement of the actual production has evaporated and the actors, directors, and producers have disappeared, the last stage of the production process begins. It is just as important as any other stage, but it occurs when everyone is tired and let down, after the tension of the shoot has eased and everyone is thinking about tomorrow.

As soon you give the order to *strike* (a term borrowed from the theater), or when the order is given by the production manager on a larger crew, all power is killed except for any work lights that are present. Then all other cables are disconnected to prevent crew members from tripping over them and pulling equipment or lighting instruments down. Each crew person is responsible for striking equipment. Cables are properly coiled and stored in their cases. Once equipment has been cleaned and returned to the proper cases, a check is made to be sure that all equipment has been packed and is ready to be loaded.

The strike should be as organized as the setup. The next use of the equipment may come the following day. Note, in writing, any damaged equipment, and notify maintenance immediately. The location has to be restored to its original condition. You should repair any damage or report it to the owners in writing and negotiate a satisfactory compensation before you leave the site (see Figure 5.25).

Equipment is then moved to the vehicle, loaded, and returned to its storage locations. Each piece of equipment needs to be carefully checked off with the person responsible, whether it is the production manager or a leasing company. Take the same precautionary measures during striking as you did during the setup. Never leave equipment or the equipment vehicle unattended until all equipment has been secured.

The "fun" part of the production has now ended for you. It consumed the shortest period of time and in many ways the least amount of effort—that is, mental and aesthetic effort. Once you have worked several EFPs, you will appreciate the physical effort required for the production process.

STRIKE LIST

1. CAP CAMERA

2. TURN OFF ALL POWER SWITCHES EXCEPT WORK LIGHTS

3. DISMISS TALENT

4. DISCONNECT ALL CABLES, BOTH ENDS

5. LOWER ALL LIGHT STANDS, MOVE GENTLY OUT OF THE WAY TO COOL

6. PICK UP AND PACK ALL PROPS, SET PIECES, LOAD SETS, LARGE SET PIECES

7. COIL CABLES PROPERLY, OVER-UNDER, NOT AROUND ELBOW

8. WIPE DOWN CABLES AND SECURELY FASTEN ENDS

9. REMOVE CAMERA FROM TRIPOD, PACK IN CASE WITH ACCESSORIES (TRIPOD PLATE, POWER PACK) WHICH BELONG IN CASE

10. PACK ALL CABLES, BATTERIES

11. PACK ALL GAFFER EQUIPMENT

12. IF COOL, DISMANTLE LAMP HEADS AND STANDS AND THEN PACK

13. INVENTORY ALL EQUIPMENT CASES AND LOOSE EQUIPMENT

14. MOVE EQUIPMENT TO VEHICLE
    ** **NEVER LEAVE ANY EQUIPMENT UNATTENDED** **

15. LOAD EQUIPMENT INTO VEHICLE

FIG. 5.25 – Strike list.

Logging and Striking

Chapter Six
The Production Process: Postproduction

The Soul of Production

As the final stage of the media production process, postproduction affords you the last opportunity to reach the goal you originally set as proposed for the client. Regardless of the saying, "Fix it in post," you cannot correct all errors in judgment, miscalculations, and poor production techniques in postproduction. If the material is not available or is technically deficient, you may not have any means of replacing it or rectifying the problems created in preproduction or production. You cannot bring out of focus shots into focus, reframe poor or incorrectly reframed shots (except by using expensive and advanced digital applications), or rezoom a poorly zoomed shot at the correct rate. You may partially correct poor lighting, but at a cost in time and energy diverted from the important work of the edit. If you forgot a shot, then you can only replace it by returning to the location and reshooting.

The Soul of Production

Editing Depends on Aesthetic and Equipment Knowledge and Skills

Most critics of editors feel the truly creative portion of a media production takes place in the editing room, and many directors and producers agree. Media editing is a complex function that requires a combination of technical knowledge and skill, a great deal of your aesthetic knowledge and sense, and unlimited patience on your part.

The technical factors depend on the capabilities of the equipment available to you for the editing session. It is possible to complete a wide variety of productions using an inexpensive, consumer central processing unit (CPU) with an amateur editing application. But the wide range of available editing equipment and the capabilities of such rapidly expanding equipment such as Final Cut Pro, Avid, and other commercial non-linear editors provide you with a nearly infinite means of editing a production at any level depending on how the material was shot. You need to know the limits of your equipment and acquire the ability to use the equipment to meet those limits without creating technical problems. Learning the specific characteristics of both the editor and the technical requirements of the final master version requires you to study, concentrate, and offer the willingness to assimilate technical characteristics of the editing process.

The aesthetic factors call on your knowledge of psychology, art, music, theater, and the rest of the performing arts. To be able to communicate to your audience, you must understand who the intended audience is. Knowledge of art provides a background for framing, color, settings, and visualization. No production exists without some music in some form. Music can be as important at setting a feeling or mood for a production as the color of the graphics or costumes. An understanding of how a theatrical production is organized and created to bring the maximum effect on the viewer is critical in your understanding of how to bring your message to your audience (see Figure 6.1).

Editing is often a long, tedious process that may stretch even the most patient people to their limits. There are no shortcuts. Editing is tedious, detail oriented, and requires tremendous concentration on both the editing process and the creation of the production itself.

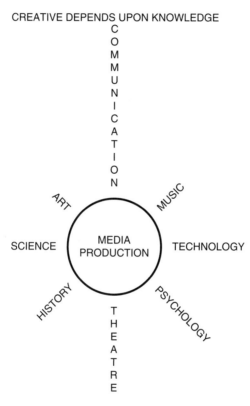

FIG. 6.1 – All artistic processes, including digital video editing, rely on a wide variety of creative fundamentals found in the basic humanities of communication, history, and psychology as well as the arts in music, theater, and fine art.

The Soul of Production

Editing Concept

Basic Process

The complexity brought about by the digital revolution has created problems with digital postproduction. On the surface, digital equipment and techniques should be a simple, straightforward, and easy approach for you to learn. Unfortunately, the simplicity of digital media has created a complex combination of technology and techniques that you must meet before shooting and before editing based partially on where you will distribute the project.

Not long ago, a video camera, regardless of its price or purpose, created an electronic signal that you could edit on any linear editor manufactured at that time. Today that is no longer true. Cameras today and, most important, the recording systems built in the camera or the means used to record the digital signal determine the type of signal available for you to edit. How the editing process may begin and proceed will depend on the method and technology of the signal you recorded. The signal generated and its form must either match your editing system or you must introduce a conversion process between the camera and the editor.

DIGITAL VIDEO SIGNAL CHARACTERISTICS

Level of Definition: High Definition (HD) or Standard Definition (SD)

Scan Type: Interlaced or Progressive

Scan Rate: 24, 30, 60. 23.976, 29.97, 59.94 or, for Europe, 25, 50 Frames Per Second (FPS)

Drop Frame DF) or Non-Drop Frame (NDF)

Frame Size: 720 × 480, 1440 × 1080

Raster Size: 1280 × 720, 1920 × 1080v

Bit Rate Quantization: 8, 10, 24 bit

Color Standard: 4:1:1, 4:2:0, 4:2:1, 4:2:2

Aspect Ratio: 4 × 3, 16 × 9

Compression Ratio: 2:1, 4:1, 5:1, 7:1, 18:1,

Format Combinations:

720p/23/976, DF	
720p/25	Europe
720/29.97	DF Flagged 59.94
720p/50	Europe
720p/59.94	DF
1080p/23.976	DF
1080/24	Film Projection
1080/25	Europe
1080i/50	Europe
1080i/59.94	DF

File Type: QuickTime, AVI, MPEG

Medium Format: Raw footage, DV, HDV, AVC-HD, Full HD, DVCam, DVCPro

Audio Rates: 16 bit, 44.1 kHz, 24 bit, 49 kHz

Audio Format: Material Exchange Format (MXF), Open Media Format (OMF) AIFF-C, WAVE

Audio Channels: 2, 4, 8 (or more)

FIG. 6.2 – The wide variety of characteristics that separate digital video signals from each other create at least 18 different formats.

Editing Concept

The exact match between your camera output and the input of your nonlinear (NLE) CPU will depend on the particular NLE program and CPU you use. This text cannot describe every NLE application and CPU combination. Make certain you carefully read the operator's manual for both the application as well as the computer (see Figure 6.2).

Process Background

Three basic electronic video editing systems exist today. The earliest, linear editing, has been supplemented almost completely by digital nonlinear editing, which is based partly on the nonlinear editing system long used in the motion picture industry (see Figure 6.3).

Nonlinear Film

Film editing is a nonlinear process. Each clip may be assembled in any order. Individual shots may be moved and combined with other shots and transitions and rearranged at will without affecting other shots because the shots are physically taped together. The sound tracks are edited separately and then combined with the picture shots in the final printing process form for distribution.

You accomplish the cutting and assembling of shots in film nonlinear editing by using a copy of the original negative film called a work print. You physically cut and splice the film together into a complete first edit, which allows you to try different combinations without harming the original negative. Once you complete the final edit, the original negative is matched to the work print edit in a process called *conforming*.

Manual Film Editing   Linear VTR Edting

FIG. 6.3 – Editing on the original professional 2-inch quadraplex video system and editing film at television stations have been replaced with nonlinear digital editing systems. (Courtesy KEPR and Ampex.)

Process Background

Linear Electronic

The first professional electronic editing of videotape required you to physically cut the tape at a precise spot between frames and splice the cut videotape with a special tape. Although shots could be moved from one position to another, the process was so primitive as to be impractical.

Another method of linear editing let you use at least one tape deck as a source tape, a computer controller to determine in and out points for shots as well as controlling the operation of both machines, and a master deck to record the final edits. You used two basic edit techniques: either you would use assemble editing to simply add one shot onto another or you would use insert editing. When using the insert editing method, you could add close-ups, add cutaways to a master shot, or add effects in the middle of the master shot. You could edit audio separately or simultaneously depending on the placement of the original audio track (see Figure 6.4).

As linear digital tape controllers became more sophisticated, you could create complex shot and sound patterns despite the linear nature of the system. Once you edited together a series of shots, a change could not be made in a shot in the middle of the sequence without changing all of the shots following the changed shot.

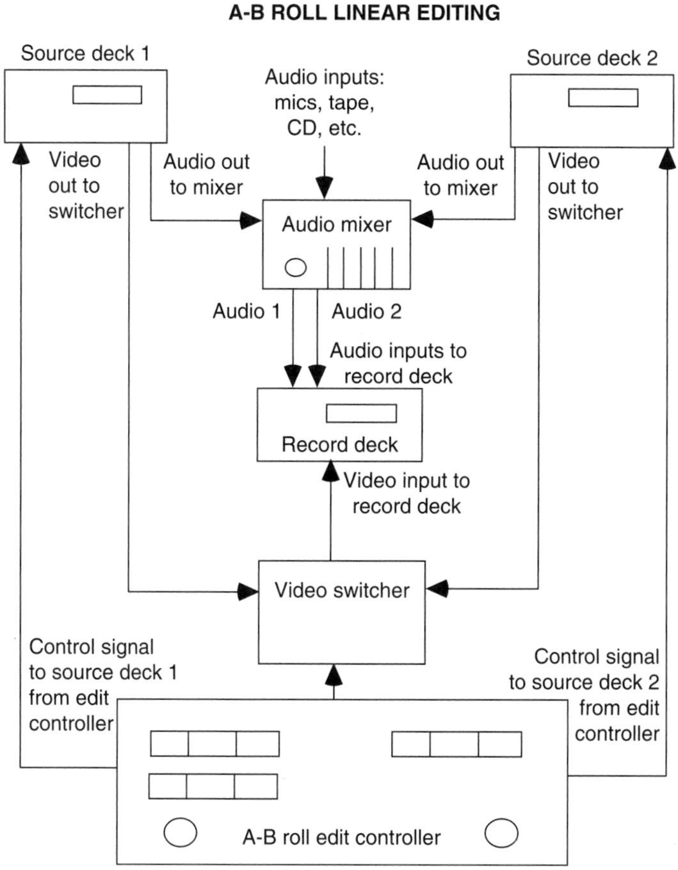

A-B ROLL LINEAR EDITING

Source deck 1

Audio inputs:
mics, tape,
CD, etc.

Source deck 2

Video
out to
switcher

Audio out
to mixer

Audio out
to mixer

Video
out to
switcher

Audio mixer

Audio 1 | Audio 2

Audio inputs to
record deck

Record deck

Video input to
record deck

Video switcher

Control signal
to source deck 1
from edit
controller

Control signal
to source deck 2
from edit
controller

A-B roll edit controller

FIG. 6.4 – Linear editing systems offer a relatively inexpensive and easy-to-operate videotape editing process. For news and simple productions, linear editing systems were popular but now have been replaced with nonlinear digital systems.

Process Background

Nonlinear Electronic

The preliminary philosophy and techniques of linear editing apply directly to nonlinear editing. Nonlinear editing allows you to both assemble and insert editing techniques for the same reasons as used in linear editing, except nonlinear editing allows for more flexibility and a wider range of easily attained techniques (see Figure 6.5).

The key to *nonlinear editing* (NLE) is the use of virtual clips, not the actual original footage. The process is based on an ability to assemble clips from a variety of sources in any order and then rearrange and modify them without affecting other clips. You accomplish all of the editing by using virtual clips, not the actual digital signal. Once you complete the editing process, then the edited virtual clips are rendered into an actual signal for distribution using the media files. The NLE process allows you maximum flexibility to assemble clips accurately without compromising the potential; you are experimenting with different combinations and selections of clips to achieve the purpose that you, the writer, producer, or director intended. This flexibility gives you the opportunity to, without destroying the original footage, modify a scene or sequence through trial and error until the best combination of clips satisfies you.

FIG. 6.5 – Modern nonlinear digital editing systems provide for the maximum in flexibility and creativity, and, with today's high-end CPUs, they offer a relatively inexpensive and easy-to-learn process to fulfill the editing needs of anyone, from the amateur to the professional. (Courtesy Advanced Broadcast Solutions and Grass Valley.)

Process Background

Hardware

Editing Equipment

Regardless of the complexity of the edited project or the editing suite, you need basic equipment in one form or another. A source of audio other than that from originally shot clips requires an audio mixing device, either an audio edit application built into the computer used as the editor, such as an external *digital audio workstation* (DAW), as a simple digital audio mixer. You may add external audio from CDs, MP3 players, cassettes, mics, or even vinyl discs (LPs) if a turntable is available. Most computer audio mixers allow multichannel mixing, so you may lay down tracks that were loaded individually and then edited within the computer.

Obviously the video must come from somewhere, but the most practical source is from the original files either recorded within the camera on tape, on disc, or to the hard drive or flash drive. You can feed the digital signal as a file directly to the hard drive of an on-set recording computer as it is shot. You also can add external video sources from film, slides, a character generator, or a graphics generator, or you can create it within the editing CPU from a built-in graphic application. Use an external video switcher to combine a complex series of shots beyond that normally handled in the editing CPU (see Figure 6.6).

Or feed the video and audio shot and recorded in the camera directly into the editing CPU as the only source of raw footage. You can finish the product with only the original material, by adding audio or video from an external source.

POSTPRODUCTION DIGITAL VIDEO HARDWARE

CPU (Mac or PC)

Minimum RAM (Random Access Memory) 2-4 GB

Speed of processor 2 GHz, but 4 GHz better

Internal memory storage, 500 GB to 2 TB

External memory storage not necessary but helpful for long projects or lengthy amounts of footage

Hard drive speed, 10K to 15K RPM hard drives and storage must be formatted for either Mac or PC, but not both simultaneously (unless dual internal drives & CPUs)

RAID ((Redundant Arrays of Independent Discs): An assortment of hard drives interconnected to provide massive amounts of alternate back-up memory internally within the RAID

CPU Connections:

Mac: Firewire (1397) 400 or 800, USB (Universal Serial Bus) 1 or 2

PC: Firewire 400, 800

FIG. 6.6 – (A) The one simple and user-friendly aspect of nonlinear editing is the hardware required. All it takes to complete a digital edit is a computer installed with an editing application. Obviously, there are choices in types and levels of equipment used in the postproduction process, but a home CPU with plenty of memory and the proper editing application will complete the job as easily as the most expensive editing suites used for editing a feature film.

Hardware

Accessories

Plugs-ins are applications that provide additional operations to an editing program. The plug-in may be for audio editing, special effects, color correction, graphics, animation, compression adjustment, or conversion application (see Figure 6.7).

You can include hardware accessories like special controllers to make editing keyboard operations faster and easier. You might also consider adding external hard drives, extra monitors, speakers, an outboard audio controller, or a digital audio workstation (DAW).

NONLINEAR DIGITAL EDITING APPLICATIONS

Windows & Mac

>   Adobe Premiere Pro, After Effects, Encore

>   Avid Media Composer, Symphony Nitris, Xpress Pro

Mac Only

>   Final Cut Express, Final Cut Pro, and iMovie

>   Media 100, HD Suite, HDe, SDe, Producer, Producer Suite

Windows Only

>   Adobe Premiere Elements

>   Avid DS Nitris

>   Edius

>   Pinnacle Studio

>   Sony Vegas Movie Studio, Sony Vegas Pro

>   Ulead Systems Video Studio

>   Windows Movie Maker

>   Womble Multimedia MPEG Video Wizard, MPEG Video Wizard DVD

FIG. 6.7 – The choices of which application to use will depend on available hardware, budget restrictions on costs of software, matching the output of cameras, and personal preferences from past experiences. Once an editor learns and becomes comfortable with a specific system, both hardware and software, it may be difficult to switch to another system.

Hardware

Software

To edit in the nonlinear mode, a computer application software specifically designed to provide the controls and functions needs to accept a variety of digital signals and render the signals into a form the application is designed to operate under. Once entered into the hard drive of the computer, the software allows you to assemble, cut, paste, and move individual shots and sequences at will. The application gives you the ability to handle audio editing, at least at the simplest level, if not multichannel and multimodification. A basic NLE application includes simple color correction, transitions, titling, and simple graphics generally.

The application must match either PC or Mac systems, as well as the camera's signal output or built-in conversion files, to make the necessary correction. The NLE must be able to read the footage signal from the camera or playback medium. If the download involves a conversion of the signal, the process may destroy the time code and also may change the frame arrangement, making frame-accurate edits impossible (see Figure 6.8).

DIGITAL CAMERA FORMATS

DV   (NTSC, miniDV, and DVCam)
4:3 720 × 480i 29.97 fps

720p   (Panasonic and JVC)
16:9 1920 × 1080p 59.94, 23.976, 29.97

1080   (Sony)
16:9 1920 × 1080i 29.97, 59.97,
Large data stream for conversion to film

1080   (Sony)
16:9 1920 × 1080p 23.976, 24, 25p, 29.97, 59.94
Requires conversion to NLE

HDV   JVC 702p, Sony 1080i, and Canon
Requires codec to NLE

FIG. 6.8 – Format choice includes definition, aspect ratio, scan choices, frame rate, line rate, and color standard.

Physical Process

Choices and Decisions

Your first critical decision requires you to match the camera specifications to the NLE application and CPU (see Figure 6.8). You should make some if not all of those decisions before shooting begins. Those decisions should be made based on the distribution plan. Once you make key technical decisions at the shooting stage, changing the technology may be difficult, time consuming, and costly. It is imperative that you thoroughly consider the possible distribution before actual shooting begins, technical standards have been established, and choices of equipment and formats have been made. Once you set those decisions, they must be accepted and dealt with at the postproduction stage because editing choices still exist at the editing stage, again depending on the plan for distribution. The following variations should be considered.

Standard definition (SD) or high definition (HD): SD is analog National Television Standards Committee (NTSC) video, 4 × 3 ratio, 535-line scan interlaced, usually recorded at 30 or 29.956 frames per second (fps). Most consumer and many prosumer cameras, as well as recording and editing equipment, are designed to work in SD. Much SD equipment also can be reset to operate in HD.

The two scan choices, interlace ("I") and progressive ("P"): These were developed separately but now may be used on the same equipment. Interlace was part of the NTSC system for the SD broadcast standard developed in the United States. NTSC developed interlace to increase resolution by scanning each frame twice, interweaving each scan line to make a full frame. Interlace is still used on high-level systems to take advantage of its superior resolution without increasing bandwidth.

Physical Process

On the other hand, progressive was developed in Europe for both the PAL and SECAM scan systems. Each frame is scanned with a complete set of lines for each frame. In retrospect, for most conditions progressive appears to be a superior system. (Some problems exist when the camera pans rapidly from side to side.) Progressive is easier to edit because each frame may be cut individually, whereas in interlaced the edit must be made at the beginning or end of a frame, not in between the fields.

The number of frames per second varies from 23.976, 24, 25, 29.97, 30, 59.97, 60 fps. Each frame represents a complete picture made up of a series of horizontal lines or a series of pixel patterns changed at the frame rate. The wide variation in rates is due to the differences between SD and HD, differences between 50 cycle and 60 cycle voltage rates, compensation for color systems, and compatibility with motion picture film systems.

Only to complicate matters further, the NTSC developed the drop-frame (DF) non-drop-frame (NDF) system. The drop-frame system was designed to compensate for the approximate 3 minutes lost in an hour's recording using the 29.76 or 59.97 frame rates. The camera, recorder, and editing equipment must be set with matching DF or NDF to make certain the final production will be correctly timed for audio and video edited on separate equipment to stay in synchronization.

The size of the fame depends on the setting of the number of lines vertically and horizontally. The two common sizes are 960 × 720 and 1440 × 1080; 720 is considered slightly lower in quality but easier to handle because of its lower bandwidth requirements (see Figure 6.2).

The other size of the frame is the aspect ratio, or the relationship between the width of the frame and the height of the frame. Today the two systems now in use are 4 × 3 and 16 × 9; 4 × 3 was the original television and film aspect ratio. Motion pictures in the 1950s expanded their width to make "wide-screen" projection. The aspect ratios in film increased to as much as 2 × 1, or the width twice the height. When the industry began designing HD, it was obvious that a wide-screen format was needed. A mathematically determined ratio of 16 × 9 was chosen. It does not exactly match any film aspect ratio, but it is close enough for relatively easy conversion between the media. The numbers 16 × 9 mean the screen is 16 units wide and 9 units high. (See Figure 5.16 for relative aspect ratios and conversion problems between ratios.)

Understanding color standards from their classifications may make sense, but it may not be necessary for you to understand why and how the standards actually work in order to understand this text. Color standards indicate the split in level of the three primary parts of the color signal. The first number (Y) indicates the strength of the luminance part of the signal, the second number (R-Y) indicates the color, and the third number (B-Y) indicates the color values. For most productions, the color standards are indicated by 4:1:1, 4:2:0, or 4:2:2. For the highest quality production, a color standard of 4:4:4 may be used.

Physical Process

Bit rates at 8, 10, and 14 of video indicate the level of quantization of the digitization of the signal. The higher the rate, the better the quality, but also the greater the bandwidth and memory requirements needed to handle the signal. The same holds true of audio: 16 bit, 44.2 kHz, or 24 bit, 49 kHz. The frequency attached to the bit rate indicates the highest workable frequency of your audio signal. The indicated frequency is actually double the best reproduced signal—that is, a 48.2-kHz signal will handle 22 kHz and their overtones without distortion; 44.1 kHz is the standard for most recordings, 48.2 kHz is used only for the highest quality signals.

The compression standards 2:1, 4:1, 5:1, 7:1, and 18:1 indicate the amount of compression you apply to the signal, either audio or video, although audio signals require far less if there is any compression. You always compress video except when you are working on extreme high-end productions using raw footage and 4:4:4 signals. Compressing signals saves bandwidth and memory requirements by reducing or removing from each frame unnecessary or repeated parts of the signal that may be replaced in the demodulation stage. The specific codec (compression-decompression) application or circuit sets the compression and restoration levels (see Figure 6.9).

POTENTIAL DISTRIBUTION GOALS FOR DIGITAL VIDEO

Standard Definition

High-Definition Wide-Screen

Disc (DVD or Blue-Ray)

Memory Cards or Drives

Hard Drive Disk

Digital Tape

Broadcast

Cablecast

Satellite

Internet

Streaming

Motion Picture Film

FIG. 6.9 – The final edited signal may be fed out to tape, disc, hard drive, memory medium, or the Web to be broadcast on television, cable, or satellite.

Technical Process

Each of the major editing applications (and the many other minor editing applications) uses its own terminology for the equipment, the icons, and the menus on the screen, and the process that works best for that individual application. Before starting an editing project, you must carefully read and comprehend the terminology, menus, and process of the application you will use.

Begin your edit session by logging on to the CPU by using your name and password. Launch the application by clicking on the application icon. Then open the editing mode. Screens will appear to show the following: *bin* or *browser, source* or *viewer, record* or *canvas monitors*, and a *timeline*. The names of the monitors vary with the NLE application, but the functions are similar in operation.

FIG. 6.10 – The parts of the edit window may be arranged for the convenience of the editor or to follow specific instructions provided in the manual for the application. (Courtesy Advanced Broadcast Solutions.)

The browser or project window serves as your home page. It lists all the bins you must open it to perform any functions of editing. Make certain you leave it open until the end of the session. Your captured or imported footage goes into bins. The footage is actually virtual footage; the actual media files are stored elsewhere on the hard drive. Name the bins to suit yourself, but think of a logical system because you may end up with many, many bins containing similar shots and you want to be able to access the individual shots easily and quickly. Each bin will contain the series of shots you recorded on a single tape, disc, or card. The bin indicates your master clips that are virtual copies of the original footage. You may manipulate these files any way you wish because you are working in a nondestructive system. If you want to change an edit or change your mind for a sequence, no footage actually is lost or permanently cut or modified until the entire project is rendered. When you click on a bin icon, the list of individual shots included in that bin appears with time code (if shot with TC). You monitor clips by clicking on different views, depending on the application. Each view shows additional information you may need to make your decisions on where to edit (see Figure 6.10).

When you double-click on a clip icon, the clip appears in the viewer or source monitor. Beneath that monitor is a position bar with an indicator. Beneath the position indicator are toolbar buttons. The toolbar buttons indicate commands that you may issue when clicked. They are the "IN" button and the "OUT" button. You use them to indicate where you want a shot to begin and where the shot will end.

Technical Process

The canvas or record monitor shows what the shots look like when edited together in a sequence. The monitor also contains a *position window, position indicator*, and a *toolbar* (see Figure 6.11).

The timeline is a graphic representation of the shots in your sequence in the form of the video and audio tracks labeled V1, A1, A2, and A3 as needed. The timeline contains viewer, source and canvas, record track selectors, scale and scroll bars, and a position indicator.

A CPU loaded with an editing application will respond to the instruction you give the CPU through the menus and keyboard. Most editing applications come with a special keyboard, key stickers, or an overlay that covers the keyboard keys and shows you the special editing commands. The keys "J," "L," "K," "I," and "O" each allows for special commands designed to speed your editing process.

Once you become familiar with all of the operations, menus, and commands of the application mounted on the CPU you use to edit, you are ready to edit your project.

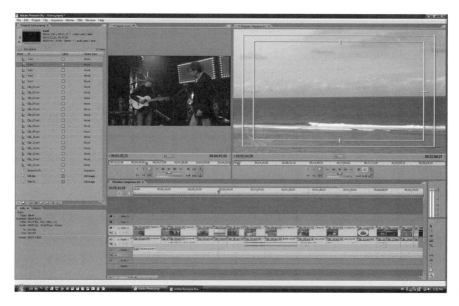

FIG. 6.11 – Each segment visible in the editor's window shows the different stages of the action required to complete an edit. (Courtesy Advanced Broadcast Solutions.)

Technical Process

Editing Operating Methods

Each studio, facility, or station lists a *standard operating procedure* (SOP) that designates exactly the format you are to use in preparing to edit, including use of color bars and tone, slate, and labeling of discs, memory media, and containers. The following section is a compilation of SOPs used that demonstrates the purposes of each segment of the operation.

Start by laying down 30 seconds to 1 minute of 1,000-Hz tone with bars as video as the first clip. If you do not set these two test signals at the exact levels to be used in the recording, they will be useless. Technicians use these test signals to prepare to play the file back, to set the playback levels, and to make electronic adjustments. Following the tone and bars, record 10 seconds or so of a slate that specifies the title, length, client, and date of recording. Your next clip needs to be a *countdown* with descending numbers from 10 down to 2, followed by a minimum of 2 seconds of clean black and silence before the beginning of the first audio and video of the first clip of your edited production (see Figure 6.12).

At the end of the production, record at least 10 seconds of a clean black and silent clip. These periods of clean black and silence furnish a guard band of neutral signals in case there are errors in switching during a playback or they provide a logical space for dubbing.

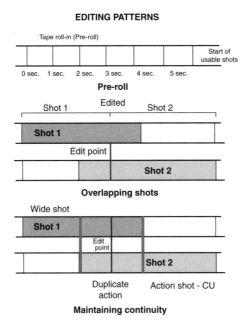

FIG. 6.12 – Every studio and station requires countdown, slate, and protection areas at the beginning and at the end of a completed edited project. Output to disc does not require such signals, but the signals should be recorded on the master file and removed for disc duplication.

Basic Editing

Your first action in beginning to edit a project is to choose the first shot from the bin containing that shot. Open that shot in the viewer or source monitor, followed by each of the shots that will follow in that sequence. The viewer or source monitor is a holding bag with a menu that shows all of the clips loaded at that time. Click on that first shot. Play the clip to make certain it is the correct take. Then on the position bar beneath the window, choose your in and out points using the "I" and "O" keys or command buttons. You will need to title this as the beginning of a sequence. Now return to the viewer or source monitor and find the next clip. Click on it; it will be placed next to the first shot in the sequence. Mark the in and out points, and you are editing.

The editing process, including transitions and audio editing, becomes much more complex from this point on, but the general steps of the process are as indicated above. Creative, aesthetic methods of editing follow in the next section.

Technical Process

Transitions

Any type of transition requires connecting two shots together. The most common transition in editing is a *cut*. In live television, it would be called a *take*. You create a cut by simply dragging one shot onto the timeline following another. An instantaneous change of picture will appear at the point of where the two shots meet when played back. The point where you want a shot change from one to another may be trimmed frame by frame at the point of connection (see Figure 6.13).

A dissolve is a type of soft transition. A dissolve involves two video timelines. The first shot is on one line, the following shot is dropped onto the second timeline slightly overlapping the first. The amount of overlap between the two shots will determine the length of the dissolve. A 1-second dissolve (not a very fast dissolve) will require at least 30 frames of each shot. The last 15 seconds of the first shot will slowly disappear, and the first 15 seconds of the second shot will slowly appear as the first shot completely disappears. A dissolve is a minor type of special effect that you should treat with care and not use carelessly but for a specific reason in the story. A dissolve must be programmed by the application used in editing. You must find the drop-down transition menu, indicate a dissolve, and click on the spot between the two shots indicating the midpoint of the dissolve.

A superimposition, or *super*, is a combination of two shots each on a different timeline but lined up so they appear simultaneously. A super is basically a dissolve stopped and frozen in midtransition.

A wipe is the next step up in transitions. A wipe is a dissolve, but instead of one shot disappearing as another appears, one shot is replaced by another with a hard line between the two shots, or one shot is "pushed" out of the frame, replaced by the second shot. The editing process is the same as for a dissolve, but the transition menu indicates what the wipe will look like. In dissolves and wipes, both shots have to be long enough to allow for the overlap plus some extra so there is no loss of signal during the transition.

You create a split screen by stopping a wipe in midstream. Again, such a transition requires enough footage of each shot to last for more than the duration of both sides of the split.

The final transition is a digital effects transition, best considered as a complex wipe. Depending on the editing application, with a digital transition, you may create a page turn; you may create multiple screen wipes in fancy, specially created shapes; or you may move screens in different directions and at different speeds. Don't attempt such a transition unless you have a great deal of time to experiment and solve problems.

FIG. 6.13 – Depending on the editor application, a variety of different functions may be accessed by searching menus visible on the screen. (Courtesy Advanced Broadcast Solutions.)

Technical Process

Titles

Titles constitute an important a part of your production's appearance. Audiences expect titles, and they expect them to be clear, fulfill a purpose, and add to the production. Your most common titles are opening and closing titles. At the very least, you tell the audience what the name of the production is, who is responsible for it (producer, director, writer, videographer, editor), and indicate what the project is all about. You may gain or lose your audience with your opening titles, so choose and design them carefully. A title is a shot. So most NLE applications have a titling segment on a drop-down menu. You can set the font size, style, color, and arrangement of the title. Keep a critical copy of the titles within the critical area of the frame. Once you create the title, save it and move on to the next page or create a series of title pages as part of one file, depending on the program used. You may use the title functions of the application as transitions and within special effects, as well as for the important closing titles that must credit everyone who contributed to your project.

Adding Audio

Audio is as important as any visual. Tests show conclusively that more than half of the information an audience comprehends from a video production comes from the audio portion of the program. Treat your audio with respect and care—poor audio will destroy a production more quickly than any one other aspect of the production. You edit audio on one or more timelines laid parallel to the video timelines. If you include audio in a shot and both were edited simultaneously, the audio track for that shot will appear in parallel to the shot on one of the audio timelines. You may add audio by dragging music, sound effects, or narration onto one of the other timelines and placing it in proper relationship to the matching video. You will find that editing audio is similar to editing copy in a word program. You may copy, drag, and place a sequence where you want it on a timeline. You raise or lower your audio levels using the tools in the audio toolbox. You also may equalize or modify the audio as required by using the tools available in the editing application (see Figure 6.14).

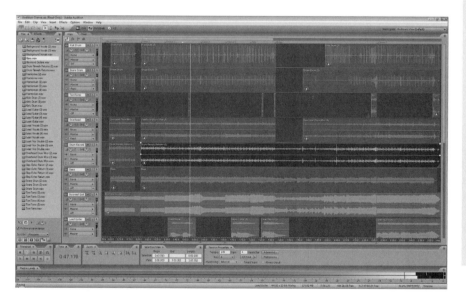

Technical Process

FIG. 6.14 – The audio timeline is a visible indication of each audio clip, its relative level, and the relationship between channels if more than one channel is used in that particular editing session. (Courtesy Advanced Broadcast Solutions.)

Rendering

You end the session by saving your final edited project. Hit Command/S on the Mac or Control/S on the PC to save all of your edits. Remember you are working on virtual files. Before moving forward, make certain both audio and video levels meet technical standards. If either your audio or video is overmodulated the signal may be distorted and or broadcast operations will not accept the program unless the technical standards are within the levels set by the Federal Communications Commission (FCC). You must convert the edited files to final digital files for outputting and storage by combining them with the original media files. This process is called *rendering* and is either a separate stage of finishing a project or may be completed automatically depending on the specific application used. When a QuickTime project is exported both types of files are combined into one complete digital file. Other editing programs require a rendering stage before exporting the completed project.

Once you render the project, it may be exported to film, a disc, a tape, or a storage medium for archiving or a later decision on distribution. If you export to film, the file must match with the film rate of 24 fps. For broadcast distribution, the project must have a leader of color bars and thousand-cycle tone, an identifying slate, and a count-down followed by 2 seconds of black. All of your projects should include several seconds of a clean black silent clip as a protection at the beginning and end of the project. Creating a disc from your files does not require the leader clips but must be in the format that matches the disc burner. Outputting to tape requires you to use the format of the signal that matches that of the tape. You may store the final combined edited file and media files on hard drives, memory media, or other digital media for archival purposes or as storage until the distribution is determined later. The signal used to feed a Web program also must have the standards set to match the requirements of that Web program. A Web feed restricts the bandwidth of the signal so a highly compressed codec is necessary for such an output.

Technical Process

Aesthetic Process

For you to assemble clips to tell a meaningful story requires your maximum energy, concentration, and creative effort. The editing stage requires the greatest amount of creativity and skill from the beginning to the end of the process of producing a media project. You may solve or compensate for some errors, mistakes, and misjudgments made during preproduction and production. But post is the last chance to make the production tell the story you intended to tell in the manner you intended to tell it. The aesthetic process consists of your assembling clips, both audio and video, in the meaningful manner you director intended. But there exists a virtual infinite number of methods you may use to assemble clips and thereby accomplish any one task (see Figure 6.15).

EDITING METHODS

Master Shot and CUs
Master Shot

Cut-away   CU

Master shot with CUs inserted at appropriate times

Shot Sequencing

Shot 1	Shot 2	Shot 3	Shot 4	Shot 5	Shot 6

Individual shots assembled one after another

Final Video Edited to Audio

Audio recorded first

Shot 1	Shot 2	Shot 3	Shot 4	Shot 5	Shot 6

Video edited to match audio

FIG. 6.15 – **Basic editing methods include combining a master shot with cut-ins and cutaways, arranging the shots in order chronologically as a series of related shots, and adding audio in the form of music, special effects (SFX), and narration, to be inserted to create a finished edited project.**

Rules have been developed over the years for how best to edit clips together, but because editing is the most creative aspect of media production, rules must either be ignored or used as a guide. The rules are based on how audiences have come to comprehend what the media tells them. Some of the rules are culturally based, others have developed to fulfill a technical limitation. Regardless of the origination of the rules, the rules help an editor avoid creating a message that the audience may totally misunderstand. Here are the rules you should consider:

1. Show everything the audience needs to see in order to understand what you are trying to say.
   a. Don't show anything the audience does not need to see. Don't use every shot recorded, regardless of how important it seemed to be when shot. During post, look at every shot as a new piece of information. Use only what is necessary to show clearly what the audience needs to see.
   b. Every shot has to have a reason. Each shot must say something that moves your story forward. Each shot must add something to the flow of information to keep the audience in tune with your program and wanting to watch more.
2. Build tension and excitement by showing critical information, but leave something for the audience's imagination. Make the audience want to keep watching to find out what is going to happen next or how the story will end. Each section of the story should build to a minor climax until a major conflict must be resolved to lead to the final dénouement.
3. Either leave the audience satisfied and fulfilled or slightly unfulfilled and wanting more of your story.

Aesthetic Process

4. Remember, there are three forms of editing movement: movement of subject(s), camera movement, or movement created by shot changes. Use each at appropriate moments in your scene, but don't overuse any of the three. Movement keeps an audience involved and watching, but movement just for the sake of movement becomes boring and confusing when you improperly apply it to a scene. Keep movement direction consistent. If subject A moves to the right on the first shot, make certain the subject keeps moving in the same direction in following shots unless there is reason to show a specific change in direction. Western cultural rules indicated a movement from left to right is a forward movement, whereas movement from right to left is backward or returning movement.

5. A corollary of movement consistency is consistency of continuity. There are two important aspects to consider: you must first maintain consistency of relationships between subjects by observing and not violating the 180-degree line. Pay close attention to small details such as hand positions, placement of props, and relationship between subjects and backgrounds. Three types of shots you might use to avoid such errors are cover shots, cutaways, and cut-ins. A cover shot is a wide shot showing all of the subjects, props, foreground, and background relationships. This is a shot that a continuity assistant should have photographed during production to use not only for shooting related shots but also to help the editor make certain that continuity is followed during post. A cut-in usually is a CU showing significant detail that is important to the scene. Such a shot can cover a movement or lack of continuity in a wide shot by forcing the audience's attention to a small and important detail. A cutaway provides the editor with an even handier tool by having a shot that relates to the scene but may not show anything significant in detail that must match continuity. An example of such a use of these three shots is a WS of a couple sitting in a park with children playing in the background (BG). An MCU of one of the two could be considered a cut-in, but if the children playing in the BG don't match the WS, you can use a CU of the couple's hands that does not show any of the BG and then cut back to an MCU of either one of the two members of the couple, even though the children have moved on.

6. Last, but not the least important, concerns your audio. Audio must be considered with as much effort you put forth to perfect the picture. Audio carries as much information as the video and in some cases makes more sense to your audience, who can more quickly comprehend the action if the sound is accurate and well edited. You use sound to support the picture, but it should not duplicate the picture. Sound can be contradictory, but not so much that it confuses the audience. Each change of sound does not have to occur simultaneously with the matching shot. You can slightly anticipate a shot change with a minimally advanced sound change that may heighten the tension and increase interest in the sequence. Use music and sound effects to create a critical sense of what is happening in a scene. Both are important, but they should be used carefully and thoughtfully.

EDITING STYLES

❖ **Single-camera dramatic**

A master shot covering the entire scene
Cut-ins and cutaways illustrating specific points and dialog
Reversals for dialog
Shots combined in postproduction with audio/SFX/music

❖ **Multiple-camera dramatic**

Three to four cameras recording simultaneously
One wide for cover
Others focused on individuals or CUs
Recording played back simultaneously and edited as if "live"
Additional editing as needed—audio/SFX/music added in post

❖ **Documentary**

Interview shot with one or two cameras
One focused on subject, second on interviewer or cut-aways
In field—one or more cameras covering subject(s) and action
Additional shots of topics and information shot separately
All shots assembled in post with narration, music, SFX

❖ **Electronic news gathering (ENG)**

Shots gathered on scene by one or more cameras
Wild sound, interviews, and cover shot as available
All shots assembled in post with narration, SFX

❖ **Commercials and other short forms**

Shots and material gathered in same pattern as dramatic
Edited in post with SFX/music/narration

Aesthetic Process

FIG. 6.16 – Editing styles vary according to the type of production, the intended audience, and, in some cases, the budget.

There are many styles, methods, and traditions of editing visual and aural media. Some are based on the traditions of Hollywood feature film editing, others on cinema verité; those two systems reveal the extreme opposites in the philosophy of editing. In between the two, news, documentary, music video, archival footage, TV commercials, film trailers, and dramatic storytelling editing provide you with various means of expressing your vision in final form. Because editing is the most creative of all stages of media production, it allows the widest range of techniques to fulfill the effort of the editor. Also, the creative nature of editing refuses to allow absolute rules and restrictions on how you may assemble the material at hand. There is only one rule: what works and tells the story best is the right way (see Figure 6.16).

Output-Distribution

Preparing to Output/Export

Before you move a production from your editor, you must make certain that the files are ready for the move. There are two types of moves: output for dubbing a finished production to tape or disc, and export for converting and copying a complete file plus file data to another computer for further treatment or processing.

For audio files, make certain all of the audio clips are adjusted to the same overall level (beyond necessary creative dynamics). Second, make certain all audio clips are at the same rate and bit depth. For example, adjust all audio clips to 48 kHz and 12 or 16 bits. If the bit rate or depth changes between clips within a single production, distortion may occur.

For video files, make sure that video clips are adjusted to the same white and black levels to avoid sudden changes in levels that will destroy the feeling you created in the edit. Also, make certain there are no missing frames or bad edit points, as those will cause a major glitch in any copy of the original, and when projected on a large screen, they will be extremely obvious and will destroy the flow of the storyline. All of the clips must be adjusted to the same frame rate, frame size, pixel rate, and aspect ratio. You may vary resolution between clips, but if possible convert as many clips to the same resolution before attempting either an output or an export. Also, the cable connection between your computer and the input device must match; Firewire to Firewire, SDI to SDI, or HD-SDI to HD-SDI. You may need a converter box between devices to complete any conversion factors.

Output-Distribution

Output Process

Of all the stages of the production process, postproduction is the one stage in which the technology of digital equipment and circuits cannot be ignored. There are some processes that you can operate without understanding the technology, but only if all of the equipment is matched by either the manufacturer or the technician supervising the editing suite. A basic knowledge of the technical standards may not be necessary, but they certainly will be helpful as you pursue a career in digital editing. Many of the technical specifications were described in previous sections of this text, and for precise instructions, study the operating manual of the editing equipment and follow its directions.

Your first step is setting and adjusting monitors, both audio and video. During the production and editing processes, viewing the clips and sequencing on a standard suite monitor may show the editor what is occurring between shots, and play the sound for easy listening. But before a project leaves the suite, you must adjust the monitors (they should be properly adjusted at all times, but may not have been) so that you can make certain the color matches between shots; that the color of each shot is correct; and that the sound is clean without distortion or noise and that any unwanted sounds are not audible on the small speakers mounted in the computer. You should use a set of studio speakers powered by a professional amplifier, or use a set of professional headsets, to monitor the audio for the entire length of the project.

A professional color monitor (not a TV set) that has been properly adjusted using color bars is required to judge accurately the value of the video signal. While adjusting the set and previewing the project, look away from the monitor periodically, glancing at a white or gray surface to allow your eyes to return to a stable level. As color changes, the human mind will adjust the appearance of colors, making you think the color remains the same when there may be a great variation in hue and chroma. Do not try to set a monitor with any signal except color bars. If professional color settings equipment is not available, then set the controls of the monitor so that the color bars appear as accurately as possible. Make certain the colors are distinct and that a pure black and a pure white are clearly visible. Only the operation manuals of the equipment in question can positively provide the answers to questions about those connections.

In general, if the production is to be sent to a postproduction or authoring house, the signal must be an uncompressed version in either QuickTime or Audio-Video Interactive (AVI) format delivered on a portable hard drive. All clips, project files, rendered files, and graphics must be on the same hard drive. If a complete QuickTime file or QuickTime conversion file has been created, including all of the assets, then that one file may be transmitted via Firewire.

If the project format does not match between equipment, you will need a software or hardware encoder to convert the signal from one format to another. Encoders compress the signal, so avoid them if possible.

The quick-and-dirty method of transfer is to create a complete final production in your editor and then feed an output signal from the editor to a tape deck. Start the deck rolling and recording, pause, and then start playing the project on the editor. This works only if the project is complete with all files and data and the tape deck can accept the signal directly from the editor.

Output-Distribution

Destination Choices

You may feed a completed project to a line-out signal to the input of a video switcher, to a tape or disc recorder, to a hard drive, or to a telecine, or you may convert the project to a motion picture film, to stream on the Web, or to feed to a mobile system. Cable, satellite, and broadcast operations will accept your production if you have properly prepared it to fit their format and technical specifications. Check with their engineering staffs to determine what they expect and will accept. Each of these sources offers a potential for earning back some of the funds you invested in and committed to in order to complete the project. There are no guarantees of return from any of these sources. Competition is strong, and demand for product from untried, new producers is slim at best. But that doesn't mean you shouldn't try to sell your work. Begin at a low, local level, be willing to accept a minimum return, and depend on some exposure to lead to greater success with future productions.

Finally, you should arrange to create an archival recording of your project. Even a backup copy placed in a safe and secure location will protect you from losing your hard work.

Chapter Seven
Your Future

Introduction

The future of electronic media, including motion pictures, is only partially dependent on the advances in the development of new equipment. Smaller, less expensive, higher-quality equipment will make a difference, but knowledge and the inventive use of communication are the keys—software and brainware, not hardware, will determine the future of electronic media, especially for you as a media producer or operator.

Regardless of your function in media production, you will need to study and follow the changes in distribution methods, because convergence now questions which one will best serve which market. Today, new technology and audience demand provide you with two extremes: high definition on a wide screen or low definition on a miniature screen. High-definition television (HDTV) and mobiles each demand a different type of technical production and as of now, there is no certainty as to what type of creative production will serve each better than the other. Today, no one knows what form the next distribution method or technology will take: tape, film, disc, or sold state. That means you must prepare yourself to work and be familiar with all forms of electronic media.

Convergence has brought about two changes in the communication industry. First is compression, not by way of bandwidth but in terms of combining the jobs, functions, duties, and responsibilities of individuals working in all communication fields. Companies that specialize in print, public relations, advertising, motion pictures, billboards, and digital games, as well as television, satellite, and cablevision companies, expect employees to be able to understand and create in all communication fields, not just an employee's chosen field.

The second aspect is the convergence of communication corporations into operations that deliver information in all areas of communication. And these companies expect their employees to be able to deliver in all areas also. Reporters must be able to research, interview, shoot, edit, and produce complete packages of news for delivering as a newspaper, TV, radio, or Web-based story. Producers, videographers, editors, and talent must think and create with the understanding that whatever they are working on will be distributed or exposed to an audience in more than one communications distribution method.

To succeed in this new world of communication, you must face increased competition for fewer jobs and for jobs that require a broad range of skills and knowledge at a professional level of expertise. To meet this challenge, you must use your best knowledge and training, combined with passion and dedication. You should approach your search for employment based on three steps:

1. Research and exploration
2. Personal and professional preparation
3. Presentation and interview preparation

The first step in your job search is to decide what you want to do, whom you want to work for, and where you want to do it. It most cases, a wide-ranging search with few limitations in each of these categories is a wise choice. You must go where the jobs are and work for the organization that will hire you to do the job you have prepared yourself for and are capable of performing at a professional entry level (see Figure 7.1).

Your search should include everyone you know in the business, family, acquaintances, classmates, and friends. Reach out in every direction, and leave no possible contact untouched. Use the Web and written sources to research possible companies. The *Broadcasting-Cablecasting Yearbook* is available in most major libraries or on the Web. It lists a wide variety of companies involved in electronic communication.

CAREER SEARCH POSSIBILITIES

❖ FAMILY

❖ FRIENDS AND THEIR FAMILIES

❖ PREVIOUS WORK CONTACTS

❖ INTERNSHIP CONTACTS

❖ PROFESSIONAL ORGANIZATIONS – STUDENT BRANCHES

❖ INDUSTRY NEWSGROUPS & BLOGS

❖ ACADEMIC CONTACTS

❖ PROFESSIONAL PUBLICATIONS

❖ NETWORKING

❖ PERSONAL RESEARCH

FIG. 7.1 – No possible area of searching for contacts should be overlooked.

The listings include the names of the managers and administrators of each company, along with mailing addresses, phone numbers, and email addresses. If you use any of the listings, call to make certain that person you are contacting still holds the position. Personnel changes, especially at the middle-management level, occur rapidly and without any apparent reason. Another source of addresses is the semiannual *Motion PictureTV and Theatre Directory*. The publisher, Motion Picture Enterprises Publications, Inc., provides copies of the directory to schools, or it is available online at MPE.net.

The next step requires you to collect every possible bit of information about yourself. You will need this file of information to write professional résumés and cover letters and to prepare yourself for the interview process. You need to create a written (computer) file of your most recent three to five jobs as well as your supervisors' names, addresses, and phone numbers (and emails, if available). You will need to write a brief description of your duties and successes at each job. You also need to list your most recent three or four residences and, if possible, the landowners' names and contact information. Once you accept a position, you might also be required to present a list of family contacts. At that time, you will also need to make decisions about health and life insurance, retirement benefits, and beneficiaries. All of these matters arrive quickly and suddenly in the final stages of accepting a position, and they will have long-range effects later in your career and life (see Figure 7.2).

PERSONAL INFORMATION FILE

- ❖ YOUR NAME YOU WANT USED PROFESSIONALLY
- ❖ BIRTHDATE – BIRTH LOCATION
- ❖ CITIZENSHIP
- ❖ SOCIAL SECURITY NUMBER
- ❖ GRADUATION DATE
- ❖ OFFICIAL DEGREE TITLE
- ❖ MAJOR AND MINORS
- ❖ LIST OF HIGHER EDUCATION SCHOOLS ATTENDED, DATES
- ❖ COLLEGE HONORS (IF MEDIA OR MANAGEMENT ORIENTED)
- ❖ LAST THREE JOBS, SUPERVISOR'S NAME, PHONE, EMAIL
- ❖ LIST JOB RESPONSIBILITIES OF EACH
- ❖ LAST THREE RESIDENCES, OWNER'S NAME, PHONE, EMAIL
- ❖ CAREER-ORIENTED SKILLS, INCLUDING LANGUAGES
- ❖ COMPUTER SKILLS, INDICATE LEVEL
- ❖ FAMILY CONTACTS, MAILING ADDRESS, PHONE, EMAIL

FIG. 7.2 – Your personal information list must include all information that a prospective employer or human resources director may ask for or that you may need in order to fill out employee forms.

Internship

A critical aspect of preparation includes your academic work, your professional work, and, it is hoped, your internship experience. An internship should be the cumulating stage of your training, combining the knowledge and skills learned in the classroom, your work experience other than media production, and your willingness to accept the responsibility of serving as an intern. An internship must be earned. Depending on the policies of your school and the companies that offer internships, there are minimum qualifications. An internship does not replace coursework. Don't expect an intern host to teach you everything you need to know to work in the field of your choice. The knowledge and skills you acquired in school should prepare you to qualify for an internship that may lead to an entry-level position (see Figure 7.3).

The best internships are competitive internships that are designed to be true beginning work experience—that is, they provide actual work experience in a variety of areas where skilled employees supervise and evaluate your work on a continuing basis. Companies, organizations, and associations that clearly understand the virtues and values of internships, to themselves and to the industry as a whole, set up

INTERNSHIP CRITERIA

❖ INTERNSHIP TYPES

Competitive

Paid (with or without academic credit)

Unpaid (must be for academic credit)

Volunteer at non-profit organization (with or without academic credit)

❖ INTERNSHIP REQUIREMENTS

Professional preparation

    At least two years of college

    Sufficient media skills and knowledge

    Mentally/physically prepared for work pressures

Approval of academic unit

Acceptance by host

❖ INTERNSHIP CAUTIONS

Remain under close faculty supervision

Maintain close relationship with the Human Resources office of host

Avoid unfulfilling non-value busywork

Accept intern-level work matching your experience/knowledge

Accept every assignment as an opportunity to gain knowledge/experience

Always present professional appearance in action, dress, relationships, and speech

Accept and understand the intern level in the hierarchy of the host

Use the experience to develop career contacts

Immediately report any physical or sexual harassment to your faculty advisor and the Human Resources office

FIG. 7.3 – An internship is not automatic. You must earn the right to serve. Meeting certain criteria will provide the basis for your acceptance in most intern situations.

competitive internships. Examples of such organizations are the Academy of Television Arts and Sciences and the Belo Corporation.

Once you obtain an internship, you must demonstrate your willingness and ability to work and perform every reasonable task, however menial the task may seem at the beginning of your internship. If you have chosen your internship well and continue to display enthusiasm for your work, you may be given a bit more responsibility and an opportunity to gain experience with a greater variety of work areas, tasks, and duties as your internship progresses.

You should wait until near the end of your academic career before enrolling in an internship program. There are two reasons for this decision. First, you need the education and background to prepare you for the internship. Second, if the internship works well and you are offered a full-time job, you don't want to have to choose between accepting the offer and quitting school before you graduate or turning the offer down because you must wait to obtain your degree. Any company that offers you a full-time position while you are completing an internship will be willing to wait if you are in your last semester of school. Also, if you accept an internship during the fall or spring semester, make certain you carry as light an academic load as possible. If you apply for an internship during the summer, expect very heavy competition, because many schools allow students to intern only during the summer.

To take full advantage of an internship, free yourself of as many obligations as possible to concentrate your energies and time on the internship. During the internship, work to prove you will make a good employee. Perform any job assigned to you, and be positive about all of the activities that your host asks you to do, even if some of them are boring, repetitious, and not at all what you thought the industry was all about. Ask questions; don't hesitate to ask if you can perform work not assigned to you, but first make certain you know what to do and then do the job well.

Be aware of two negative incidents that may occur during an internship. First, if your assignments consist of only clerical work—answering telephones, getting coffee, running errands, or sitting around just watching people work—you have the right to report this to your school's intern supervisor, your supervisor on the job, or the company's human resources (HR) office. Expect to be assigned to low-level jobs during an internship, but an internship is also an educational activity; if there is no potential for learning, it is of limited value to you. Your school needs to be aware of your insufficient work assignment. The second is the more serious matter of sexual harassment. If you feel threatened at any time or are approached by an employee in an offensive manner, report the incident immediately to the HR department and your school's intern supervisor. At the same time, make certain you dress appropriately and act professionally toward all employees at all times.

The Application Process

Once you have completed your internship and are close to collecting your diploma, your next step is to begin the process of finding, applying for, and earning your first paying job in the communications field. As suggested at the beginning of this section, the first step in this process is gathering information about yourself and about any potential employers.

Résumé Writing

Once that process is completed, then it is time to write your résumé and cover letter. Even though the cover letter actually precedes the résumé in the process, you should prepare the résumé first. The résumé is a concise description of who you are; the cover letter states where you are going. The résumé should list your academic record, your work record, and a list of references. A well-written résumé should run no longer than one page; you may add a second page for references, but your potential employer should be able to read the first page at a glance. The reader should be able to make a judgment about your experience and capabilities (see Figure 7.4).

If a potential employer is impressed, the next step will be checking your references. You need to list at least three, better five, people who know you well, will speak honestly about you, and can be reached from the contact information that you list on your reference page. Make certain all of the contact information—the person's name, title, telephone number, email address, and mailing address—is accurate and complete. Also, always ask permission to list someone as a reference, and it might be helpful to send each person an updated copy of your résumé so that he or she will be able to give you an accurate reference. It is best not to list a reference from a religious organization. Such a person is highly unlikely to say anything negative about you, and a potential employer does not necessarily only want to hear the good things.

Composing a Cover Letter

The cover letter needs to be written individually for each job you apply for. The letter should briefly summarize who you are, but leave the details to the résumé, which should be attached to the cover letter. The rest of the cover letter should highlight your knowledge of the company and explain why you would make an excellent employee (see Figure 7.5). Again, make the sentences concise. Leave creative writing for other tests, not for either the résumé or the cover letter. The final paragraph of the letter should indicate that you will call the potential employer in a week or 10 days, and then make certain that you do so. Don't necessarily expect an immediate answer; you may be one of hundreds of first-timers applying for the one job, and it will take time for the human resources department to read applications and check references

Composing a Cover Letter

	Megan O'Brien	
816-532-3625	2835 Granite	sjones@comcast.net
	Kansas City, MO	
	64131	

EDUCATION The University of Missouri-Kansas City   June, 2010
Bachelor of Arts
Major: Communication
Minor: Computer Graphics
GPA 3.6

EXPERIENCE Brandon, Fife and Lewis, Advertising   Kansas City, MO
May 2008-present Receptionist
Handled telephone and guest duties
Entered data and typed letters, proposals and scripts

May 2007-May 2008 Outback Steakhouse   Overland Park, KS
Waiter/bartender
Accurately handled cash register, tended bar, and waited tables
Trained income employees

HONORS AND Communication School Scholarship, two years
ACTIVITES Member Omicron Delta Kappa Honorary
Writer, Producer, Director UH TV
Volunteered for various community fundraisers
Internship, WDAF-TV

ADDITIONAL Proficient with both PC and Mac Operating systems, MS Word, Excell,
INFORMATION Power Point, FileMaker Pro, Photoshop, Illustrator.
Final Cut Pro and other editing systems.
Attended NAB conference, completed media production workshops,
          and attended broadcast lectures and panels

REFERENCES

Michael J. Brandon   Wendy Adair
Partner   Manager
Brandon, Fife, and Lewis, Advertising   Outback Steakhouse
1235 North Loop West   2100 195th St.
Kansas City, MO 64105   Overland Park, KS, 66207
816-862-1860   913-3650-4122
mjbrandon@att.net   wadair@outback.com

Jennifer Ayles, Ph.D.
Director, School of Communication
UMKC
Kansas City, MO 68108
713-743-2108
jayles@umkc.edu

FIG. 7.4 – A résumé must be concise, accurate, error free, and provide the critical information a potential employer needs to make a decision as to your ability to fit the requirements for the position.

Megan O'Brien
2835 Walnut
Kansas City, MO
64131
816-532-3625
mobrien@comcast.net

May 20, 2010

Mr. Charles Profiot
Operations Manager
KGFO-TV
P. O. Box 7777
Kansas City, MO
64555

RE: Production Associate Position

Dear Mr. Profiot:

My media production experience and academic training provide the basis for consideration as a Production Associate at KGFO-TV. I will graduate this month with honors in Communication and a minor in Computer Graphics. While at the University I worked all positions at the student operated television station including writing, producing, and directing a weekly public affairs program.

I spent last semester as an intern at WDAF-TV as a Production Assistant operating studio equipment and assisting the directors and producers. I suggested ideas for programs at channel four where they were accepted and aired successfully. During that time I watched your operation and believe I could be of benefit to you and KGFO-TV.

I feel my broad liberal arts education including study of theatre, art, and music as well as the study of media history, communication law, and audio, video, and computer graphics production courses with a GPA of 3.6 prepares me for a career in media production.

I worked part time while attending school, paying for part of my education and gaining valuable work experience. My former employers and references will honestly evaluate my work habits and potential for a career in electronic media.

I look forward to meeting you and will call on Monday May 25th to discuss my application and for an interview. Thank you for your consideration.

Sincerely,

Ms Megan O'Brien
816-532-3625
mobrien@comcast.net

Enc: Resume, references

FIG. 7.5 – A cover letter must be written for a specific job application; do not expect a general letter to cover all application situations.

Composing a Cover Letter

and other cross sources. Remember, your potential employer can and will read anything you have placed on the Web in any social network. Clean out or delete information that indicates you are anything but a mature, intelligent, and hard-working individual. That includes information about you that your "friends" have listed on their sites.

The Portfolio

A portfolio is not an afterthought. It is a succinct and engaging summary of your best work, and it is the culmination of several years of accomplishments. Throughout your academic career, you should be designing, planning, and completing short works of high quality that help build your portfolio. You should submit these works to student film, video, audio, and Internet contests, screenings, festivals, and exhibitions where your work might receive some kind of recognition or awards. You need a means to show what you are capable of doing and have accomplished in the past. Your portfolio allows you to do just that.

The approach you use for your portfolio may follow two different paths: (1) prepare a portfolio that shows at least one example of each type of production that you are capable of, or (2) create a portfolio that contains only one type of work. The latter selection is best used if you are applying for a specific job, such as an editor or a news videographer for a television station. Some jobs require a range of work, from short spots or news clips to lengthy documentary or longer dramatic shooting. A portfolio for that type of job should include as wide a range of samples as possible (see Figure 7.6).

An important consideration requires that you include only your best work. The impulse to include every piece that you like or have an emotional attachment to creates a mediocre portfolio. It is better to have one excellent example of your work rather than one good one and several mediocre ones. The viewer will remember the mediocre samples. Choose wisely and critically as if you are looking at someone else's work, not your own. If there were production restrictions beyond your control, you may explain, but do not rationalize or excuse poor or mediocre work—just don't include it in the portfolio. Once you have chosen your work, use only clean copies, preferably on a DVD or some other ubiquitous digital disc format. Media formats change, but most operations today can review a standard burned DVD or CD. Check every clip for production errors or bad edits. Make certain each video clip is carefully dubbed with color bars and slate, and make sure that it is professionally formatted. Each clip slate should have your name on it. Few examiners will look at the entire portfolio, so make certain the first few clips are the very best and will entice the viewer to look further into the samples.

All written material should be mounted in some type of loose-leaf binder if more than one page. The DVD or CD case should have a clean, professional appearance; again, save your creativity showcase for what's inside the DVD or CD, not the case itself. But it needs to be carefully labeled both on the front surface and on the disc. The label needs to be visible and contain your name and contact information. If your presentation does not grab the viewer within the first 30 seconds, your work may never receive full consideration.

PORTFOLIO PREPARATION

1. Research Company

    Know who will view portfolio

    Learn what they will look for

    Choose works that fit the job

2. Choose Selections

    Review all of your work

    Select ONLY the best

    Select ONLY Professional quality examples

3. Create Portfolio

    At this time DVD is the best format

    Clean each selection: no bad edits, clean audio, black in and out

    Begin recording with Slate:

        Name, email address, phone numbers, mailing address

        Table of contents: title, length, medium each selection

    End recording with repeat of slate

    Restrict recording to ten minutes, maximum, better a tight five minutes

4. Mounting

    Clearly label disc

    Clearly label disc sleeve

    Place in foam shipping pack with slate label on outside

    Include a self addressed return label inside pack

    Expect to leave cover letter, resume with disc

    Do not expect the disc to be returned.

The Portfolio

FIG. 7.6 – A portfolio must illustrate the best aspect of you and your capabilities. It needs to show only your best work, and it should be presented in a format that is easily accessed and clearly identifies you as the creator.

Every portfolio won't appeal to every interviewer; you need to redesign the portfolio for each different type of job that you apply for. Often your portfolio will not be viewed until you have been given an interview, and as a part of that interview you will be given the opportunity to show your portfolio. If you have prepared it well, your portfolio should speak for itself; you will need only to make explanations or provide more detail about your experience. If you mail your portfolio, make certain you keep original copies of all of the work contained in the package. Carefully package the DVD or CD and accompanying material to make certain it will not be damaged in shipment and will arrive at its destination on time. A little money spent at this point will pay dividends in the long run. Also include a prepaid, self-addressed return-shipping label if you expect the portfolio to be returned. Maintain a portfolio demo reel online on your web page for continual updates and additions of your works.

The Interview

For most people, including those who have gone through the process more than once, interviewing for a job can be uncomfortable. It doesn't have to be, if you prepare yourself and your materials well. Remember, both you and the interviewer have a common goal—to find out if you fit the requirements the interviewer has for a position. The session need not be a confrontational battle, but a give and take during which you explain who you are, what you are capable of doing, and how it fits with the needs of the company. If there is no fit, then don't take the rejection personally. It is better if you don't accept a position that doesn't match your interests or capabilities than to end up on a job that will make you unhappy and not allow your creativity to blossom.

Concentrate during the interview by giving the impression that you are a dedicated and task-driven potential employee. Be willing to start at or near the bottom of the rank and file. Of course, no one wants to stay in that position very long—more than two years in an entry-level position may mean that there is no possibility of moving up and it's time to look for a position at another company. The amount of money you make should not be the major motivating factor in the choice of your first position. Find work that gives you the opportunity to prove yourself, get experience, and develop those all-important networking contacts.

Thoroughly research the company, the job you want, and the work you may be expected to perform. Be prepared to answer questions that reveal your knowledge of all of those subjects. You may not be asked detailed questions at the first interview, but knowing what you have learned from your research will give you confidence in talking intelligently about the company, and confidence is one of the best characteristics to show during an interview. Arrive on time fully prepared for both the face-to-face part of the interview and, depending on the size of the company, a stack of forms to fill out. To prepare for the forms as part of your research—research yourself. Arrive with every possible bit of information about your past that the potential employer might be interested in (see Figure 7.7).

Depending on the company and what position you are applying for, you may be asked to submit to an examination or test. If you are applying for a job as an editor, you may be asked to quickly cut a story, commercial, or treatment with basic information provided. The interviewer may intentionally ask you to complete another test or application in your handwriting, or she or he may give you access to a computer. Your portfolio should provide samples of your ability to work under pressure, but some companies will want to see if you can work with basic information against a deadline.

THE INTERVIEW

- ❖ RESEARCH THE FIRM, THE POSITION, AND THE INTERVIEWER
- ❖ PREPARE YOUR INTERVIEW FILES
- ❖ PREPARE YOUR PORTFOLIO
- ❖ ARRANGE FOR THE INTERVIEW
- ❖ ARRIVE ON TIME
- ❖ ARRIVE DRESSED AND APPEARING AS A PROFESSIONAL
- ❖ REVIEW ALL OF YOUR INFORMATION AND RESEARCH
- ❖ PREPARE FOR QUESTIONING
- ❖ KNOW WHO YOU ARE AND WHAT YOU ARE PREPARED TO SELL
- ❖ DELIVER A SALES PITCH THAT IS MEANINGFUL TO THE INTERVIEWER
- ❖ IF OFFERED A POSITION, NEGOTIATE PAY, WORKING CONDITIONS, SCHEDULES. AND BENEFITS
- ❖ LEAVE THE INTERVIEW ON A POSITIVE NOTE, WHETHER OFFERED A POSITION OR NOT
- ❖ IF NO POSITION IS OFFERED, ASK ABOUT OTHER POSITIONS
- ❖ FOLLOW UP WITH AN EMAIL OR A PHONE CALL WITHIN 2 WEEKS
- ❖ DON'T GIVE UP, PERSISTENCE IS THE KEY TO SUCCESS

The Interview

FIG. 7.7 – Prepare yourself for an interview by making an appearance that indicates you are a mature professional. Prepare all the information for any question you may be asked during the interview. Approach the situation with a clear head and an open mind.

Negotiating pay and benefits is a difficult challenge for all new employees, but even more so for creative applicants. We all know what we think we are worth, but it is difficult to face someone across a desk in a suit and demand that figure. Again, begin this part of the process with research. Find out what that company or similar companies in the same market size pay beginning employees in the position for which you are applying. Don't be afraid to ask for that figure if you are offered less. Knowing your own value again shows confidence, but don't argue. If you are told the figure is the maximum the company is willing to pay, don't walk out the door. Explore other perquisites (perks) such as car or clothing allowances, equipment, overtime pay, moving expenses, or a signing bonus. Don't take rejection personally; try to assume a pleasant negotiating stance, not an argumentative position. If you cannot come to terms satisfactory to you, don't hesitate to thank the interviewer for her or his time and for considering you for the position.

Sending blind inquiries may yield a result, but be prepared to send hundreds if not more to get one or two responses. Never send unsolicited portfolios. They will be returned unopened or destroyed. Unsolicited résumés and cover letters may receive some limited attention.

Summary

The best job search philosophy requires a three-step plan. First, conduct a detailed search based on research you have gathered on the companies who might be hiring, and develop contacts from friends, family, and your internship. An internship is one of the most beneficial activities you as a soon-to-graduate student can engage in to prepare yourself for building contacts and learning on a practical level what a job in the field of your choice actually is like.

Once you have established a reasonable goal, your next job is to prepare the paperwork you will need in order to apply for and gain worthwhile employment. You must write a cover letter tailored for each individual company and position, create a résumé that describes you completely but succinctly (who you are and what you are capable of giving to an employer), and put together your portfolio. Each must be carefully and professionally prepared, because they represent who you are and what you are capable of doing. Ideally, an interview will follow, and again you need to do background research into the company, what the company produces, what its pay scales are, and how your skills may be attractive to the person doing the hiring.

The field of media production is highly competitive and at times frustrating. Many people prepare for careers in the field, and many simply believe they can enter the field without the necessary knowledge, skills, and experience that help provide the basis for a serious attempt at entering the industry. If you really have the desire and are willing to offer the energy, sacrifice, passion, tenacity, and hard work to succeed, you will enter the narrow range of qualified and successful applicants who have finally found their place.

Summary

Glossary

A/B ROLL Editing process using two separate rolls (cassettes or reels) of tape. Each cassette contains alternate shots of the sequence, enabling the editor to use transitions other than straight cuts between shots.

ABSTRACT One of three basic media aesthetic choices. Abstract goes beyond realism as seen in the way some music videos and science fiction dramas stretch the audience's imagination and sense of reality.

ADDITIVE The colors used in mixing light and upon which both film and video signals are based: red, blue, and green.

ADVANCED TV SYSTEMS COMMITTEE (ATSC) An American professional group formed to set standards for television broadcasting beyond analog NTSC, including high-definition and digital television standards.

AESTHETIC ASPECT One of two choices that need to be made during any media session. Aesthetic covers the creative, artistic values; the other considerations are the practical choices.

AMBIENT Prevailing environment; in audio, the background noise present at a location.

AMPLITUDE The instantaneous value of a signal; the electronic equivalent of level or loudness in audio.

ANALOG Electronic signal that is constantly varying in some proportion to sound, light, or a radio frequency.

APERTURE (IRIS) The size of the lens opening, measured in f-stops.

APPLE BOX A series of various sized boxes used to stand on and carry production items. Manufactured in standard sizes with holes on two sides to ease carrying them about the set or location.

ASA EXPOSURE INDEX Numerical system that refers to the ability of a film stock to react to light. Set by the American National Standards Institute.

ASPECT RATIO The measurement of width to height of the visual frame—4:3 in NTSC, 16:9 in HDTV.

ASSEMBLE EDIT Sequential arranging of shots in a linear manner. Can be accomplished on raw tape without previously recording a control track.

ATSC-DTV The digital video broadcast standard set by the Federal Communications Commission (FCC) for the United States.

ATTENUATE To lower the level of an electronic signal.

AUDIO The sound portion of the videotape. Frequencies within the normal hearing range of humans.

AURAL Having to do with sound or audio.

AUTOMATIC GAIN CONTROL (AGC) Circuit that maintains the audio or video gain within a certain range. Prevents overdriving circuits, which causes distortion but can increase signal-to-noise ratio.

AUTOMATIC LEVEL CONTROL (ALC) Circuit that maintains set levels at the output of an audio compressor to set the proper level for the next stage.

AVAILABLE LIGHT Illumination existing at a location.

BACK FOCUS The distance the lens must be mounted from the focal point for maximum focus.

BACKLIGHT Lamp placed behind the subject, opposite the camera; usually mounted fairly high and controlled with barn doors to prevent light shining directly into the camera lens.

BALANCED LINE An audio cable constructed with two conductors and a shield designed to provide the best protection from outside interference.

BARN DOOR Movable metal flap attached to lighting fixtures to allow control over the area covered by the light from that lamp.

BARREL A cable adapter designed to connect two cables ending in similar plugs.

BARS/GAIN SELECTOR A switch that allows the camera operator to record color bars or change the gain setting of the internal video amplifier.

BASE LIGHT The minimum amount of light required to provide an acceptable picture.

BASIC THREE-POINT LIGHTING Basic three-point lighting is designed to satisfy the need for basic lighting to create an image and provide a realistic setting for a scene. This design derives its name from the three lighting instruments used to achieve satisfactory levels and appearance: key lights, fill lights, and backlights.

BASS The low end of the audio spectrum.

BEL Basic unit of audio measurement. Usually too large for normal usage, so decibels ($\frac{1}{10}$ bel) are used instead.

BETACAM One-half-inch professional videotape format developed by Sony specifically for use in a camcorder. Betacam replaced ¾-inch U-matic as the predominant news-gathering video format. Now upgraded to digital Beta.

BIDIRECTIONAL Microphone that picks up sound from the front and back but rejects most sound from the sides. The pickup pattern appears in the shape of a figure eight.

BIN (BROWSER) A section of the editing screen that shows the files or clips ready to be edited.

BIT Smallest digital measurement; 8 bits = 1 byte.

BLACK BURST A composite video signal including sync and color signals, but the video level is at black, or minimum.

BLACK LEVEL The normal level for pedestal or video black in a video signal. See also SETUP.

BLEED Space beyond the critical or essential area that may be seen on some television receivers but not on others.

BLOOM The effect seen when a video signal exceeds the capabilities of the system: white areas bleed into darker areas.

BNC A type of twist-lock video connector, now the most common for professional equipment.

BODY MIC A microphone concealed or hung directly on the body of the performer, sometimes called a lapel or lavalier mic.

BODY MOUNT A method of holding and controlling a camera without the use of a tripod or other fixed mounting. Most common is the Steadicam, which uses a series of gyroscopes, springs, and counterweights.

BOOM Movable arm from which a microphone or camera may be suspended to allow for movement to follow the action.

BOOST To raise the level of an electronic signal.

BRIGHTNESS The luminance value of a video picture.

BROAD A type of open-faced fill light, usually rectangular in shape.

BUBBLE Leveling device mounted on a tripod pan head consisting of a tube containing liquid with a bubble of air trapped inside. Centering the bubble on a circle or cross-hair indicates that the pan head is level.

BUST SHOT The composition of framing a human from slightly above the waist to the top of the head.

BYTE A measurable number of bits treated as a unit. Also a convenient measurement of digital memory.

CAMCORDER Camera-recorder combination. Designed originally for news coverage, but now becoming popular for EFP and other productions.

CARDIOID MIC Specialized unidirectional microphone with a heart-shaped pickup pattern.

CASE Style of letters. Uppercase letters are capital letters; lowercase letters are small letters.

CASSETTE Prepackaged container of either audio or videotape containing a specific length of tape stock, a feed reel, and a take-up reel. BetaSP, S-VHS, miniDV, and Hi-8 systems use incompatible videocassettes.

CATHODE RAY TUBE (CRT) The large picture tube used as video monitors and television receivers replaced by LED, PDP, and plasma monitors.

CD-ROM (COMPACT DISC READ-ONLY MEMORY) A permanently recorded digital compact disc.

CENTRAL PROCESSING UNIT (CPU) The main control and operating circuits of a computer.

CHARACTER GENERATOR (CG) Computerized electronic typewriter designed to create titles or any other alphanumeric graphics for use in video.

CHARGE-COUPLED DEVICE (CCD) A solid-state element designed to convert light to electronics; replaces the pickup tubes in video cameras.

CHIAROSCURO LIGHTING Lighting accomplished with high-contrast areas and heavy shadows.

CHIP A semiconductor integrated circuit. Depending on its design, a chip can replace tubes, resistors, and other electronic components.

CHROMINANCE The portion of the video signal controlling color.

CINEMATOGRAPHER Its narrowest definition is the operator or supervisor of a motion picture camera. Over the years, the job description of a cinematographer has, to some, come to include the field of operating a video camera.

CLIP A single shot of a sequence to be edited in an NLE system.

CLOSE-UP (CU) The second tightest shot in a sequence. Camera framing showing intimate detail, often a tight head shot.

CLOSURE Psychological perceptual activity that fills in gaps in the visual field.

CODEC Short for COmpressionDECompression. The process or type of equipment that modifies digital signals between types of formats or compression ratios.

COLOR BARS Electronically generated pattern of precisely specified colors for use in standardizing the operation of video equipment.

COLOR TEMPERATURE CONTROL A series of filters enabling the camera operator to compensate for the variations in Kelvin temperature of the location.

COLOR TEMPERATURE See KELVIN TEMPERATURE.

COMPLEMENTARY METAL OXIDE SEMICONDUCTOR (CMOS) A type of solid-state element designed to convert light to electronics.

COMPRESSION In the digitizing process, certain unnecessary or redundant portions of the signal are not digitized, saving precious storage memory.

CONDENSER MIC Transducer that converts sound waves by conductive principle. Requires a built-in amplifier and a power source. Also called electrostatic or capacitor mic.

CONNECTOR PANEL Usually a section on the rear of a piece of equipment where the jacks are located.

CONTINUITY (1) A depiction of continuous action, location, direction, or time. (2) Script written for spots—commercials, public service announcements, or promotional announcements.

CONTINUITY ASSISTANT (CA) The member of the crew who follows the shooting script, keeps track of the logs, and checks to make certain shots will match later in the editing process between shots.

CONTRAST RANGE Ability of a camera to distinguish between shades of reflected black-and-white light: in TV, 30:1; in film, 100:1; with the human eye, 1,000:1.

CONTRAST RATIO The mathematical comparison of the measured light value reflected from the brightest part of the picture with detail and the darkest part of the picture with detail.

CONTROL TRACK Synchronizing signal recorded onto a videotape to align the heads for proper playback.

CONTROLLER A specialized computer designed to accurately maintain control over a series of videotape decks during the linear editing process.

COOKIE See CUKALORIS.

COPY The words on a script or to duplicate a signal or file.

COUNTDOWN A timed sequence of events leading to the beginning of a production. Numbered frames from 10 to 3, then 3 seconds of black.

COUNTER A meter designed to indicate either a position on a reel of tape or the amount of tape already used. May be calibrated in revolutions, feet, meters, or time.

COVER SHOT Any one of several shots, usually close-ups, designed to give the editor a means of preserving continuity. See also CUTAWAYS and CUT-INS.

CRAB DOLLY A small platform large enough for a tripod and camera operator. It usually has four wheels, two designed to provide a means of steering the dolly. Usually pushed by a crew member; sometimes set on tracks for a tracking shot.

CRANES One of the support systems used for single-camera production. Cranes are designed to permit the camera to be raised and lowered over a wide range as well as to swing back and forth for 360 degrees when necessary.

CRITICAL AREA (ESSENTIAL AREA) Space occupying approximately 80 percent of the center of the video frame. This area is seen with relative surety by the majority of the television receivers viewing that particular program. The 10 percent border outside of the critical area may not be seen by many receivers.

CROSS-KEY LIGHT A single instrument used to provide key light for one subject and, at the same time, fill light for another subject.

CUE (1) Signal to start talking, moving, or whatever the script calls for. (2) To ready material to be played back or edited by running and stopping a tape, film, record, and so on, at a specified spot.

CUKALORIS A pattern inserted into an ellipsoidal spotlight to throw a mottled design onto the background. Also known as a cookie or gobo.

CUT (TAKE) (1) Cue to stop an action, and the like. (2) An instantaneous change in picture or sound. *Cut* is considered a film term, and *take* is considered a video term, but they have become interchangeable.

CUTAWAY Close-up shot of an image related to, but not visible in, the wider shot immediately preceding or following it.

CUT-IN Close-up shot of an image visible in the wider shot immediately preceding or following it.

CYCLE Time or distance between peaks of an alternating voltage. Measured in hertz (Hz).

DECIBEL (dB) Logarithmic unit of loudness. A dB is $\frac{1}{10}$ of the original unit, the bel.

DECK In media, this term refers to a machine that plays or records audio or video signals.

DEGRADATION Lowering the quality of a signal from transporting, storing, or modifying the signal.

DEMODULATOR Separates audio and video signals in a cable.

DEPTH OF FIELD (DOF) The range of distances from the camera within which subjects remain in acceptable focus.

DIALOGUE Speech between performers, usually seen on camera.

DICHROIC Filters designed to reflect certain colors of light and pass others.

DIGITAL AUDIO WORKSTATION (DAW) A computer designed specifically to manipulate and edit digital audio signals.

DIGITAL Binary-based, constant-amplitude signals varying in time.

DIGITAL CINEMA (DC) Formerly known as electronic cinema. A video format designed to rival the quality of 35-mm film.

DIGITAL SUBSCRIBER LINE (DSL) A standard telephone line set up to carry broadband signals.

DIGITAL VERSATILE DISC (DVD) A high-density version of the CD.

DIGITAL VIDEO CAMERA (DVC) A half-inch digital videotape format. Various versions range from DVCam (prosumer level) to DVCPro (professional broadcast level), and PVCProHD (professional high-definition level). Some compatibility between levels and manufacturers.

DIN (DEUTSCHE INDUSTRIE NORMEN) The German standards organization. DIN usually refers to a type of plug or jack.

DIRECTOR Commands the creative aspects of a production. In the field, the director makes creative decisions. In the studio, the director calls the shots on live productions. In the editing room, the director provides opinions.

DISC A digital recording medium. May be either magnetic or optical. Ranging from the 3.5-inch floppy to 5-inch CD-ROMs and DVDs, and large hard drives.

DISSOLVE Transition of one image fading into and replacing another. If stopped at the midpoint, it is a superimposition. Also called a lap.

DISTORTION An undesirable change in a signal.

DISTRIBUTION AMPLIFIER (DA) Electronic amplifier designed to feed one signal (audio, video, or pulses) to several different destinations.

DOLLY (1) Three-wheeled or four-wheeled device that serves as a movable camera mount. (2) Movement in toward a subject (dolly in) or back away from a subject (dolly out).

DOWNLINK Transmission path from a satellite to a ground station. Sometimes used to describe the ground station capable of receiving a satellite signal. See also UPLINK.

DRAG The back pressure designed to make panning and tilting a camera head smooth and controlled. The drag can be created by friction, fluid, spring, or geared mechanisms.

DROP FRAME The frames omitted to allow color NTSC to stay in step with actual time.

DUAL-COLUMN FORMAT A scripting format used primarily for live or tape-to-live video and television productions. Developed over the years from radio and audio/video formats. All video and movement instructions are located in the left-hand column, all audio in the right-hand column.

DUB (1) Copying a recorded signal from one medium to another. (2) Replacing or adding voice to a preexisting recording; now called automatic dialogue replacement (ADR).

DVB-T (Digital Video Broadcast-Terrestrial) The high-definition technical standard developed by European on-air broadcasters.

DYNAMIC MIC Transducer designed to convert sound to electronics by using an electromagnetic coil attached to a lightweight diaphragm.

DYNAMIC RANGE Loudness range from the softest to the loudest that can be reproduced by any system without creating distortion.

DYNAMICS Refers to the difference between the loudest and the quietest passage.

EDGE ATTRACTION THEORY When an object appears to move toward the edge, even if it remains stationary in the frame.

EDGE BLEED AREA The 10 percent border around a frame, which may be visible to some viewers.

EDIT DECISION LIST (EDL) List of precise locations of edit points. May be generated manually or by computer.

EDITOR Tape or film specialist charged with assembling stories from footage and recordings to create the final production.

EIAJ (Electronic Industries Association of Japan) Standards-setting organization of Japan. At one time, EIAJ referred to a specific ½-inch open-reel videotape system.

ELECTRONIC ASPECT The editing criteria to be considered that affects the signal itself, not the visual or aesthetic criteria.

ELECTRET A small condenser mic often used as a lavalier or mic built in to equipment.

ELECTRONIC FIELD PRODUCTION (EFP) Process of researching, shooting, and editing materials to be utilized in non-news productions.

ELECTRONIC NEWS GATHERING (ENG) Process of researching, shooting, and editing materials to visually report on occurrences of interest, utilizing video cameras and electronic editing specifically for newscasts.

EQUALIZATION Process of compensating for required changes in frequency, level, or phase of an audio or video signal.

EXTERIOR (EXT) A setting or location outdoors.

EXTREME CLOSE-UP (ECU or XCU) The tightest shot in a sequence. Usually reserved for an effect. A very close view of a product would be an ECU.

EXTREME CLOSE-UP (ECU or XCU) Tightest framing of a shot in a sequence, for example, just the eyes or hands of a subject.

EXTREME WIDE SHOT (EWS or ELS) The widest shot of a sequence, for example, a shot from a blimp.

EXTREME WIDE SHOT (EWS or XWS) Widest shot of a sequence, for example, an entire city block or football stadium.

F A type of connector for a cable intended to carry a modulated signal or signals. See also RF.

FACILITIES (FAX) Technical equipment, lights, cameras, microphones, and so on.

FACSIMILE (FAX) Transmission of information by optical/electronic system through telephone lines.

FADE, IN OR OUT A gradual change in signal, either from zero to maximum or maximum to zero. Can apply to either audio or video.

FAY A series of fixed-focus lamps mounted in a bank. A FAY has a color temperature of 5,400 degrees Kelvin. See also PAR.

FEDERAL COMMUNICATIONS COMMISSION (FCC) Federal agency charged with the supervision and regulation of all electronic communication media in this country.

FIELD OF VIEW The range of subjects and settings that a camera shows in a single shot.

FIELD One-half of a complete interlaced television picture; 262.5 lines of the 525 NTSC system occurring once every 60th of a second. Two interlaced fields make a complete frame. One complete progressive video field may consist of from 360 to 1040 lines in a single fame.

FILL LIGHT Soft, shadowless light used to reduce contrast and lighten shadow areas. Usually placed on the opposite side of the camera from the key light and low enough to remove harsh shadows.

FILTER A colored element placed in front of or behind a lens.

FIREWIRE (IEEE 1394) Also known as iSync or iLink. A standard for transmission of data between digital equipment. A high-performance standard becoming one of the preferred methods of moving data in the media production world.

FISHPOLE Handheld expandable mic boom.

FIXED FOCUS INSTRUMENTS One of the three basic types of field lighting instruments. Fixed-focus instruments are designed around a lamp similar to an auto headlight. (See PAR and FAY.)

FLAG An opaque piece of material hung between a light and subject or set to control light or throw a shadow.

FLASH DRIVE A small, portable digital memory device designed to connect to a USB outlet to operate as portable hard drive. Also known as a thumb drive, pen drive, key drive, or USB drive.

FLASH FRAME An unwanted frame between two edited shots.

FLOODLIGHT A nonlensed instrument that provides soft, diffused light.

FLUORESCENT LIGHT Gas-filled tube that emits light when an electrical current ionizes the gas. It does not emit light of a specific Kelvin temperature, but is bluish green in color.

FLYING ERASE HEAD Erase head mounted on the rotating head mount of a helical recorder. Designed to allow precise editing of the video signal without losing sync between shots.

FOCAL LENGTH Theoretical distance from the optical center of the lens to the focal plane. Determines, with the size of the image surface, the angle of view, depth of field, and image size.

FOCAL POINT The position behind the lens where the image is concentrated.

FOCUS The ability of a lens to create the sharpest image of a subject.

FOCUSING SPOTLIGHTS One of the three basic types of field lighting instruments. Focusing spotlights are either open faced without a lens or lensed with a Fresnel or plano-convex lens. Focusing spots are essential for critical creative lighting.

FOLEY SESSION Named for Jack Foley, an early sound operator in film. A studio designed to create sounds in postproduction.

FOOT-CANDLE Older measurement of illumination. Originally, the amount of light from one candle, falling on an area one foot square, one foot from the candle.

FORMAT, VIDEOTAPE Specifications of a specific type of videotape. There are approximately 23 different formats in use today.

FRAME (1) Complete video picture, made up of two 262.5-line interlaced scanned fields. There are 30 frames per second in the NTSC system. (2) In HDTV 360 to 1040 lines in the progressive system at a rate of from 24 to 60 fps. (3) The outline of the available area in which to compose a video picture. Today's NTSC standard is a frame 3 units high by 4 units wide, HDTV 9 units high, 16 units wide.

FREEZE FRAME Stopping a single frame within a moving sequence.

FREQUENCY Number of complete cycles an electrical signal makes in one second. Measured in hertz (Hz).

FREQUENCY RESPONSE A measurement of a piece of equipment's ability to reproduce a signal of varying frequencies.

FRESNEL A spotlight equipped with a stepped lens that easily controls and concentrates light.

FRONT FOCUS Creating the sharpest picture by adjusting the lens.

F-STOP A measurement of the size of opening that allows light to pass through an iris or aperture.

FUSE BOX (CIRCUIT BREAKER BOX) The location of alternating current power distribution with individual switches or fuses (in older locations), which protect each circuit from having too much current drawn from it.

GAFFER Senior electrician on a crew.

GAIN The amount of amplitude of an electronic signal. Usually measured in dB.

GAIN CONTROL An electronic control in a camera, usually located internally.

GEN-LOCK Abbreviation for synchronous generation locking. Electronically connecting all circuits together so that synchronizing will remain stable.

GENRE A type of programming (e.g., western, comedy, drama).

GIGAHERTZ A measurement of frequency, one billion hertz.

GIRAFFE Small mic boom mounted on a tripod on wheels, usually designed for limited mic movement.

GOBO (1) In video, a set piece that allows a camera to shoot through it, such as a window. (2) In audio, a movable sound reflector board. (3) In film, a movable freestanding pattern cutout similar to a cookie. (4) On stage, the equivalent of a cookie.

GRAPHIC WEIGHT (GRAPHIC FORCE) The perceived value of any item within the picture frame.

GRAPHICS GENERATOR A digital unit designed to create and combine pictures with type. Sometimes called a paintbox.

GRAY SCALE Multiple-step intensity scale for the evaluation of a picture. Ranges between television white and television black in a series of calibrated steps.

GRIP A stagehand, a crew person who moves sets, props, dollies, and so forth. The head stagehand is the key grip.

HAND PROPS Items small enough to be picked up and handled, but for the most part, they are items that need to be handled by the talent during the production.

HARD DRIVE A magnetic disk drive designed to store large amounts of digital information. Most computers have at least one hard drive installed internally, but hard drives can also be connected externally to digital equipment.

HEAD A pan head supports the camera and is designed to allow both horizontal and vertical movement of the camera.

HEAD SHOT A composition of framing the human just above the shoulders to above the top of the head.

HELICAL Videotape with multiple recording heads that record information in long slanting tracks; each track records one field of information.

HELICAL RECORDING (see HELICAL)

HERTZ (Hz) Measurement of frequency. Number of complete cycles completed in one second.

HI-8 Semiprofessional digital 8-mm videotape format developed by Sony for the prosumer market.

HIGH-DEFINITION TELEVISION (HDTV) One of several subcategories of advanced TV (ATV). Attempt at creating a video system nearly equal to 35-mm film in resolution and aspect ratio.

HIGH HAT A minimal platform designed to mount a pan head, allowing for shots close to the ground or to mount the camera on a car, boat, or airplane.

HIGH IMPEDANCE A measurement of resistance to current flowing through a cable. High-impedance lines generally are designed to carry signals amplified to at least midlevel to prevent noise being added. Some mics are rated as high impedance, but they must be connected to short cables to prevent picking up extraneous noise.

IDIOT CARD A prompting device made of large bold key words written on cards held next to the camera lens for the talent's benefit.

IMAGE ORTHICON (I-O) An early video camera tube. The development of the I-O opened the way for reasonably mobile studio and remote cameras.

IMPEDANCE Apparent AC resistance to current flowing in a circuit. Measured in ohms.

INCANDESCENT LIGHT Inert, gas-filled electric lamp emitting light and heat from a glowing filament. A typical lamp is the tungsten-halogen lamp used in most production instruments.

INCIDENT LIGHT Illumination from a light source. Measured in foot-candles or lux by pointing the light meter at the light source.

INPUT Signal entering a system or an electrical unit.

INSERT EDIT Assembling a video production by adding video and audio signals to a master that already has had control track recorded on it. Insert edits also can be made over existing edited files.

INTEGRATED SERVICE DIGITAL BROADCAST (ISDB) The digital broadcast standard set for Japan.

INTERIOR (INT) Setting or location inside of a building or structure.

INTERLACED SCANNING The method of combining two fields of scan lines into one frame.

INTERNAL GAIN CONTROL A potentiometer that allows continuous gain settings on a camera.

INTERVALOMETER A control that sets the number of frames per second at which the recorder will operate. This compresses the action in any time elapsed required for the production.

INTRO Abbreviation for introduction.

INVERSE SQUARE LAW A mathematical analysis of changes in alternating energy. The amount of energy is inversely proportionate to the change in distance. The formula is easily applied to calculations of lighting and audio levels.

IRIS See APERTURE.

IRIS FADE-IN/FADE-OUT An iris fade-in or fade-out is created by placing the iris control on manual and setting the iris opening stopped all the way down. With the recorder rolling, the iris may be slowly opened up and brought to the proper setting. This creates a fade-in. A fade-out is created by reversing the procedure: A scene is started with the recorder rolling and the iris set properly. At the right moment, the iris is stopped down until the picture fades to black. Neither of these effects works well unless the light level is low enough so that the iris is nearly wide open at the proper setting.

IRIS INST. CONTROL A camera control designed so that you can zoom in on the surface that is reflecting the average amount of light for that scene, such as the face of the subject. Press the iris inst. control, which locks the iris at that setting, and then zoom back or pan to whatever framing is needed or to the beginning of that scene.

IRIS MODE CONTROL Allows you to choose between setting the iris manually or letting the camera's automatic iris circuits set the iris.

ISDB-T The Japanese digital video standard.

JACK A cable connector mounted on equipment.

JARGON Terminology and slang of a particular field.

JUMP CUT Any one of several types of poor edits that either break continuity or may be disturbing to the audience.

KELVIN TEMPERATURE Measurement of the relative color of light. Indicated as degrees Kelvin. The higher the temperature, the bluer the light; the lower the temperature, the redder the light. Also known as color temperature.

KEY LIGHT Apparent main source of light. Usually from one bright light above and to one side of the camera.

KICKER A light focused from the side on the subject or on a particular section of the set.

KILOHERTZ (kHz) A measurement of alternating energy, 1,000 hertz.

LAG That characteristic of a sensor in which a picture trails its own images as the camera moves. Lag varies depending on the quality of the sensor.

LAPTOP A portable computer designed small enough to fold and carry. Also a term for laptop editor. A single unit portable nonlinear editor.

LAVALIER (LAV) Microphone worn around the neck. Also sometimes called a lapel mic when clipped to a tie or front of the clothing.

LAYING DOWN CONTROL TRACK The process of recording a sync signal. It requires a video signal, a set of sync signals, but no audio is needed. Usually records color bars or a video black signal.

LEAD ROOM Extra space in front of any moving object in the camera frame.

LENS Glass or plastic designed to focus and concentrate light on a surface to form an image.

LENS CAP Opaque covering to slip over the end of a lens to protect the surface from damage and to protect the image device from excessive light.

LEVEL Relative amplitude or intensity. Used to indicate light audio, video, and other electronic signals.

LIGHT METER (EXPOSURE METER) Instrument used to measure the intensity of light. May be calculated in foot-candles, lux, or f-stops.

LIGHT-EMITTING DIODE (LED) A solid-state component that emits light when a small voltage is applied. Useful as a level or operating condition indicator.

LIGHTING RATIO A numerical value comparing the amount of incident light provided by the fill lights alone against the amount of incident light provided by the combination of key plus fill light. The standard ratio is 2:1.

LINE LEVEL Signal amplified enough to feed down a line without fear of degradation. A microphone level is lower than line level; speaker level is higher.

LINEAR In a straight line.

LIQUID CRYSTAL DISPLAY (LCD) (1) A flat-screen video monitor. (2) A source of flat, even light balanced to daylight.

LOCAL AREA NETWORK (LAN) A set of wires designed to carry digital signals between several peripherals or computers.

LOCATION Area or site of a production. Usually refers to sites away from studios.

LOG Listing of shots as they are recorded on tape.

LONGITUDINAL Lengthwise. In media, refers to the method of recording audio and control track signals.

LOOPING The process of rerecording audio during postproduction. Also now called automatic dialogue replacement (ADR).

LOUDNESS Perceived intensity of audio. Depends on the intensity and saturation of the sound, as well as the sensitivity of the listener to a range of frequencies.

LOW IMPEDANCE A measurement of resistance to current flow. Low impedance circuits often are at a low level. High-quality mic lines are low impedance with two conductors and a shield to prevent noise entering the circuit.

LUMINANCE The brightness component of a video signal.

LUX European measurement of light intensity. There are approximately 10 lux per 1 foot-candle.

MASTER SHOT Extended wide shot establishing the scene and often running the entire length of the sequence. Intended to be broken down in the editing process.

MATTE BOX A mounting mechanism on the front of a lens designed to hold filters, sun shades or other accessories used in electronic cinematography.

MEDIUM CLOSE-UP (MCU) Relative average framing for a shot, often framed from the waist up.

MEDIUM SHOT (MS) Wider than an MCU, often framed head to toe.

MEMORY CARD A thin combination of solid-state circuits designed to store digital signals. Also known as a flash drive or flash card.

MENUS A series of operational options that can be read in the viewfinder of a camera or on the face of a recorder. The options may be modified by watching the menus while adjusting the equipment.

METAL OXIDE SEMICONDUCTOR (MOS) A type of solid-state element designed to convert light to electronics; replaces the pickup tube in video cameras.

MICROWAVE High-frequency carrier for both audio and video signals. Operates only on a line-of-sight path.

miniDV A narrow-gauge digital tape recording medium. May be used to record either or both audio or video, SD or HD signals.

MINI-PLUG (⅛-INCH) Audio connector designed for small equipment. Scaled-down version of ¼-inch phone plug.

MIXED LIGHTING A set lit with light of various Kelvin temperatures.

MIXER A piece of electronic equipment designed to combine several signals. Usually refers to an audio board or console.

MODULATOR An electronic component designed to impress one signal on another, usually of a higher frequency.

MONITOR (1) To listen to or watch audio or videotapes or off-air programs. (2) Device used to view video signals, much like a TV receiver, but usually of much higher quality and generally does not have an RF section for off-air monitoring.

MORGUE Library, reference files, storage for used scripts, tapes, maps, and other reference material.

MOS A film term indicating a shot was recorded silent, or it is said, as the early German film directors said, "Mit out sound."

MPEG (MOTION PICTURE EXPERTS GROUP) A series of compression standards used in digitizing visual media.

NAT SOUND Ambient sound that exists on location, recorded as a story happens. Often used as background for a voiceover. Sometimes called wild sound.

NEUTRAL An aesthetic level without any specific genre or setting, often used for newscasts.

NEUTRAL DENSITY (ND) A type of filter that decreases light passage without changing the color value of the light.

NOISE Any undesirable additions to a signal.

NON-DROP-FRAME (NDF) Timing system that follows clock time precisely as opposed to drop frame that must compensate for color signals.

NONLINEAR (NLE) The storage and editing of video and audio digital signals. Comparable to film editing in that edits can be made in any order without disturbing previously edited sequences; also nonevasive, in that the original footage is not handled during the editing process.

NOSE ROOM The extra space allowed for in front of the face when framing the human head if facing in a specific direction.

NOTAN A lighting style similar to Japanese watercolors: high-key, few shadows, evenly lit.

NTSC (NATIONAL TELEVISION STANDARDS COMMITTEE) (1) The organization charged with setting television standard in the United States in the early days of television. (2) The television standard now in use in North America, much of South America, and Japan.

OFFLINE Using the lowest quality and lowest cost editing system suitable for a particular project.

OMNIDIRECTIONAL Microphone pickup pattern that covers 360 degrees around the mic.

ONLINE Using the highest quality and highest cost editing system suitable for a particular project.

OPEN UP The process of increasing aperture size in a lens. The f-stop number decreases in size.

OPERATOR Person whose main responsibility is to operate equipment, as contrasted with technicians, whose main responsibility is to install, repair, and maintain equipment; and engineers, whose main responsibility it is to research, design, and construct equipment.

OPTICS/OPTICAL Having to do with lenses or other light-carrying components of a video or film system.

OSCILLOSCOPE Test equipment used to visualize a time factor system, such as a video signal. Shows a technician what the picture looks like electronically. May also be used to analyze audio or other signals.

OUTPUT Signal leaving a system or electrical unit.

OVER-THE-SHOULDER (OS) A typical news interview shot in which part of the interviewer's shoulder appears in the foreground and the person being interviewed faces the camera.

P2 A solid-state digital card designed by Panasonic for their cameras. The card records digital media in the same manner as flash drives.

PAN Horizontal movement of a camera; short for panorama.

PAN HEAD Mechanism designed to firmly hold a camera on the top of a tripod, pedestal, or boom while allowing for smooth, easily controlled movement of the camera horizontally (pan) and vertically (tilt). May be mechanical, fluid, geared, or counterbalanced.

PAR A series of fixed-focus lamps mounted in a bank. A PAR has a color temperature of 3,200 degrees Kelvin. See also FAY.

PARABOLIC MIC Focused, concave, reflective, bowl-shaped surface with a mic mounted at the point of focus. Used to pick up specific sounds at a distance. Commonly used during sporting events.

PEDESTAL (1) Electronic calibration between blanking and black level. (2) Hydraulic, compressed-air, or counterbalanced studio camera mount; designed to permit the camera to be raised straight up or down effortlessly and smoothly.

PEDESTAL CONTROL Changes the black level or contrast of the picture.

PERAMBULATOR A large, wheeled, platform-mounted boom that a mic boom operator rides. Capable of swinging a mic over a large area.

PERIPHERAL Accessories connected to digital equipment—printers, decks, hard drives.

PHANTOM POWER The 48 volts required by condenser mic preamplifiers located in the mic. If the mic does not carry its own battery power, phantom power may be supplied through the mic line by the mixer or recorder.

PHASE The relationship of two signals differing in time but on a common path.

PHASE ALTERNATIVE LINE (PAL) A television system developed in England using 625 lines and 50 frames rather than the 525–60 system of NTSC. Used in many countries around the world.

PHOTOGRAPHER Originally, a person taking still photographs. In some markets, the term *photographer* was applied to news cinematographers, and even today, the term sometimes is applied to videographers.

PITCH The perception by humans of frequency.

PITCH SESSION A verbal presentation of a concept to a producer, funding source, or sponsor to gain funds and permission to proceed with the production.

PIXEL A short version of "picture element." A single sample of digital color information.

PIXILATION A process of removing a certain number of frames from a sequence so that the objects appear to be jumping about or suspended and moving in space.

PLASMA DISPLAY PANEL (PDP) Flat-screen video monitor.

PLOSIVE SOUNDS Vocalization made by the human voice that tends to pop a microphone. Sounds beginning with the letters "p" and "b," among others.

PLOT A scale drawing of the location of a shoot.

PLUG A connector on the end of a cable.

PLUG-INS Applications added to a computer to expand the capabilities and operations of the original application.

PODCASTING Streaming media intended for mobile reception.

POINT-OF-VIEW (POV) A camera angle giving the impression of the view of someone in the scene.

POSITION MONITOR, INDICATOR An monitor tool used to locate clips in the nonlinear editing process.

POWER SELECTOR SWITCH A control on a camera or tape deck used to switch the power source from either a battery or external AC power.

PRACTIAL ASPECT The editing criteria to be considered that must meet the needs of the system used within the available material.

PREAMPLIFIER (PREAMP) Electronic circuit designed to amplify weak signal to usable level without introducing noise or distortion.

PRIME LENS A fixed focal length lens.

PRISM A glass or plastic block shaped to transmit or reflect light into different paths.

PRODUCER Person in charge of a specific program.

PROGRESSIVE SCANNING A video frame constructed of a series of lines continuously forming a single frame before starting another scan sequence.

PROMPTER Device used to provide the talent with the copy as they perform on camera. Can be handheld copy beside the camera or a signal fed to a monitor mounted with mirrors to project the copy in front of the camera lens so the anchor can look directly into the camera. This signal may come from a signal fed directly from a computer.

PROPOSAL A concise summary of a project intended as a sales tool to accurately describe a production and to sell a sponsor on funding.

PROSUMER A category of producer and equipment that falls below that of professional quality but higher than consumer quality.

PUBLIC ADDRESS (PA) Sound-reinforcing system designed to feed sound to an audience assembled in a large room.

PULLING FOCUS The process of changing focus in the middle of a shot. Also known as rack or rolling focus.

PULSE CODE MODULATION (PCM) A digital recording system based on sampling an analog signal at regular intervals (usually audio).

QUADRAPLEX (QUAD) First practical professional videotape format. Quadraplex used 2-inch tape pulled across four heads to achieve a high-quality signal. No longer manufactured.

QUANTIZATION The measurement of a signal indicating the number of discrete levels of analog measured in the conversion process to a digital signal.

QUARTER-INCH PLUG (PHONE) Audio connector used for many years for high-impedance signals. Still used in some consumer equipment and patch panels.

QUARTZ-HALOGEN A lamp designed to provide a fixed color temperature of 3,200 degrees Kelvin.

RACK, ROLL FOCUS Changing focus in the middle of a shot. See also PULLING FOCUS.

RASTER The complete sequence of lines that make up the field of lines creating a video picture.

RCA The U.S. corporation that promoted the NTSC video system, the developer of many early television inventions, and the original owner of NBC radio and television networks.

RCA PLUG (PHONO) Audio and video connector designed originally for use only with the RCA-45 revolution per minute record player. Now used as a consumer audio and video connector. Some professional equipment uses this plug for line level audio. Not to be confused with the phone (¼-inch plug).

REALISTIC An aesthetic value of production creating as lifelike a setting as possible.

RECORD, CONVAS MONITOR The screen in NLE that shows what a series of clips look like after editing.

RECORDER DECK In a linear editing system, the deck that records the final edited sequence. See also EDITOR.

REFLECTANCE VALUES The amount of light reflected from the brightest and darkest objects in the picture used to determine contrast ratio.

REFLECTED LIGHT Illumination entering a lens reflected from an object. Measured with a reflected light meter pointing at the object from the camera.

REFLECTORS Large foam boards covered on one side with a variety of surfaces: plain white, colored, or textured. These are used to throw a soft fill light into areas not easily reached with instruments or to provide light when an instrument is not available or would cast an additional shadow.

REGISTRATION The alignment of either electronic or physical components of a system. Especially important in tube cameras.

RELEASE (1) Legal document allowing the videographer to use the image and/or voice of a subject. (2) Public relations copy.

RENDER Combining digital signals to follow a preordered virtual signal into the file's final form.

RESOLUTION Ability of a system to reproduce fine detail. In video, determined by the number of vertical lines; in film and computers, the number of pixels per line.

RETURN VIDEO OR VTR RETURN CONTROL A button on the camera that, when pressed, feeds the picture being played back from the tape deck into the viewfinder, allowing the videographer to observe the images already recorded.

REVERSING POLARITY Electronically changing video light values from dark to bright and colors to their opposites.

RF (1) Those frequencies above the aural frequencies. (2) A type of plug attached to a cable designed to carry a modulated signal. Also called F plug.

RIBBON MIC A transducer utilizing a thin gold or silver corrugated ribbon suspended between the poles of a magnet to create an electrical output.

RIDING GAIN The manual process of maintaining specific levels of electronic signals.

ROLL The command given by the director to start tape or the film camera recording.

ROLLING OR PULLING FOCUS Changing focus on a camera while recording.

RULE OF THIRDS The composition and framing theory that the visual frame may be split into nine sections by the intersection of two vertical lines and two horizontal lines, each one-third of the way into the frame.

SAMPLING In the process of converting an analog signal to digital, the number of times per second the signal is measured to determine the equivalent digital signal.

SATELLITE Geostationary orbiting space platform with transponders to pick up signals from the Earth and retransmit the signals back down to Earth in a pattern, called a footprint, that covers a large area of the earth.

SATURATION Intensity of a signal, either audio or video, but especially used as the third of three characteristics of a color video signal.

SCAN AREA The portion of the subject that the camera converts into an electronic signal.

SCENE A series of related shots, usually in the same time and location.

SCENE SCRIPT A full script without individual shots indicated.

SCRIM A metallic or fabric filter placed over a lighting instrument to diffuse and soften the light.

SCRIPT Complete manuscript of all audio copy and video instructions of a program.

SEQUENCE Individual shots edited into scenes, and individual scenes edited together to make a story.

SEQUENTIAL COLOR WITH MEMORY (SECAM) The color television system developed by the French and in use in many countries around the world.

SERVO LOCK An electronic synchronization signal that keeps recording devices running at the proper rate and in step with other signals.

SET The physical space within a studio for the production of a visual scene.

SET DESIGN The process of creating on paper the environment for a visual production.

SET LIGHT A lamp focusing on the area behind the talent or objects to provide a pattern on the background or to wipe out unwanted shadows.

SET PIECES A type of dressing for a set: furniture, wall hangings, and objects too large or fixed in place to be handled by performers.

SET UP The assembly of equipment and people in preparation for rehearsing a production.

SETUP Same as pedestal and black level; electronic calibration between blanking and black level.

SHOOTING LIST (SHOT SHEET) A listing of all shots in the order they are to be made, regardless of their order in the script.

SHOOTING SCRIPT A script complete in all details, including specific shot descriptions.

SHOT One continuous roll of the recorder; the smallest unit of a script.

SHOT SHEET Also known as shooting list. A listing of all shots in the order they are to be made, regardless of their order in the script.

SHOTGUN Ultra-unidirectional microphone designed to pick up sound at a distance by excluding unwanted sound from the sides of the mic.

SHUTTLE Movement of videotape back and forth while searching for edit points. Usually done at speeds faster or slower than real time.

SIGNAL-TO-NOISE RATIO (S/N RATIO) The mathematical ratio between the noise level in a signal and the program level. The higher the ratio, the better the signal.

SINGLE-COLUMN FORMAT A script format derived from stage script format now used in both feature film and some types of video productions. All instructions and dialogue are arranged down the middle of the page with various margins and placement of copy indicating instructions, character's names, settings, and dialogue.

SITE SURVEY A detailed listing of all the information needed to shoot on location at a certain site.

SLANT TRACK Another name for helical recording.

SLATE Several frames identifying the shot, tape reel number, or other logging information. Usually recorded at the beginning of the tape.

SOCIETY OF MOTION PICTURE AND TELEVISION ENGINEERS (SMPTE) A professional engineering organization that sets visual and aural standards in this country.

SOFTLIGHT A large light fixture that emits a well-diffused light over a broad area.

SOLARIZATION An in-camera effect created by varying the pedestal and gain to remove portions of the picture or expand other portions.

SOURCE DECK In an editing station, the deck playing back the original footage.

SOURCE, VIEWER MONITOR A screen that shows the first frame of a clip to be edited in an NLE editing system.

SPEED The response the camera operator and sound operator give to the director to inform her or him that both of their machines are running at the proper rate before starting to record the shot.

SPLITTER BOX Device used to feed an input signal to more than one output. Commonly used at news conferences to avoid a jumble of microphones by splitting the feed from one mic to all those covering the event.

SPOT METER A light meter designed to read a very small area of reflected light.

SPOTLIGHT A lamp designed to provide a hard-edged controllable field of light. Fresnels and ellipsoidals are typical spotlights.

STANDARD DEFINITION (SD) A video signal of lower quality than high definition (HD).

STANDARD OPERATING PROCEDURE (SOP) Predetermined methods of accomplishing tasks. Often set by corporate or upper management policy.

STANDBY The command a director gives to warn the crew, cast, and others in the studio or on location that a camera is about to roll.

STICKS Another name for a tripod.

STOCK New, unused tape or film before it is exposed to light.

STOP DOWN Decreasing the amount of light passing through a lens. Stopping down increases the f-stop number.

STORYBOARD A series of drawings indicating each shot and accompanying audio in a production.

STREAMING Distributing a video or audio program continuously on the Web.

STRIKE To tear down and pack up equipment and settings from a shooting location.

SUPERIMPOSITIONS (SUPERS) Two or more simultaneously fed video signals, stopping a dissolve at the halfway point.

S-VHS PLUG A plug that carries video signals split into two separate signals, Y and C, for higher-quality transmission of video than standard VHS.

SWISH PAN A rapid horizontal movement of the camera while recording. May be used as a transition device.

SWISH ZOOM A pan shot accomplished by starting on a scene and at the end of the shot, quickly panning the camera at a high enough rate so that the image is blurred.

SWITCHER (1) In multicamera or postproduction, a device used to change video sources feeding the recording tape deck. (2) The person operating the video switcher.

SxS CARD A solid-state card designed by Sony for their cameras. The card records digital media in the same manner as flash drives.

SYNC PULSES Signals created either in the camera or in a sync generator and added between the fields and between the lines. They are part of the recorded signal, and the receiver locks onto those pulses when the tape is played back or the signal is broadcast. The pulses can be corrected if there are errors in their timing by running the signal through a time base corrector (TBC).

SYNCHRONOUS (SYNC) Signals locked in proper alignment with each other; sound and picture locked together, all the various video signals in their proper relationship to each other.

TENT An opaque sheet of material suspended over a subject to diffuse and soften the light.

THREE-SHOT A camera composition focused on three people or objects.

TILT The vertical movement of a camera on a pan head.

TIMBRE The perception of a musical note that differentiates the same note from a piano or clarinet.

TIME BASE CORRECTOR (TBC) Electronic device used to lock together signals with dissimilar sync. May also be used to correct for phase, level, and pedestal errors in original recordings.

TIME CODE Time-based address recorded on videotape to allow for precise editing. SMPTE time code is the time code most universally used at present.

TIMELINE (1) The calendar schedule of a production, with each step of the production from beginning to end set as goal dates to be met to keep the production progressing on schedule. (2) A visual indication of either or both the audio and video signals in timed segments on an NLE system.

TONE A sound created by generating a single frequency for test purposes and for setting standard levels on recordings.

TRACKING Movement of a camera to the left or right, parallel to the subject, usually while mounted on a set of tracks for maximum smoothness and control.

TRANSDUCER Any device used to convert any form of energy to another form: a camera transduces light to video; a microphone transduces sound to electronics; a speaker transduces electronics to sound.

TRANSFORMER Magnetic voltage-changing or impedance-changing device.

TREATMENT A narrative description of a production. It should read more like a novel than a script, because it is intended for a nonmedia person.

TREBLE High frequencies of the audio band.

TRIPOD Three-legged portable camera support. (Also called "sticks.")

TRUCK A side-to-side movement of the entire camera mounted on a tripod, dolly, or pedestal mount.

TUNGSTEN LIGHT Relatively efficient gas-filled light source of approximately 3,200 degrees Kelvin temperature.

TWO-SHOT A camera composition focused on two people or objects.

UHF (ULTRA HIGH FREQUENCY) (1) Frequency band for television broadcasting channels 14 to 69. (2) An older, large, threaded type of video connector.

UMBRELLA LIGHT A means of creating a soft, defused light by focusing a spotlight on the inside of an umbrella designed with a reflective interior surface.

UNBALANCED A circuit usually consisting of a single conductor and a shield.

UNIDIRECTIONAL Microphone pickup pattern from a single direction. Comes in a variety of degrees of pickup angle, from cardioid to super unidirectional (shotgun).

UNIVERSAL SERIAL BUS (USB) A bidirectional digital circuit designed to connect a series of digital peripherals with a computer to create an efficient system.

UPLINK Transmission path from an Earth-based station up to a satellite. Sometimes used to describe the ground station capable of sending a satellite signal. See also DOWNLINK.

VARIABLE FOCAL LENGTH LENS (ZOOM) A lens that can have its focal length changed while in use.

VCR (VIDEOCASSETTE RECORDER) A recording system that uses tape contained in closed cassettes.

VECTORSCOPE Electronic test equipment designed to show the color aspects of the video signal.

VERTICAL INTERVAL TIME CODE (VITC) Time address recorded within the vertical interval blanking instead of on a separate linear track.

VHS, S-VHS JVC-developed consumer VCR system. VHS stands for Video Home System. The "S" in S-VHS stands for "separate," as it is a semicompatible component recording system rather than a composite system.

VIDEO (1) Picture portion of an electronic visual system. (2) All-inclusive term for electronic visual reproduction systems; includes television, cablevision, corporate media, and video recording.

VIDEOGRAPHER The proper term for the operator of a video camera.

VIDICON A type of video camera tube that replaced the Image Orthicon. It is lighter, smaller, and more durable, and it provides higher resolution.

VIEWFINDER The miniature video monitor mounted on the camera so the operator can see what is framed by the camera.

VIRTUAL A copy of an original signal of file. Used to manipulate the signal before rendering the final signal. A nonvolatile signal.

VISUAL The video portion of the program.

VOICE-OVER (VO) Story that uses continuous visuals, accompanied by the voice of an unseen narrator.

VOLT An electronic measurement of the pressure available at a power source. In North America, the standard is 110–120 V.

VOLUME The measurable loudness of a sound signal.

VOLUME UNIT (VU) Measurement of audio level. Indicates the average of the sound level, not the peak.

VTR (VIDEOTAPE RECORDER) A system that uses tape mounted on open reels.

VTR SELECTOR SWITCH Enables your camera to operate with a variety of different recorders manufactured by someone other than the manufacturer of your camera.

VTR START SWITCH A switch that may be mounted on the camera body, but more than likely it is mounted on the lens handgrip close to the thumb for easy use. This switch allows you to start and stop the recorder without leaving the camera or taking your eye from the viewfinder.

WAIST SHOT A composition framing a human from just below the waist to the top of the head.

WATT Measurement of power used in a piece of electrical or electronic equipment.

WAVEFORM MONITOR An electronic measuring tool; both oscilloscopes and vectorscopes are waveform monitors.

WEDGE Plate fastened to the bottom of a camera that allows it to be quickly mounted to a tripod equipped with a matched slot.

WHITE BALANCE Electronic matching of the camera circuits to the color temperature of the light source.

WHITE LEVEL (GAIN) Level of maximum voltage in a video signal.

WIDE SHOT (WS or LS) The second widest shot in a sequence. A WS is often used as an establishing shot to identify the environment and set the scene.

WILD SOUND Ambient background sound. See also NAT SOUND.

WINDOW DUB A low-quality copy of original footage with the time code signal visible in the frame.

WIPE Electronic special effects transition that allows one image to be replaced by another with a moving line separating the two pictures. Stopping a wipe in mid-movement creates a split screen.

WORK FLOW The process of moving audio and video signals from one production stage to another from inception through manipulation to distribution.

WRATTEN A series of filters originally designed for photography but adapted for use in cinematography and videography.

X-AXIS The plane running horizontally to the camera.

XLR PLUG Professional audio connector that allows for three conductors plus a shielded ground. Special types of multi-pin XLR plugs are used for headsets and battery power connectors.

Y-AXIS The plane running vertically to the camera.

YOTTAHERTZ (yHz) One septillion, or 1,000,000,000,000,000,000,000,000 hertz. Useful for indicating digital storage.

Z-AXIS The plane running away or toward the camera.

ZOOM See also VARIABLE FOCAL LENGTH LENS.

ZOOM LENS CONTROL Usually a rocker switch, which allows you to press one end to zoom in and the other end to zoom out. The harder you press, the faster the lens zooms. A gentle touch produces a slow, smooth zoom. On some cameras, an additional control allows you to set the speed range of the zoom control from very slow to very fast.

ZOOM MODE CONTROL Allows the operator to either zoom the lens manually or use its motorized control to zoom the lens.

Further Reading

Alten, Stanley R. *Audio in Media,* 9th ed. Belmont, CA: Wadsworth, 2010.

Arntson, Amy E. *Graphic Design Basics,* 5th ed. Belmont, CA: Wadsworth, 2007.

Benedetti, Robert. *From Concept to Screen: An Overview of Film and Television Production.* Boston: Allyn & Bacon, 2002.

Benedetti, Robert, Michael Brown, Bernie Laramie, and Patrick Williams. *Creative Postproduction: Editing, Sound, Visual Effects, and Music for Film and Video.* Boston: Allyn & Bacon, 2004.

Bermingham, Alan. *Location Lighting for Television.* Boston: Focal Press, 2003.

Billups, Scott. *Digital Moviemaking 3.0.* Studio City, CA: Michael Weise Productions, 2007.

Box, Harry C. *Set Lighting Technician's Handbook,* 3rd ed. Boston: Focal Press, 2003.

Browne, Steven E. *High Definition Postproduction Editing and Delivering HD Video.* Boston: Focal Press, 2007.

Burrows, Thomas D., Lynne S. Gross, James C. Foust, and Donald N. Wood. *Video Production: Disciplines and Techniques,* 9th ed. Boston: McGraw-Hill, 2005.

Compesi, Ronald J. *Video Field Production and Editing,* 7th ed. Boston: Allyn & Bacon, 2007.

Crowell, Thomas A. *The Pocket Lawyer for Filmmakers: A Legal Toolkit for Independent Producers.* Boston: Focal Press, 2007.

Debreceni, Todd. *Special Makeup Effects for Stage and Screen.* Boston: Focal Press, 2009.

DiZazzo, Ray. *Corporate Media Production,* 2nd ed. Boston: Focal Press, 2004.

Eargle, John. *The Microphone Book.* Boston: Focal Press, 2001.

Elkins, David E. *The Camera Assistant's Manual,* 5th ed. Boston: Focal Press, 2009.

Evans, Russell. *Practical DV Filmmaking.* Boston: Focal Press, 2006.

Ferrara, Serena. *Steadicam: Techniques and Aesthetics.* Boston: Focal Press, 2001.

Fowler, Jaime. *Editing Digital Film: Integrating Final Cut, Avid, and Media 100.* Boston: Focal Press, 2001.

Friedmann, Anthony. *Writing for Visual Media,* 2nd ed. Boston: Focal Press, 2006.

Gloman, Chuck, and Tom LeTourneau. *Placing of Shadows: Lighting Techniques for Video Production,* 3rd ed. Boston: Focal Press, 2005.

Gloman, Chuck, and Mark Pescatore. *Working with HDV: Shoot, Edit, and Deliver Your High Definition Video.* Boston: Focal Press, 2007.

Goodman, Robert M., and Patrick McGrath. *Editing Digital Video: The Complete Creative and Technical Guide.* New York: McGraw-Hill, 2003.

Grant, August E., and Jennifer N. Meadow. *Communication Technology Update,* 11th ed. Boston: Focal Press, 2008.

Grant, Tony. *Audio for Single Camera Operation.* Boston: Focal Press, 2003.

Gross, Lynne S., and Larry Ward. *Digital Moviemaking,* 7th ed. Belmont, CA: Wadsworth, 2009.

Harrington, Richard. *Photoshop for Video.* Boston: Focal Press, 2007.

Hartwig, Robert L. *Basic TV Technology: Digital and Analog,* 4th ed. Boston: Focal Press, 2005.

Holman, Tomlinson. *Sound for Digital Video.* Boston: Focal Press, 2005.

Holman, Tomlinson. *Sound for Film and Television,* 2nd ed. Boston: Focal Press, 2001.

Honthaner, Eve Light *Hollywood Drive: What It Takes to Break In, Hang In, and Make It In the Entertainment Industry.* Boston: Focal Press, 2005.

Irving, David, and Peter W. Rea. *Producing and Directing Short Film and Video.* Boston: Focal Press, 2006.

Jackman, John. *Lighting for Digital Video and Television.* San Francisco: CMP Books, 2002.

Kauffmann, Sam. *Avid Editing: A Guide for Beginning and Intermediate Users,* 4th ed. Boston: Focal Press, 2009.

Kellison, Catherine. *Producing for TV and New Media: A Real-World Approach for Producers,* 2nd ed. Boston: Focal Press, 2009.

Kindem, Gorham, and Robert Musburger. *Introduction to Media Production: The Path to Digital,* 4th ed. Boston: Focal Press, 2009.

Maes, Jan, and Mars Vecommen. *Digital Audio Technology, CD, MiniDisc, SACD, DVDA, MP3,* 4th ed. Boston: Focal Press, 2001.

Mamer, Bruce. *Film Production Technique: Creating the Accomplished Image,* 5th ed. Belmont, CA: Wadsworth, 2009.

McClean, Shilo T. *Digital Storytelling: The Narrative Power of Visual Effects in Film.* Cambridge, MA: The MIT Press, 2007.

Millerson Gerald, and Jim Owens. *Television Production Handbook,* 14th ed. Boston: Focal Press, 2009.

O'Steen, Bobbie. *The Invisible Cut: How Editors Make Movie Magic.* Studio City, CA: Michael Wiese Productions, 2009.

Pearlman, Karen. *Cutting Rhythms: Shaping the Film Edit.* Boston: Focal Press, 2009.

Rabiger, Michael. *Directing the Documentary,* 5th ed. Boston: Focal Press, 2009.

Rayburn, Dan. *Streaming and Digital Media: Understanding the Business and Technology.* Boston: Focal Press, 2007.

Roberts-Breslin, Jan. *Making Media: Foundations of Sound and Image,* 2nd ed. Boston: Focal Press, 2008.

Rose, Jay. *Audio Postproduction for Film and Video,* 2nd ed. Boston: Focal Press, 2009.

Rose, Jay. *Producing Great Sound for Film and Video,* 3rd ed. Boston: Focal Press, 2008.

Rosenthal, Alan. *Writing, Directing, and Producing Documentaries,* 4th ed. Carbondale, IL: Southern Illinois University Press, 2007.

Schneider, Chris. *Starting Your Career in Broadcasting: Working On and Off the Air in Radio and Television.* New York: Allworth Press, 2007.

Simpson, Wes, and Howard Greenfield. *IPTV & Internet Video Expanding the Reach of Television Broadcasting,* 2nd ed. Boston: Focal Press, 2009.

Skidgel, John. *Producing 24p Video.* San Francisco: CMP Books, 2005.

Spotted Eagle, Douglas. *Vegas Pro 9 Editing Workshop.* Boston: Focal Press, 2010.

Sterling, Christopher, ed. *Focal Encyclopedia of Electronic Media.* CD-ROM. Boston: Focal Press, 1998.

Thompson, Roy, and Christopher Bowen. *Grammar of the Edit,* 2nd ed. Boston: Focal Press, 2009.

Thompson, Roy, and Christopher Bowen. *Grammar of the Shot,* 2nd ed. Boston: Focal Press, 2009.

Tolputt, Bob. *DV Filmmaking,* 2nd ed. Boston: Focal Press, 2006.

Uva, Michael. *The Grip Book,* 4th ed. Boston: Focal Press, 2009.

Viers, Ric. *The Sound Effects Bible: How to Create and Record Hollywood Style Sound Effects.* Studio City, CA: Michael Wiese Productions, 2008.

Watkinson, John. *The Art of Digital Audio,* 3rd ed. Boston: Focal Press, 2000.

Watkinson, John. *The Art of Digital Video,* 4th ed. Boston: Focal Press, 2008.

Weynand, Diana. *Final Cut Pro 6: Professional Editing in Final Cut Studio 2.* Berkeley, CA: Peachpit Press, 2007.

Wheeler, Paul. *High Definition Cinematography,* 3rd ed. Boston: Focal Press, 2009.

Wiese, Michael, and Deke Simon. *Film and Video Budgets,* 3rd ed. Boston: Focal Press, 2001.

Wolsky, Tom. *Final Cut Express 3.54: Editing Workshop.* Boston: Focal Press, 2007.

Yoop, Jan Johnson, and Kathy McAdams. *Reaching Audiences: A Guide to Media Writing,* 4th ed. Boston: Allyn & Bacon, 2007.

Zettl, Herbert. *Sight-Sound-Motion,* 6th ed. Belmont, CA: Wadsworth, 2010.

Zettl, Herbert. *Television Production Handbook,* 10th ed. Belmont, CA: Wadsworth, 2006.

Zettl, Herbert. *Video Basics 2,* 6th ed. Belmont, CA: Wadsworth, 2010.

Index

Note: Numbers followed by *f* indicates figures and *t* indicates tables.

A

A-B roll linear editing, 203*f*
AAC codec, 20*t*
aberrations
 audio signals, 16
 video signals, 22
abstract lighting, 141
AC power connectors, 71, 71*f*
AC power sources, 96, 97
AC power switch, 54
AC-3 codec, 20*t*
accessories (hardware), editing, 208, 209*f*
"action" (director's cue), 160, 161*f*
action, continuity of, 182, 183*f*, 230
actors. *See* cast and crew
adjusting monitors, 234
Advanced TV Systems Committee (ATSC)
 signals, 24, 28, 29*f*
aesthetics of editing, 181, 196–197, 197*f*,
 228–232, 231*f*
afternoon, lighting to indicate, 154
AIFF codec, 20*t*
amperage available, calculating, 140
 Ohm's law, 96, 97*f*
amplitude of audio signals, 16, 17*f*
analog signals, digitized, 17*f*, 19
aperture, 48, 48*f*
applications, digital editing, 208, 209*f*
applying for jobs, 242–243
 cover letter writing, 243–246, 245*f*
 interviewing, 248–250, 249*f*
 portfolios, 246–248, 247*f*
 résumé writing, 243, 244*f*
arc (camera movement), 174
archival recordings, 236
art of editing. *See* aesthetics of editing
aspect ratio, 166, 167*f*, 168, 213
ATSC signals, 24, 28, 29*f*
attenuating audio levels, 18
audio (in general)
 adding to digital video, 225, 225*f*
 choosing tracks, 88
 continuity of location, 183, 183*f*

 editing into digital video, 225, 225*f*, 231
 outputting/exporting, 233–236
audio connectors, 72–73
audio equipment, 78–88
 choosing audio tracks, 88
 electronic impedance, 79, 87
 element construction, 80, 81*f*
 field preparation, 134, 135*f*
 microphones, 79
 mounting devices, 84–85, 86*f*, 177*f*
 nonmicrophone audio sources, 87
 pickup patterns, 82–83, 83*f*
audio signals, 14–16
 amplitude, 16
 compression, 20–21, 214
 distortion and noise, 16, 87*f*
 frequency, 14–16
 measuring, 18–19
 recording, 64
 synchronization, 24–28
automatic gain controls (AGCs), 18
automatic level controls (ALCs), 18
auto-white button. *See* white balance
autumn, lighting to indicate, 154

B

back focus, 47, 48*f*
backgrounds. *See* sets for production
backlight ratio, 101
backlights, 148
 multiple or moving subjects, 153*f*
 sun as, 146
 three-point lighting, 151*f*
backup copies, 236
banana plugs, 73*f*
bandwidth requirements, 214
bars/gain selector, 52
base light, 101
batteries as power source, 96
 checking, 133
benefits, negotiating, 250
benevolent dictator, director as, 159
bidirectional audio pickup, 82, 83*f*

bit rates, 214
blooming (light contrast), 102
BNC connectors, 74, 75*f*
body mounts, 57, 57*f*, 177*f*
boom-mounted microphones, 84, 86*f*, 133
breaker circuits, 74
 determining at site survey, 124
brightness controls for viewfinder, 51
broadcast cameras, 37*f*, 41, 41*f*
broads (spotlights), 90
budget for production
 determining, 106, 110
 summary page, 111*f*
bust shots, 162

C

cables and connectors. *See* connecting
 equipment
camera controls, 52, 53*f*
 bars/gain selector, 52
 color temperature control, 53
 miscellaneous, 54, 55–56
 white balance, 54–55, 142, 143
camera movement, 174, 175*f*, 230
camera setup, 132–133, 133*f*
camera supports, 56–61, 57*f*
 cranes, dollies, and pedestals, 58–59
 hands, 60–61
 tripods and body mounts, 56–57, 132–133,
 133*f*
cameras, 36–43
 choosing among, 36
 formats for digital cameras, 210*f*
 in-camera effects, 186–188, 189*f*
 types of, 37
candlelight (color temperature), 98
cardoid microphones, 83, 83*f*, 84
career possibilities, 237–252
 cover letter writing, 243–246, 245*f*
 internships, 240–242, 241*f*
 interviewing, 248–250, 249*f*
 job application process, 242–243
 portfolios, 246–248, 247*f*
 résumé writing, 243, 244*f*
 searching for, 238, 239*f*
CAs (continuity assistants), 190
cast and crew
 continuity assistants (CAs), 190
 directing and rehearsing, 156–159

organizing, paperwork for, 126
 prompting devices, 136, 137*f*
 shooting locations and, 122
 site survey and, 124
CCDs (charged-coupled devices), 22, 34, 44–45
CD codec, 20*t*
CD deck controls, 67
charged-coupled devices (CCDs), 22, 34, 44–45
checklists. *See* documents, preproduction
chiaroscuro lighting, 154
chips, 22, 44–45
 CCDs (charged-coupled devices), 22, 34,
 44–45
 CMOS (complimentary metal oxide
 semiconductor), 22, 34, 44–45
chroma adjustment (monitors), 234
circuit-breaker boxes, 74
 determining at site survey, 124
close-up shots, 163, 164*f*
closure, 165*f*
CMOS (complimentary metal oxide
 semiconductor), 22, 34, 44–45
codecs, 20–21, 20*t*
coiling cables, 70, 70*f*, 192
cold weather, equipment and, 131
color, weight of objects and, 178
color adjustment (monitors), 234
color bars, 51
color bars and tone, 220
color standards, 213
color temperature control, 98–99, 142–143,
 143*f*
 camera controls for, 53
 various light sources (list), 99*f*
color video signals, 26
communicaiton industry, convergences in, 238
communication with talent, 156
complex lighting plots, 153*f*
complex wipes, 223
complimentary metal oxide semiconductors
 (CMOS), 22, 34, 44–45
compression (data)
 of audio signals, 20–21
 standards for, 214
 of video signals, 32, 33*f*
compression of Z axis, 46, 46*f*
condenser micrphones, 80, 81*f*
connecting equipment, 69–77
 audio connectors, 72–73
 cable coiling, 70, 70*f*

checking and taping, 133
digital connectors, 76–77
placing for shooting, 140
power connectors and plugs, 71, 71*f*
striking, 192
video connectors, 74–75
consistency of continuity, 230
contingency item (budget), 110
continuity, managing, 182, 183, 183*f*, 230
logging process, 181
continuity assistants (CAs), 190
contrast ratio, 102–103, 146
control controls for viewfinder, 51
convergences in communicaiton industry, 238
cookies, spotlights with, 155*f*
cool colors, 178
copyrighted works, permissions for, 112
countdown, 220
cover letters, writing, 243–246, 245*f*
cover shots, 184, 185*f*
CPU requirements for editing, 207*f*
crab dollies, 58–59
cranes, 58–59, 174
creative lighting, 154
creativity of editing. *See* aesthetics of editing
crew. *See* cast and crew
critical area (framing), 167*f*, 168
cross-key light, 152
CU shots, 163, 164*f*, 228*f*
cue cards, 136
cukaloris patterns, 155
cultural values attributed to movement, 173, 173*f*
"cut" (director's cue), 160, 161*f*
cutaway shots, 184, 185*f*
combining with master shot, 228*f*
cut-in shots, 184, 185*f*
combining with master shot, 228*f*
cuts (transitions in editing), 222
cycles (audio signals), 14, 17*f*

D

data compression. *See* compression
date, lighting for, 154–155
daylight, 142
daylight (color temperature), 98, 99
DC cameras. *See* digital cinema (DC) cameras
DC power connectors, 71, 71*f*
decibels, 16
decoration, set. *See* sets for production

demodulators, 74
depth of field (DOF), 46, 49, 49*f*
desk-mounted microphones, 86*f*
digital audio workstations (DAWs), 206
digital cinema (DC) cameras, 37*f*, 42, 42*f*
digital connectors, 76–77
digital effects transitions, 223
digital in-camera effects, 188
digital media production. *See entries at*
production
digital recording equipment, 63–67, 63*f*
operation, 66–67, 67*f*
digital subscriber line (DSL), 76
digital technology. *See entries at* technology
Digital Video Broadcast-TV (DVB-T), 28, 29*f*
digital video signals, characteristics of, 199*f*
digital world, different from real world, 12–13
equipment limitations, 12–13, 13*f*
dimmers, 144
DIN connectors, 71, 74, 76
directing and rehearsing, 156–159
hand and verbal cues, 161*f*
direction, continuity of, 182, 183*f*
disc-based recorders, 64, 67
dissolve (transition), 222
distortion
audio signals, 16, 87*f*
video signals, 22
distribution of completed project, 106, 215*f*
destination choices, 236
preparing for, 233–236
documents, preproduction, 106–112
legal considerations, 112
location-related, 122, 123*f*, 124
organizing forms, 120–126
proposal document, 106, 107*f*
treatment, 108–110, 109*f*
DOF. *See* depth of field
dollies, 58–59
dolly in/back (camera movement), 174, 175*f*
double-spacing in scripts, 116
drag controls (tripod), 132
drop-frame (DF) system, 212
DSL lines, 76
dual-column format (scripts), 118–119, 119*f*
DVB-T signals, 28, 29*f*
DVD deck controls, 67
D-VHS cables, 76
dynamic microphones, 80, 81*f*
dynamics, audio, 19

E

ear, limitations of, 12–13, 13*f*
early morning, lighting to indicate, 154
ECU shots, 163
edge attraction (framing), 169
edge bleed areas, 168
editing, 181–184, 198–199
　cover shots, 184, 185*f*
　equipment for
　　hardware and accessories, 206–208, 207*f*
　　software, 209*f*, 210
　in-camera effects, 186–188, 189*f*
　linear electronic, 202
　managing continuity, 182, 183, 183*f*, 230
　shooting to edit, 181
　technical process
　　audio, adding, 225, 225*f*, 231
　　rendering, 226–227
editing process
　aesthetic process (guidelines), 228–232, 231*f*
　basic process, 198–199
　knowledge and skills, 196–197, 197*f*
　linear, 200, 201*f*
　linear electronic, 203*f*
　nonlinear. *See* nonlinear editing
　physical process, 211–214
　preparing for output and
　　distribution, 233–236
　technical process, 216–227
　　basic editing, 221
　　operating methods, 220
　　titles, 224
　　transitions, 222–223
EFP. *See* field production
1/8-inch phone plugs, 72
electronic aspect of editing, 181
electronic impedance, 79, 87
electronic news gathering. *See* ENG
electronic tubes, 44
ellipsoidal spotlights, 155*f*
energy spectrum range, 15*f*
ENG (electronic news gathering)
　batteries as power source, 96
　equiment for, 35*f*
equalization, 16
equipment, 34–104, 101
　audio equipment, 78–88
　camera supports, 56–61, 57*f*
　cameras. *See* cameras

chips, 44–45
connecting. *See* connecting equipment
development of, 34
for digital recording, 63–67, 63*f*
　operation, 66–67, 67*f*
for editing
　hardware and accessories, 206–208, 207*f*
　software, 209*f*, 210
field preparation, 131
identifying requirements for shoot, 126, 157*f*
image sources and optics, 44–49
lenses. *See* optics
lighting. *See* light control; lighting
limitations of, 12–13, 13*f*
monitors, adjusting, 234
organizing forms, 126
prompting devices, 136, 137*f*
striking, 192–193
tubes, 44
viewfinder, 51*f*, 52
essential area (framing), 167*f*, 168
Ethernet connectors, 76, 77*f*
EWS (extreme-wide shots), 163
expenses. *See* budget for production
exporting files, 227, 233–236
　destination choices, 236
extra close-up shots, 163, 164*f*
extra-wide shots, 163, 164*f*
extreme heat, equipment and, 131
extreme shots, 163
extreme-wide shots, 163
eye, limitations of, 12–13, 13*f*

F

F connectors, 74, 75*f*
fade-in and fade-out, 186
fall, lighting to indicate, 154
FAY lamps, 93
female plug, about, 69
field floods. *See* floodlights
field production
　color temperature control, 99
　equiment for, 35*f*
　lighting power sources, 96
　microphone element construction, 80
　microphone mounting, 85
　scouting for locations, 122, 123*f*.
　　See also location choices
　site surveys, 124, 125*f*

script formats for, 116
studio production vs, 8–9, 8*f*
field production, stages of, 129–194
directing and rehearsing, 156–159
editing. *See* editing
lighting preparation, 140–155
color temperature control, 142–143, 143*f*
contrast ratio, 146
creative and mood lighting, 154
intensity control, 144, 145*f*
kicker and set lights, 150
for multiple or moving subjects, 152–153, 153*f*
three-point lighting, 148, 149, 151*f*
logging and striking, 190–193, 191*f*, 193*f*
setting up, 129–139
audio preparation, 134, 135*f*
camera setup, 132–133, 133*f*
field equipment considerations, 131
prompting devices, 136, 137*f*
sets and properties (props), 138–139, 139*f*
shooting, 160–165
creating movement, 172–178, 230
framing, 166–170
framing and, 162
list of shot names, 163–165, 164*f*, 165*f*
files, outputting/exporting, 233–236
fill lights, 149
multiple or moving subjects, 153*f*
three-point lighting, 151*f*
film editing, 200, 201*f*
filter selector (camera), 53
filters, to control light intensity, 144
FireWire connectors, 77, 77*f*
fish poles, 84
five-point lighting, 151*f*
fixed-focus lighting, 93
FLAC codec, 20*t*
flaring (light contrast), 102
flexibility, budget, 110
FL-M filter, 53
floodlights, 90, 91*f*
fluorescent lighting, 93, 99, 142
focal length, 46, 46*f*
focal point, 47
focus, 47, 48*f*
depth of field (DOF), 46, 49, 49*f*
roll or rack focus, 187
focusing spotlights, 88, 92*f*, 155*f*
forklifts, 59

formats for digital cameras, 210*f*
forms, preproduction, 106–112
legal considerations, 112
location-related, 122, 123*f*, 124
organizing forms, 120–126
proposal document, 106, 107*f*
treatment, 108–110, 109*f*
4:3 aspect ratio, 166, 168, 213
four-point lighting, 151*f*
frame ratio. *See* aspect ratio
"framed" (director's cue), 160
frames per second (fps), 212
framing, 165*f*
describing in shooting script, 114
principles of, 166–170, 167*f*, 171*f*
scan choices, 211
shooting and, 162
standard shot names, list of, 163–165, 164*f*, 165*f*
freeze frames, 188
frequency, bit rate and, 214
frequency of audio signals, 14–16
frequency spectrum chart, 15*f*
Fresnel lenses, 92
front focus, 47, 48*f*
f-stops, 48, 48*f*
funding, preproduction paperwork helpful for, 106, 108, 110

G

gaffe equipment, 93*f*
gaffer, defined, 93*f*
gaffer hooks, handing microphones from, 84
gain selector, 52, 66
generators, portable, 96
giraffe (microphone boom), 84
glass-sided elevator, 59
goals-oriented analysis, 4–5, 4*f*
gobo patterns, 155
graphic force movement, 178, 179*f*

H

H.261 video compression, 33*f*
H.264 video compression, 33*f*
1/2-inch videotape, 34
hand cues (direction), 161*f*
handheld cameras, 38
support considerations, 60–61, 61*f*
handheld microphones, 84, 86*f*

handheld prompters, 136
hard drives, 65
hardware, editing, 206–208, 207*f*
HDV cameras, 37*f*, 38*f*, 39–40, 40*f*
head shots, 162
head-to-toe shots, 163
hertz, 14
high hats, 59
high-definition (HD) cameras, 37*f*
aspect ratio, 166
deciding on, 211
lighting design for, 141
miniature HD cameras, 43
set and prop design for, 138
high-definition television (HDTV), 26
high-impedance microphones, 79, 87
hot colors, 178
hue adjustment (monitors), 234
human limitations, 12–13, 13*f*
humidity, equipment and, 131

I

idiot cards, 136
IEEE 1394 connectors. *See* FireWire connectors
iLink connectors. *See* FireWire connectors
image sources and optics, 44–49
aperture, 48, 48*f*
focal length, 46, 46*f*
focus, 47
impedance, electronic (audio), 80, 81*f*, 87
in-camera effects, 186–188, 189*f*
digital, 188
incandescent fixtures, 142
incident light, defined, 100, 100*f*, 102*f*
instruments. *See* equipment
intensity of lighting
controlling during field production, 144, 145*f*
measuring, 100
interlace scan, 211
international video transmission standards, 28, 29*f*
internships, 240–242, 241*f*
interpersonal communication with talent, 156
interviewing for jobs, 248–250, 249*f*
inverse square law, 144, 145*f*
iris fades, 186
iris inst. control, 55
iris mode control, 55
iris setting. *See* aperture
ISDB-T signals, 28, 29*f*

J

jack, defined, 69
job application process, 242–243
cover letter writing, 243–246, 245*f*
interviewing, 248–250, 249*f*
portfolios, 246–248, 247*f*
résumé writing, 243, 244*f*
JPEG compression, 32, 33*f*

K

Kelvin temperatures, 98, 142
various light sources (list), 99*f*
key lights, 101, 149
multiple or moving subjects, 153*f*
three-point lighting, 151*f*
kicker and set lights, 151*f*
kicker light, 150

L

lamps on digital recorders, 66
late afternoon, lighting to indicate, 154
lavalier unidirectional mirophones, 84, 86*f*
lead room (framing), 169
LED banks, 90
LED meters, 18, 18*f*
legal considerations, 112. *See also* documents, preproduction
lens (lens mount) controls, 55–56
lenses. *See* optics
light control, 95
color temperature. *See* color temperature control
contrast ratio, 102–103, 146
intensity control, 100, 144, 145*f*
lighting ratio, 101
power sources, 96–97, 124
three-point lighting, 148, 149
light emitting diodes (LEDs), 26
light meters, 100, 100*f*, 102*f*
light-emitting diodes (LEDs), 18, 18*f*
lighting, 89–103
continuity of location, 183, 183*f*
fixed-focus instruments, 93
floodlights, 90, 91*f*
focusing spotlights, 88, 92*f*, 155*f*
gaffe equipment, 93*f*
intensity of, 100, 144, 145*f*
plotting for rehearsal, 157*f*
preparation, 140–155

color temperature control, 142–143, 143*f*
contrast ratio, 146
creative and mood lighting, 154
intensity control, 144, 145*f*
kicker and set lights, 150
for multiple or moving subjects, 152–153, 153*f*
three-point lighting, 148, 149, 151*f*
lighting ratio, 101
line level, 87*f*
line spacing in scripts, 116
linear editing, 200, 201*f*
linear electronic editing, 202, 203*f*
linear workflow systems, 6*f*
line-scanning systems, 28
liquid crystal displays (LCDs), 26
loading areas, determining, 124
location, continuity of, 183, 183*f*
location, lighting for, 154–155
location choices, 8–9, 8*f*
  scouting, 122, 123*f*
  site surveys, 124, 125*f*
"locked in" (director's cue), 160
logging, 190–193, 191*f*
loudness. *See* amplitude of audio signals
low-impedance microphones, 79, 87

M

male plugs, about, 69
master shot, editing, 228*f*
matching continuity, 181, 182, 183, 183*f*
  logging process, 181
MCU shots, 163, 164*f*
measuring audio signals, 18–19
measuring video signals, 30–32
media production jobs. *See* job application
  process
medium close-up shots, 163, 164*f*
medium shots, 163, 164*f*
memory requirements for signals, 214
merry-go-rounds, 59
metal oxide semiconductors, 22, 34, 44–45
metric prefixes, 15*f*
microcameras, 43
microphones, 79
  alternative audio sources, 87
  electronic impedance, 79
  element construction, 80, 81*f*
miniature HD cameras, 43
miniplugs, 72

mixed lighting, 99
modulators, 74
monitor adjustment, 234
mood lighting, 154
morning, lighting to indicate, 154
Motion-JPEG compression, 33*f*
mounting devices
  audio equipment, 84–85, 86*f*
  camera body mounts, 57, 57*f*, 177*f*.
    See also camera supports
movement (perceived), shooting and, 172–178,
  230
  camera movement, 174, 175*f*
  graphic force movement, 178, 179*f*
  movement through zooms, 174
  subject movement, 172–173, 173*f*
  z-axis movement, 176–177, 177*f*
movement of camera. *See* camera supports
movement through zooms, 174–175, 230
moving coil microphones, 80, 81*f*
moving subjects, lighting for, 152–153, 153*f*
MP3 codec, 20*t*
MPEG compression, 32, 33*f*
  MPEG-4 systems, 32
MS (medium shots), 163, 164*f*
multiple subjects, lighting for, 152–153, 153*f*

N

names for standard shots, 163–165
narrative description of production.
    See treatment
nat (natural) sound, 82
National Television Standards Committee
    (NTSC) signals, 24, 28, 29*f*
ND filters, 53
neutral density (ND) filters, 53
neutral lighting, 141
night lighting, 146
NLE. *See* nonlinear editing
no-filter position (color temperature), 53
noise
  audio signals, 16
  video signals, 22
non-drop-frame (NDF) system, 212
nonlinear editing (NLE), 181
  electronic, 204, 205*f*
  with film, 200
  hardware for, 206–208, 207*f*
nonmicrophone audio sources, 87
nose room, 169

Notan lighting, 154
NTSC signals, 24, 28, 29f, 211
numbering shots in scripts, 118
numbering shots in storyboards, 121f

O

Ohm's law, 96, 97f
omnidirectional audio pickup, 82, 83f
1/8-inch phone plugs, 72
1/2-inch videotape, 34
1/4-inch plugs, 64, 73f
one-column format (scripts), 116, 117f
open up (aperture), defined, 48
open workflow systems, 6f
operating methods (editing), 220
optics, 45
    aperture, 48, 48f
    focal length, 46, 46f
    focus, 47
organizing forms
    for equipment and crew, 126
    location scouting, 122, 123f
    site surveys, 124, 125f
    storyboards, 120–121, 121f
OS shots, 163, 164f
oscilloscopes, 30
outputting files, 233–236
    destination choices, 236
overhead (budgeting), 110
over-the-shoulder shots, 163, 164f

P

P64 video compression, 33f
PAL signals, 24, 212
pan (tripod), 56, 132
    lead room (edge attraction), 169
panning left/right (camera movement), 175f
panning with handheld camera, 61
paperwork, preproduction, 106–112
    legal considerations, 112
    location-related, 122, 123f, 124
    organizing forms, 120–126
    proposal document, 106, 107f
    treatment, 108–110, 109f
PAR lamps, 93
parking, 124
pay, negotiating, 250
PCM signals, 88
peak-to-peak meter, 18

pedestaling, 174, 175f
pedestals, 58–59
perambulators, 84
perceived movement, shooting and, 172–178, 230
    camera movement, 174, 175f
    graphic force movement, 178, 179f
    movement through zooms, 174–175
    subject movement, 172–173, 173f
    z-axis movement, 176–177, 177f
perception, human, 12–13
permissions, 112, 123f
    location-related, 122, 124
personal information, collecting, 239, 240f
personal property, permissions for, 112
personnel. *See* cast and crew
phantom power, 80
Phase Alternative Line (PAL) signals, 24
philosophy of production, 2–11
    goals-oriented analysis, 4–5, 4f
    production process, 2, 3f
    studio vs. field production, 8–9, 8f.
        See also field production
    technology, importance of, 10–11
    workflow, importance of, 6
phone plugs. *See* 1/4-inch plugs
phono plugs. *See* RCA connectors
pickup patterns, 82–83, 83f
pictures, in storyboards, 120, 121f
pitch (audio), 14
pixilation, 65, 188
planned vs. unplanned productions, 10f
plano-convex lenses, 92
plasma display panels (PDPs), 26
playback audio requirements, 134
plotting location site. *See* site surveys
plotting set, 157f
plug, defined, 69
plug-ins, editing, 208
point-of-view shots, 163, 164f
polarity, reversing, 188
portable generators, 96
portfolios, buliding, 246–248, 247f
postproduction, 2, 195–236
    editing. *See* editing
    tasks of, 3f
POV shots, 163, 164f
power connectors and plugs, 71, 71f, 133
    placing for shooting, 140
    striking and, 192
power selector switch, 54

power sources
  checking, 133
  determining at site survey, 124
  for lighting, 96–97
  striking and, 192
practical aspect of editing, 181
preliminary forms, 106–112
  legal considerations, 112
  proposal document, 106, 107*f*
  treatment, 108–110, 109*f*
preproduction, 2, 105–128
  organizing forms, 120–126
  preliminary forms, 106–112
  script formats, 112–119
  tasks of, 3*f*
production, 129–194
  directing and rehearsing, 156–159
  editing. *See* editing
  lighting preparation, 140–155
    color temperature control, 142–143, 143*f*
    contrast ratio, 146
    creative and mood lighting, 154
    intensity control, 144, 145*f*
    kicker and set lights, 150
    for multiple or moving subjects, 152–153,
      153*f*
    three-point lighting, 148, 149, 151*f*
  logging and striking, 190–193, 191*f*, 193*f*
  setting up, 129–139
    audio preparation, 134, 135*f*
    camera setup, 132–133, 133*f*
    field equipment considerations, 131
    prompting devices, 136, 137*f*
    sets and properties (props), 138–139, 139*f*
  shooting, 160–165
    creating movement, 172–178, 230
    framing, 166–170
    framing and, 162
    list of shot names, 163–165, 164*f*, 165*f*
production, studio vs. field, 8–9, 8*f*
production goals, 4–5, 4*f*
production jobs. *See* job application process
production process, 2, 3*f.*
    See also postproduction; preproduction
  tasks of, 3*f*
progressive scan, 211, 212
prompting devices, 136, 137*f*
properties (props), 138–139, 139*f*
proposal document, 106, 107*f*
  treatment and, 108, 109*f*

Pulse Code Modulation (PCM) integrated
  signal, 88

Q

quadraplex videotape, 34
quantization, 19, 214
QuickTime format, 235
"quiet" (director's cue), 160

R

rack focus, 187
range of human perception, 12–13
RCA connectors, 73, 73*f*, 74, 75*f*
reading time code (TC), 66
real world, different from digital, 12–13
  equipment limitations, 12–13, 13*f*
RealAudio codec, 20*t*
realistic lighting, 141
record start switch, 54
recording equipment, 63–67, 63*f*
  operation, 66–67, 67*f*
recording logs, 190–193
references, listing on résumé, 243
reflectance values, 146
reflected light, defined, 100, 100*f*, 102*f*
reflectors, 95
rehearsing, 157–159
releases, 112, 123*f*
  location-related, 122, 124
rendering, 226–227
résumé writing, 243, 244*f*
return video control, 55
reversing polarity, 188
RF connectors, 74, 75*f*
ribbong micrphones, 80, 81*f*
riding gain, 18
roll focus, 187
"roll tape" (director's cue), 160, 161*f*
rule of thirds (framing), 170, 171*f*

S

salary, negotiating, 250
sampling, 17*f*, 19
scan choices, 211
scan systems, 28
scene lighting. *See* lighting
scene scripts, 112, 113*f*
scouting for locations, 122, 123*f.*
    See also location choices
  site surveys, 124, 125*f*

scrims, 144
script formats, 112–119
    professional layout options, 114, 116,
        117*f*, 119*f*
    scene script, 112, 113*f*
    shooting script, 114, 115*f*
searching for careers. *See* career possibilities
seasons, lighting to indicate, 154
SECAM signals, 212
semiconductors (CMOS), 22, 34, 44–45
sensitivity, 12–13
    camera control for, 52
set lights, 150, 151*f*
sets for production, 138–139, 139*f*
    plotting for rehearsal, 157*f*
    striking, 192
setting up for shooting, 129–139
    audio preparation, 134, 135*f*
    camera setup, 132–133, 133*f*
    field equipment considerations, 131
    prompting devices, 136, 137*f*
    sets and properties (props), 138–139, 139*f*
shooting lists, 126, 157*f*
shooting locations, 8–9, 8*f*
    scouting, 122, 123*f*
    site surveys, 124, 125*f*
shooting process, 160–165
    creating movement, 172–178, 230
    framing, 162, 166–170
    hand and verbal cues, 161*f*
    list of shot names, 163–165, 164*f*, 165*f*
    shooting to edit, 181
shooting scripts, 114, 115*f*
Shorten codec, 20*t*
shot names, list of, 163–165, 164*f*, 165*f*
shot numbers, in script, 118
shot numbers, in storyboards, 121*f*
shot rundowns (shot sheets), 126, 157*f*, 158
shotgun microphones, 82, 83*f*, 84, 86*f*
shoulder mounts, 61*f*
signal characteristics (digital video), 199*f*
silent hand cues (direction), 161*f*
single-camera production. *See entries at*
    production
single-column format (scripts), 116, 117*f*
single-spacing in scripts, 116, 117*f*
site surveys, 124, 125*f*
16:9 aspect ratio, 166, 168, 213
size, frame, 212
slate, 220, 220*f*

softlights, 90
software, editing, 209*f*, 210
    how it works, 216–227
solarized effects, 188
solid-state recorders, 63*f*, 65, 67
sound. *See entries at* audio
special effects
    built into camera, 65
    in-camera effects, 186–188, 189*f*
specialized digital cameras, 43
spectrum of frequencies, 15*f*
"speed" (director's cue), 160, 161*f*
split screen, 223
spotlights. *See* focusing spotlights
spring, lighting to indicate, 154
stability of camera. *See* camera supports
stages of production, 2
    tasks of, 3*f*
"stand by" (director's cue), 160, 161*f*
stand microphones, 84, 86*f*
standard operating procedures (SOPs), 220
standard-definition (SD) cameras, 37*f*
    aspect ratio, 166
    deciding on, 211
    set and prop design for, 138
stop down (aperture), defined, 48
storyboards, 120–121, 121*f*
striking, 192–193, 193*f*
studio production, field production vs, 8–9, 8*f*.
    See also field production
styles of editing, 231*f*
subject movement, 230
subject movement (perceived), 172–173, 173*f*
subminiature cameras, 43
summary page, budget, 111*f*
summer, lighting to indicate, 154
superimposition (transition), 222
supports for cameras. *See* camera supports
survey of shooting locations, 124, 125*f*
S-VHS cables, 75, 75*f*, 76
swish pans, 187
swish zooms, 187
synchronization, 24–28
    scan systems, 28

T

takes (transitions in editing), 222
talent. *See* cast and crew
tape-based recorders, 64
TC (time code), 66

technology, 12–33
  audio signals, 14–16
  gap between real and digital, 12–13
    equipment limitations, 12–13, 13*f*
  importance of, 10–11
television script format, dual-column, 118–119, 119*f*
temperature, equipment and, 131
tents (for controlling light), 95
Terrestrial Integrated Digital Broadcasting (ISDB-T), 28, 29*f*
test signals, 220
three-point lighting, 148, 151*f*
three-shots, 163
360-degree crane shots, 59
three-step production process, 3*f*
tilt (camera movement), 174, 175*f*
tilt (tripod), 56, 132
  lead room (edge attraction), 169
timbre (audio), 14
time, lighting for, 154–155
time code (TC), 66
timeline
  audio, 225*f*
  video, 218
timeline for production, determining, 106, 126, 127*f*
titles, 224
tone. *See* frequency of audio signals
tracks (audio), choosing, 88
transducers
  audio (microphones), 80, 81*f*
  chips. *See* chips
  video (electronic tubes), 44
transducing process, 22–23
transfer. *See* outputting files
transitions (editing), 222–223
treatment, 108–110, 109*f*
tripods, 56–57, 57*f*, 132
  adding wheels to, 58–59
  microphone support, 84
truck left/right, 174, 175*f*
tubes, 44
12-volt connectors, 71, 71*f*
2-inch videotape, 34
two-column format (scripts), 118–119, 119*f*
two-shots, 163

U

UHF connectors, 75*f*
umbrella lighting, 90

unidirectional audio pickup, 82, 83*f*
universal serial bus. *See* USB connectors
unplanned vs. planned productions, 10*f*
uppercase type in scripts, 116
USB connectors, 77, 77*f*

V

variable-directional audio pickup, 83
vectorscopes, 32
vehicles
  parking, 124
  supporting camera in, 58
verbal cues (direction), 161*f*
video connectors, 74–75
video files, outputting/exporting, 233–236
video production. *See entries at* production
video signals, 22–23
  compression, 32, 33*f*, 214
  digital, characteristics of, 199*f*
  distortion and noise, 22
  measuring, 30–32
  synchronization, 24–28
  transducing process, 22–23
viewfinder, 51*f*, 52
visualizations of production. *See* storyboards
volume (audio), 16
VU meter, 18, 18*f*

W

waist shots, 162
walking shots, 61
warning lamps on digital recorders, 66
wattage available, calculating. *See* Ohm's law
WaveForm codec, 20*t*
waveform monitors, 30
weather, equipment and, 131
weight of objects, perceived, 178
white balance, 54–55, 142, 143
white light, defining, 98
wide shots (WS), 163, 164*f*
wild sound, 82
winter, lighting to indicate, 154
wipe (transition), 223
wired and wireless microphones, 85
workflow, 6, 6*f*
WS (wide shot), 163, 164*f*

X

X axis, focal length and, 46
X-axis movement, 172

XCU shots, 163, 164*f*
XLR connectors, 71, 72, 73*f*
XWS (extra-wide shots), 163, 164*f*

Y
Y-axis movement, 172

Z
Z axis, focal length and, 46, 46*f*

z-axis movement, 176–177, 177*f*, 230
zoom lens control, 55, 175
zoom lenses, focusing, 47
zoom mode control, 55
zooms
    movement through, 174–175, 230
    swish zooms, 187